Successful businesses understand that they need to engage their employees, bottom-up, with ways to tackle social problems as well as building long-term economic value. Social intrapreneurism is a helpful and valuable way to capture the essence of that engagement.
Harvey McGrath, Chairman, Heart of the City; former Chairman of Prudential plc, Man Group plc, and the London Development Agency

We know that businesses can have a major positive impact in the world. Until now though, not enough attention has been paid to the people within companies driving change. This book is an important contribution to our collective understanding of the growing intrapreneurism movement. For people on the inside, it's a practical how-to guide for enhancing your impact. For people on the outside, it's an inspiring tale of human progress.
Lindsay Levin, Founder and Managing Partner, Leaders' Quest

Unipart wants all our 10,000 employees to be change-agents. *Social Intrapreneurs and all that Jazz* gives plenty of how to tips for companies like ours that want to harness the energies and creativity of our people.
John Neill CBE, Executive Chairman, Unipart Group of Companies

Making an impact doesn't have to be extracurricular: *Social Intrapreneurship and All That Jazz* is an inspiring take on what's possible in the working world.
Liz Maw, CEO, Net Impact

Social Intrapreneurism and All That Jazz offers a distinctive perspective on social entrepreneurialism within commercial enterprises (with the added twist of some themes and insights from the world of jazz music). It also suggests a fascinating range of ways in which international NGOs can partner effectively with businesses to move them towards a stewardship model for future success.
David Nussbaum, Chief Executive, WWF UK

At last a book that highlights how we can be "entrepreneuring" wherever our career paths take us. For the last 15 years we have celebrated social entrepreneurs as the rock stars of the development world. This book expands and enriches the practice of entrepreneurship by including a heretofore unrecognised actor – the "intrapreneur", who, working from within established institutions, combines innovation, opportunity and resourcefulness to drive critical and large-scale changes in corporate practice aimed at improving social and environmental conditions, while meeting financial goals. The book is realistic about the challenges these entrepreneurs face, and provides guidance on how to turn those challenges into advantages. Bravo!
Dr Pamela Hartigan, Director, Skoll Centre for Social Entrepreneurship, Said Business School - University of Oxford

Impact Hubs make up a global network of people, places and programs that inspire, connect and catalyze impact. Traditionally, we focused on entrepreneurs with social innovation projects and business plans. In the messy process of social innovation we discovered, however, that there are change agents inside corporations who want to live their values at work. Their innovations leverage corporate structures to create social impact. This book not only provides inspiring examples of social intrapreneurs but also tools and strategies that help to turn social innovation projects into practice.

Henrique Bussacos, Chairman of Impact Hub Global Association & Pablo Handl; Co-founder of Impact Hub São Paulo

This is a vitally important book. As corporate sustainability rightfully shifts beyond policy into everyday business activity, we are now seeing the creation of better products and services as a result. There's a real and pressing need to show how innovation within large companies can be supported and turned into genuine sustainable advantage. In *Social Intrapreneurism And All That Jazz*, David Grayson, Melody McLaren and Heiko Spitzeck have done just that. Nothing helps make the business case better than genuine stories of success. This book will be foremost on management bookshelves for years, and I look forward to the second edition.

Tobias Webb, Founder, Ethical Corporation and Innovation Forum

Social intrapreneurs are living the common purpose values and I hope this book encourages many more people to emulate the examples told here.

Julia Middleton, Founder, CEO Common Purpose

Social Intrapreneurism and All That Jazz offers an exciting insight into the world of individuals striving to create social and commercial value in larger structures such as companies. It also teaches us what companies could do in order to create an enabling environment for these innovation drivers to emerge. Anyone interested in social entrepreneurship should not miss this publication on social intrapreneurship, which shows that change and social impact can also come from within larger structures.

Markus Hipp, Executive Director, BMW Foundation

Social Intrapreneurism and All That Jazz
How Business Innovators are Helping to Build
a More Sustainable World

SOCIAL INTRAPRENEURISM AND ALL THAT JAZZ

How business innovators are helping to build a more sustainable world

David Grayson, Melody McLaren and **Heiko Spitzeck**

Greenleaf
PUBLISHING

© 2014 Greenleaf Publishing Limited

Published by Greenleaf Publishing Limited
Aizlewood's Mill
Nursery Street
Sheffield S3 8GG
UK
www.greenleaf-publishing.com

Jazz photographs © Melody McLaren
Cover by LaliAbril.com

Printed in the UK on environmentally friendly, acid-free paper
from managed forests by CPI Group (UK) Ltd, Croydon

British Library Cataloguing in Publication Data:
   A catalogue record for this book is available from the British Library.

   ISBN-13: 978-1-78353-051-9 [paperback]
   ISBN-13: 978-1-78353-065-6 [hardback]
   ISBN-13: 978-1-78353-052-6 [PDF ebook]
   ISBN-13: 978-1-78353-072-4 [ePub ebook]

To change-makers everywhere, whoever you are.

Contents

Figures, tables and boxes

Figures

Tables

Box

Social intrapreneurs help business hit the top notes

John Elkington

'Here's to the crazy ones. The misfits. The rebels. The troublemakers. The round pegs in the square holes. The ones who see things differently,' ran Apple's 1997 'Think Different' ad campaign. Once heard or read, the words were hard to get out of your head. And they didn't end there. 'They're not fond of rules,' we were told. 'And they have no respect for the status quo. You can quote them, disagree with them, glorify or vilify them. About the only thing you can't do is ignore them. Because they change things. They push the human race forward. And while some may see them as the crazy ones, we see genius. Because the people who are crazy enough to think they can change the world, are the ones who do.'

Sadly, Steve Jobs has now left the stage, but potentially disruptive change agents continue to bounce into view. They are endlessly fascinating, whether pioneering electric cars, smart grids, malaria-busting vaccines or ethical microfinance. Having spent decades working with such people, I know that, like Jobs, they project reality distortion fields. The impossible becomes possible. They help us all hit those hard-to-reach top notes.

When SustainAbility—and later also Volans—attracted a three-year grant from the Skoll Foundation to help build the field of social entrepreneurship, we found that all the world's leading social entrepreneurs were desperately keen to find ways of working with mainstream business. So in our second study, *The Social Intrapreneur*, we identified, researched and celebrated their counterparts inside the business mainstream, in companies as diverse as Accenture, Banco Real, Coca-Cola, Ford, Morgan Stanley and Nike.

We were surprised to find that many of these people were struggling to find a common identity, even if they shared a common purpose. So it is exciting to see new initiatives, including the League of Intrapreneurs, playing into this space—and to see first-rate academic research developing. I warmly welcome this timely and thought-provoking book from David Grayson, Melody McLaren and Heiko Spitzeck. The analysis is rigorous, but the presentation is often playful, as when they riff off concepts like soloing, paying your dues and woodshedding.

As a Visiting Professor at the Doughty Centre for Corporate Responsibility, this fascinating investigation of the genius of top social intrapreneurs makes me even prouder of my links with the Cranfield School of Management.

John Elkington is co-founder and Executive Chairman of Volans (www.volans .com), co-founder of SustainAbility (www.sustainability.com) and co-author, with Pamela Hartigan, of *The Power of Unreasonable People: How Social Entrepreneurs Create Markets That Change the World*, Harvard Business School Press, 2008. He blogs at www.johnelkington.com and tweets at @volansjohn.

Acknowledgements

We would like to thank all our interviewees for their time and input with this project. They include the individuals listed below, as well as others who requested anonymity:

Gregory Abendroth, Kenan Aksular, Virginia Alfenas, Elisa Alkmim, Michael Anthony, Mandar Apte, Naty Barak, Mike Barry, Richard Bennett, Moram Ben-Ziv, Bruno Berthon, Ana Biglione, Roberto Bocca, Vicky Bullivant, Gib Bulloch, Henrique Bussacos, João Vitor Caires, Armelle Carminati-Rabasse, Marcelo Cardoso, Emma Clarke, Josh Cleveland, Russ Conser, Marianne Dagevos, Jo da Silva, Leonardo Vitoriano da Silva, Raylla Pereira de Andrade, Tamara Rezende de Azevedo, Maggie De Pree (née Brenneke), Katy Dobbs, James Dorling, Ian Drew, John Elkington, Paul Ellingstad, Richard Ellis, Jennifer Emery, Justin Evans, Julika Erfurt, Julie Fabian, Karl Feilder, Amy Fetzer, Carrina Gaffney, Jonas Gebauer, Andreas Gollan, Joanna Hafenmayer, Jost Hamschmidt, Pablo Handl, Erik Hansen, Chris Harrop, Martin Herrndorf, Adrian Hodges, Lance Howarth, Jill Huntley, James Inglesby, Jo Kelly, Paul Kerssens, Stefan Koch, Dr Beatrix Kuhlen, Charmian Love, Ian Mackintosh, Priscila Matta, Patricia Lagun Mesquita, Nancy McGaw, Cassiano Mecchi, Celia Moore, Dorje Mundle, Colin Mutchler, Clara Navarro, Andre Nijhof, Juliana Nascimento, Louis Notley, William Parsons, Arun Pande, Liliane Pellegrini, Yvonne Remmits, Julian Richardson, Hugh Saddington, Regan Schegg, Ralf Schneider, Mark Siebert, Camila Silvestre, Norma Snell, Mark Spelman, Nicolai Tewes, Mark Thain, Lara Toensmann, Lucas Urbano, Tom van den Nieuwenhuijzen, Wilco van Elk, Dominic Vergine, Andy Wales, Marijn Wiersma, Ingrid Zeegers.

Particular thanks to Dr Elisa Alt of the Anglia Ruskin University who collaborated with Heiko on the academic literature review on the enabling environment for social intrapreneurism and subsequently co-authored the second Doughty Centre Occasional Paper; Fuji Marlen Kimura Gomez for her help on the section on collaboration with NGOs; and to Yasmin Mahmood, whose work for a Cranfield International Human Resource Management MSC course paper forms the basis and much of the text for the Vodafone M-PESA social intrapreneurial journey described in Chapter 2.

We give especial thanks to Ron Ainsbury, Maggie De Pree, Heidi Kikoler and Andre Nijhof who generously read the early version of the manuscript and provided valuable feedback and suggestions.

We are especially grateful to Stephen Keogh and the other musicians of the Global Music Foundation (http://www.globalmusicfoundation.org) whose work inspired us; Arnie Somogyi (http://www.arniesomogyi.com), musician, composer and Birmingham Conservatoire jazz lecturer who, along with Stephen, provided feedback on our manuscript; and to Lionel Bodin of Accenture Development Partnerships, who shared our enthusiasm for applying the lessons of jazz to social intrapreneurism. While we have done our best to apply the metaphors of jazz intelligently to our analysis of the work of social intrapreneurs and their colleagues, we should emphasise that we are not experts in the jazz field. Any shortcomings in our understanding of jazz music or the musicians who inspired us are the responsibility of the authors and not the musicians. We particularly wanted to communicate the energy and vitality that we have experienced in the social intrapreneurs we have met. To help us do this and also to reinforce the parallels between social intrapreneurism and the world of jazz music, Melody has generously opened up her library of the photographs she has taken at jazz events. Her fellow authors enormously appreciate this and the alacrity with which venues and artists gave their permission for us to use these photos.

This book is based on a research project and two Occasional Papers of the Doughty Centre, Cranfield School of Management, and we appreciate the opportunity that the Centre and the School have given us to develop our ideas.

Among the team at Greenleaf Publishing, we would like to thank John Stuart who has championed the book from the beginning and provided wise counsel and encouragement; Monica Allen for her editorial prowess; Dean Bargh who has, once again, worked his production magic; and Rebecca Macklin, Anna Comerford and Sadie Gornall-Jones for their invaluable help.

Finally, to our family, friends and colleagues who must sometimes have felt they have lived the evolution of *Social Intrapreneurism and All That Jazz* vicariously, thank you for your patience and support.

David Grayson, Melody McLaren, Heiko Spitzeck, January 2014

Introduction

There are those that look at things the way they are, and ask why?

I dream of things that never were, and ask why not?

Robert Kennedy, based on George Bernard Shaw, *Back to Methuselah*

Many of us, from time to time, have imagined a world that is better than the one we have now. It is quintessentially human to see our world as it is—riddled with poverty, war, disease, environmental degradation and all the other ills we have wrought upon it through the course of our history—and envision in its place a world of beauty in which we have put an end to these myriad afflictions and learned to live in harmony with the earth and with each other.

None of us is quite sure how we might create that world. But most of us would not think immediately of harnessing the innovative powers of business as a means to getting there. A growing number of people, however, are doing precisely that—devising new products and services that are improving the quality of human life, and helping to mitigate climate change and other adverse environmental impacts—crucially, while creating commercial value for their companies.

Those people are called social intrapreneurs.

We define social intrapreneurs as 'people within a large corporation who take direct initiative for innovations that address social or environmental challenges while also creating commercial value for the company'.

The first recorded use of the terms 'intrapreneur', 'intrapreneuring' and 'intrapreneurship' dates from a paper written by Gifford and Elizabeth Pinchot (Pinchot and Pinchot 1978). Later the term was credited to Gifford Pinchot by Norman Macrae in *The Economist* (1982).

The term 'social intrapreneur' was first defined by SustainAbility (2008) as:

1. Someone who works inside major corporations or organisations to develop and promote practical solutions to social or environmental challenges where progress is currently stalled by market failures

2. Someone who applies the principles of social entrepreneurship inside a major organisation

3. One characterised by an 'insider–outsider' mind-set and approach

Other definitions include the following:

> Social intrapreneurs ... are responding to perceived shortcomings in society and utilize the resources of the firm to provide market based solutions to address them (Bode and Santos 2013).

> Employees who identify opportunities for social innovation within their corporation or organisation, playing a part in making businesses better from the inside out (Mitchell 2013).

> A new breed of business professional ... finding creative—and in many cases disruptive—ways to tackle some of society's toughest problems and create long-term value for their companies as well (McGaw 2013).

> Two thirds changemaker, one third troublemaker (Bulloch 2013).

Typically, as Josh Cleveland who has written and championed the concept with the student movement Net Impact says, social intrapreneurs are 'going against the grain a bit'.[1] They are looking to create what Harvard strategy guru Michael Porter describes as 'Shared Value' (Harvard Business Review 2011. This value-creation process typically engages individuals or organisations beyond the boundaries of their companies in unusual cross-border alliances. Deborah Leipziger, corporate responsibility consultant, and Cheryl Kiser, Director of Babson Social Innovation Lab, explore how entrepreneurial leaders in companies develop such alliances, even co-creating partnerships with competitors, to generate profits and social value in *Creating Social Value* (Kiser and Leipziger 2014).

Social intrapreneurs are challenging their organisation, questioning the status quo to develop and implement commercially attractive sustainability solutions. Hence another description: 'corporate provocateurs'. Often, at least initially, their intrapreneurial activity is not part of their job. This is why some social intrapreneurs talk of their day job and their job that they do in their spare time at weekends and night-time: 'moonlighting' for their own employer! We think the distinctive features of social intrapreneurs are that they:

- Work for for-profit enterprises[2]

---

1   From interview with Josh Cleveland, 9 June 2010.

2   While we acknowledge, as our colleague Maggie De Pree has pointed out, that 'there are intrapreneurs working in government and NGOs as well', we have focused on the work of social intrapreneurs within companies in this book.

- Treat social or environmental problems as business opportunities

- Drive innovations that create value for business and society

The value of studying social intrapreneurs lies in their potential to develop solutions to our global challenges by virtue of their positions in organisations that manage significant resources and power. Social intrapreneur Gib Bulloch at Accenture explains: 'Affecting even small change in large organisations can lead to significant positive social impact' (SustainAbility 2008).

Unlike their 'close relatives', such as corporate volunteers, corporate responsibility (CR) champions or green team members inside companies who are also furthering social and environmental goals, social intrapreneurs aim to generate entirely new forms of commercial value through significant innovations in products, services, processes or business models for their employers. However, as will become evident from the examples in our book, these diverse members of the corporate 'family' may find themselves working together as an 'ensemble' to enhance the sustainability performance of their companies.

In contrast with social entrepreneurs, social intrapreneurs can leverage existing infrastructures and organisational capabilities to deliver social value on a large scale. That fact alone tips the odds in favour of social intrapreneurs achieving large-scale social change, as *The Economist* (2008) suggested in a review of a book about social entrepreneurs:

> The greatest agents for sustainable change are unlikely to be the well-intentioned folk described in this book, interesting though they are. They are much more likely to be the entirely reasonable people, often working for large companies, who see ways to create better products or reach new markets, and have the resources to do so.

At the 2008 World Economic Forum in Davos, Bill Gates called on business leaders to support the work of social innovators in their own companies:

> I hope corporations will dedicate a percentage of their top innovators' time to issues that could help people left out of the global economy. This kind of contribution is even more powerful than giving cash or offering employees time off to volunteer. It is a focused use of what your company does best. It is a great form of creative capitalism, because it takes the brainpower and makes life better for the richest, and dedicates some of it to improving the lives of everyone else (Gates 2008).

However, many companies do not yet recognise this. Sharon Parker is a professor in organisational psychology at the University of Western Australia's Business School. Her recent research projects on proactive behaviour and responses to it have explored the motivations of social intrapreneurs and how they generate change in organisations. She notes:

> Trying to effect change gives an individual meaning and purpose. It enhances their learning and is exciting—and it's a great way to develop networks. But at the same time it's quite risky behaviour. Usually there's some resistance from somewhere and you can't anticipate what's going

to happen. Businesses are set up to deliver profit and that's their dominant logic, so anyone trying to make profit and be a social intrapreneur is
going to potentially come up across resistance (Knowledge@Australian
School of Business 2011).

Emma Stewart, Head of Sustainability Solutions at Autodesk and professional
faculty at University of California, Berkeley, adds that:

> Social intrapreneurs are employees who, in lieu of starting their own
> social enterprise, brave the stormy landscape of corporate politics to
> get their disruptive ideas to market and to more customers sooner, and
> therefore with greater environmental or social impact. It was social
> intrapreneurs who first conceived GE's Ecomagination product lines,
> Intel's super-efficient water reuse programmes, and Levi's Water<Less™
> jeans (Stewart 2013).

We began studying this fascinating but rare 'species', described first in a 'field
guide' produced by our colleagues at SustainAbility (2008). Why? At the Doughty
Centre for Corporate Responsibility, our purpose is to research, and to teach and
advise current and future business people on building and developing more responsible, sustainable businesses. But we are interested in how people at all levels of
a company, whether they are working at senior director level or elsewhere in the
organisation, become interested in trying to build sustainable businesses in the first
place. And we are particularly interested in discovering why and how inventive business people are using the power of their companies to help tackle wide-ranging issues
such as climate change, poverty and disease—big global problems that previous generations would not have believed businesses could, or even should, try to address.

So what do social intrapreneurs do?

Here is a small selection of what our research interviews, with over 40 social
intrapreneurs as well as with others who have studied and supported their work,
revealed that social intrapreneurs and their allies have already achieved:

- Creation of microinsurance products for low-income people and businesses
  unable to afford conventional insurance schemes (Allianz)

- Start-up of a business unit within a large parcel delivery corporation to improve
  operational efficiency while ameliorating climate change impacts (DHL)

- Introduction of a marketing strategy to help clients reduce their carbon footprint
  by promoting use of the company's information technology services (Telstra)

- Reduction of a large brewing company's production costs to improve competitiveness in developing countries through partnerships with local growers
  (SABMiller)

- Development of a micro-energy project within a major energy generation corporation to boost productivity and address poverty in developing countries (E.ON Energie)

- Launch of an alternative energy business within a major oil company to service customers in emerging markets (BP)

- Establishment of a 'green' advertising network as a new business stream within a major media company (The Guardian)

- Development of 'sustainable IT' service streams at a major engineering company (Siemens)

- Creation of a coalition within a major energy provider to address problems of fuel poverty (E.ON UK)

- Development of ethically produced sustainable product lines at a landscape paving company through partnerships with overseas suppliers (Marshalls)

- Creation of dialogue with a Brazilian community to develop a supply chain relationship at a personal care products company (Natura)

- Development of a commercially viable business unit within an engineering consultancy to address third-world poverty issues (Arup)

- Engineering of environmentally sustainable production processes at a global chemicals company (BASF)

- Development of sustainability strategy and network at a nuclear engineering company (Cavendish Nuclear)

- Creation of a specialty risk reinsurance company focused on climate change and carbon trading exposures (Marsh)

- Capacity-building and creation of partnerships to leverage and develop management expertise for international development (Accenture)

- Development of a commercially sustainable strategy for marketing pharmaceutical products to low-income customers in developing countries (Novartis)

In this book we present a selection of their stories and what we, and they, have learned from their journeys. We hope to inspire others to follow in their pioneering footsteps and join a growing movement of individuals who are helping to build a better, more sustainable world through their 'day jobs'.

Why are these stories important? Because they prove that work can, and should be, more than 'just a job'; it can be a fulfilling means to making the world a better place. Social intrapreneurism, we believe, is a gateway to an entirely new way of doing business: creating value, not just for investors, but for society as a whole. Businesses need to be recognised for what they truly are—not isolated entities operating in bubbles but value-generating (and potentially value-destroying) communities, interconnected with the wider world through networks of employees, suppliers, customers and others. We look forward to a future era in which it will be commonplace for inventive minds to design products and services that are not only commercially profitable but also address the world's most pressing social, environmental and economic challenges.

Perhaps you, a reader of this book, will be a leader in that future. If so, we look forward to meeting you and learning more about the great work you will be doing.

What does jazz have to do with social intrapreneurism?

Our references to jazz music, both in the title of this book and at various points in the text, have emerged from discoveries we made during the course of our research that paralleled the experiences of two amateur jazz pianists in our extended working community: Melody McLaren, a Doughty Centre research associate co-authoring this book, and Lionel Bodin, a senior manager at Accenture Development Partnerships, supporters of the League of Intrapreneurs.[3]

As Melody describes it:

> During the period of our Doughty Centre team's research on social intrapreneurs I was, by coincidence, also spending a lot of time with great jazz musicians. Whether I was listening to their performances in concerts or jam sessions, being tutored by them in jazz workshops or just conversing with them, I was struck by their aliveness, their connectedness with other musicians and the power of their musical 'storytelling'. When I was in a room with these people, I didn't want to leave.
>
> I had similar experiences when I was interviewing social intrapreneurs. Their accounts of their lives and the development of their projects conveyed a strong sense of connectedness, not only with what was happening in their businesses, but also with issues and events in the wider world including poverty, social exclusion and environmental degradation, along with their innovative practical solutions for tackling them. Whether they were describing project successes or failures or simply describing their day-to-day experiences, I had the sense that these people were very much alive. I could have listened to them for hours without losing interest in what they had to say.
>
> That sense of aliveness was the initial common thread between these two groups. Later on it became apparent that they shared other qualities—a strong sense of curiosity that emboldened them to take risks, a history of hard work to learn and perfect their 'craft', astute listening and observational powers, an ability to communicate with others in a compelling way and, above all, a passion for 'quality'.

---

3   http://www.leagueofintrapreneurs.com/.

During many discussions between the authors, Melody would often explain a point she was making with reference to her jazz experiences. To communicate these ideas to the research team in a more concise way, she began using terms such as 'woodshedding' (solitary practice to improve technical skills), 'comping' (accompanying, or providing support for, others), 'soloing' (putting your own ideas forward), 'being a sideman' (contributing to a group in which you are not the official leader but a supporting team member) and 'paying your dues' (contributing to your immediate team/community, thereby earning the trust of others). While some of these jazz colloquialisms, which are numerous,[4] are no longer in current use by jazz musicians, they nevertheless resonated with our team, other colleagues and social intrapreneurs with whom we shared our ideas.

When we began to analyse in great depth the interviews with individual social intrapreneurs and later on with their colleagues who helped create the 'enabling environment' for social intrapreneurism, parallels between the worlds of jazz musicians and social intrapreneurs became increasingly explicit. While some of the terms we use in this book (e.g. godparent) have, to our knowledge, no equivalents in the jazz lexicon, the resonances between the worlds of jazz and social intrapreneurism were sufficiently strong that we decided to introduce jazz metaphors to describe many of the ideas that emerged from our research.

1. Social intrapreneurism is not a solo act

Our interviews underscored the point that successful social intrapreneurism is a *group* (vs. individual) activity. Intrapreneurism and entrepreneurism are distinctly different in this respect. Nothing of significance can be achieved by a single person working alone inside a company, however heroic their efforts. There is simply too much to do.

Although the first phase of our research focused on individual social intrapreneurs (Grayson, McLaren and Spitzeck 2011), it became evident when we reviewed our first-round interviews, as well as during our second-phase research into the enabling environment for social intrapreneurism (Grayson, Spitzeck, Alt and McLaren 2013), that an intrapreneur had to secure the continuing support of others in order to bring a project to fruition inside a large company. For this reason, we altered the language in our second-phase research report to highlight the importance of colleagues supporting the enabling environment for social intrapreneurism.[5]

---

4   See the list on the All About Jazz website: http://www.allaboutjazz.com/php/article.php? id=1404&pg=4&page=1, accessed 6 December 2013.

5   We are aware that other colleagues working in this field use the term 'social *intrapreneurship*', which places greater emphasis on the work of the individual social intrapreneur. While we have opted for 'social intrapreneurism' to highlight the importance of the ecosystem in fostering innovation that produces social and commercial impacts, we are treating the terms 'intrapreneurship' and 'intrapreneurism' as being largely interchangeable.

While there is a Western business stereotype that celebrates the heroic efforts of the intrepid business *entrepreneur*, a successful social *intrapreneur*, although perhaps originating an intrapreneurial project idea of their own, must learn to work in, and then help to create, 'ensembles' of like-minded individuals with complementary skills and ideas, as happens with jazz musicians who are 'jamming' or performing together, in order to succeed.

If the number of individuals involved is sufficiently large (i.e. the intrapreneurial project requires assembling a 'big band' with a diverse range of talents), the proportion of orchestral 'scoring' required relative to the amount of free improvisation may need to increase to grow a corporate project to a large scale.

And, as with jazz ensembles, the mere presence of other players is not enough. We found that the quality of the 'conversation'—the collaborative relationships—between social intrapreneurs and their colleagues both inside and outside their organisation (often partners in external not-for-profit organisations) was instrumental in determining whether an idea could get off the ground and secure support in a company.

It was particularly helpful if the intrapreneur was able to find an individual who could act as:

- A power broker to provide access to resources and create a protected 'space' or 'air-cover' in which the intrapreneur could develop a project, often 'under the radar' of the rest of the organisation

- An effective networker who could connect the intrapreneur with useful contacts and help rally support for a project

- An effective translator of an intrapreneur's ideas who could highlight the links between a project and corporate purpose and values

- A skilled listener and coach/mentor who could help develop not only the project idea but also the intrapreneur to a point where they could play a leadership role in the project and become an effective advocate for sustainability within the organisation

- Someone generally open to challenge by the intrapreneur, as well as others

- An intelligent risk-taker who was prepared to bend rules to enable experimentation to achieve 'proof of concept' for an intrapreneurial project

We labelled such individuals 'godparents'. Although we recognised that this term refers to a religious role within the Christian tradition and sought a more secular synonym, we did not find a fully satisfactory alternative.[6] A 'mentor', for example, shares many of the attributes of a godparent but does not capture the full range of attributes listed above. We subsequently discovered a precedent for

---

6 When we checked the synonyms for 'godparent' on thesaurus.com, the principal synonyms were 'sponsor' and 'underwriter'. Other synonyms included advocate, backer, benefactor, patron, promoter, supporter, angel, guarantor, mainstay, surety, sustainer, another adherent, grubstaker.

using the term 'godparent' in a secular context: in the Chinese tradition the role of a godparent is largely non-religious in nature.

2. 'Woodshedding' hones skills for playing in corporate 'bands'

Many people, particularly non-musicians, believe that jazz musicians simply sit down and start producing music spontaneously without serious preparation. Nothing could be further from the truth. All jazz musicians must do their share of 'woodshedding'—developing a wide spectrum of technical skills. Jazz musicians often describe their practice as 'woodshedding' inasmuch as a musician would frequently go out to a woodshed to hone their skills in private. 'I'd had years of training as a classical pianist', says our team member Melody McLaren,

ALTO SAXOPHONIST TONY KOFI IS SHOWN PERFORMING A TRIBUTE SET TO THELONIOUS MONK WITH HIS QUARTET AT THE 2013 HERTS JAZZ FESTIVAL. KOFI EXEMPLIFIES AN EXPERIENCED SOLOIST WHO HAS DONE HIS 'WOODSHEDDING', HAVING ACQUIRED A DEEP UNDERSTANDING OF MONK'S DISTINCTIVE HARMONIC AND RHYTHMIC STYLE, BUT THEN CREATES UNIQUE MUSICAL LINES THAT REFLECT BOTH MONK'S INFLUENCE AND THE ONGOING MUSICAL 'CONVERSATION' WITH OTHER MEMBERS OF THE QUARTET (JONATHAN GEE, PIANO, BEN HAZLETON, BASS, WINSTON CLIFFORD, DRUMS).

but I had to develop a completely new set of skills for jazz—particularly listening and developing a more accurate sense of rhythm and pulse as well as getting my ear used to completely new harmonic forms—before I could join in a jazz conversation properly. It's taken me years and I'm still having to work at it.

As Stephen Keogh, a professional jazz drummer and educator who directs the Global Music Foundation says:

Jazz is a language ... one has to learn a vocabulary and grammar. Then there can be a conversation ... there are principles that must be learned, lived, memorised, and an instrument that must be mastered, plus attention to sound, pulse, intonation, repertoire, etc. This is all training and it never stops.

Arnie Somogyi, a professional bass player, bandleader and lecturer at Birmingham Conservatoire, adds:

A successful improvising musician should develop the technique required to communicate their musical 'language'. Bill Evans, for example, has a very different piano technique to Monk's, which was seen by some as primitive. But they make very different sounds on the piano. Monk's technique was integral to both his piano playing and composing.[7]

Like jazz musicians, successful social intrapreneurs have invested considerable time in technical practice of various kinds. They often have an appetite for learning that develops at an early age and continues into adulthood. As Malcolm Gladwell wrote in *Outliers: The Story of Success* (2008), 'Practice isn't the thing you do once and you're good. It's the thing you do that makes you good.'

Practice also helps you develop the intuition that enables you to 'play'—whether it's a musical instrument or performing your day-to-day job in the workplace—without having to think constantly about everything you do. Drawing on Gladwell's *Blink* (2005), our management consultant colleague Lionel Bodin has observed:

You have to work on your gut feeling. People tend to spend millions of hours looking at best option—at the end they pick their intuitive option first. People train their intuition every day ... they still need to think but still need to get confident in their intuition ... there is a link with intrapreneurship ... Intuition is listening to the environment.

Arnie Somogyi notes that this 'intuitional training' occurs 'often subconsciously. In fact we are improvising continuously in our day-to-day lives.'

Long before they become great improvisers, the best jazz musicians have spent time and effort in developing individual technical skills. Mastering an instrument requires many hours of playing scales, arpeggios and riffs to play notes fluently, in correct time and with good sound; learning about rhythm and harmonic forms and

7 See more about contrasting jazz piano styles in 'Jazz Notes – Howard Eiland', http://lit.mit.edu/lit2005-2006/spotlightarticles/jazz.html, accessed 6 December 2013.

composition structure; and internalising the shared jazz repertoire of compositions, known as jazz standards. Standards 'are an important part of the musical repertoire of jazz musicians, in that they are widely known, performed, and recorded by jazz musicians, and widely known by listeners'[8] although there is no definitive list. While classical musicians practise the works of Bach, Mozart, Beethoven and Bartok, jazz musicians practise the adapted works of Broadway theatre composers such as Irving Berlin, Cole Porter, George and Ira Gershwin, Richard Rodgers, Lorenz Hart and Oscar Hammerstein; bebop composers such as Charlie Parker, Dizzy Gillespie and Thelonious Monk; more contemporary artists such as Miles Davis, John Coltrane, Herbie Hancock and Wayne Shorter; and many others.

Arnie Somogyi adds: 'Most good jazz musicians have a varied and eclectic taste in music, which crosses genres. To paraphrase Ellington, there are two sorts of music: good and bad.'[9]

Successful social intrapreneurs have spent time learning skills associated with their own corporate specialism, whether it's marketing/communications, engineering, procurement, finance or some other business profession or function, as well as gaining an intuitive sense of how businesses work generally. They have 'learned the ropes' of how things get done in their own company, internalised the company's values (what matters most) and, crucially, how, when and where to communicate ideas in the language of their corporate peers, developing a robust 'business case' for their project ideas. They have also mastered the delicate art of balancing the behaviours of risk-taking entrepreneurs and rule-following employees within a large organisation.

3. Great intrapreneurs know how to 'jam' well with others

For jazz musicians, solitary practice is not sufficient. Jazz musicians have to develop their listening and improvisational skills by playing in groups with others—an activity known as 'jamming'—where they can try out unfamiliar harmonic or rhythmic lines with their fellow musicians in the relative safety of an informal setting.

Arnie Somogyi, an experienced composer, notes that truly novel ideas may be generated before being aired in a jam session, 'either by individuals or in rehearsals with a band where ideas are open to interpretation and "workshopping"'.

However, in preparation for 'jamming', musicians have to have done their share of 'woodshedding', as described above. Playing in a 'jam' requires a deep knowledge of jazz standards, along with a general knowledge of musical 'form'—the rhythmic and harmonic structure of jazz compositions—and, most importantly, the capacity to listen with focused attention to the music being played by other musicians in the ensemble and, in response, to communicate relevant ideas in appropriate ways. Over time, a musician who is seen to be proficient at exchanging

8 See http://en.wikipedia.org/wiki/Jazz_standard.
9 See http://jazz-quotes.com/artist/duke-ellington/.

ALTO SAXOPHONIST PERICO SAMBEAT AND PIANIST ALBERT SANZ (SHOWN WITH BASSIST ALEX DAVIS) LISTEN INTENTLY TO A DRUM SOLO BY STEPHEN KEOGH DURING THEIR QUARTET'S PERFORMANCE AT PIZZA EXPRESS DEAN STREET IN LONDON. SAMBEAT, SANZ AND KEOGH HAVE MANY YEARS' EXPERIENCE PLAYING TOGETHER IN DIFFERENT ENSEMBLES AND HAVE DEVELOPED AN INTIMATE UNDERSTANDING OF, AND TRUST IN, EACH OTHER'S PLAYING.

and transforming musical ideas will gain the trust of other musicians. They will be invited to more jam sessions or even be asked to perform in public with, and perhaps join, an ensemble.

Social intrapreneurs, like great jazz musicians, excel at exchanging and developing new ideas in informal exchanges with colleagues. Like Nobel laureate Linus Pauling, they recognise that 'The best way to have a good idea is to have lots of ideas'.

To participate successfully in the corporate equivalent of a 'jam'[10]—perhaps a brainstorm or other collective gathering (face to face or even online) where new ideas are being considered for corporate action—the social intrapreneur needs to have mastered the appropriate 'form' for exchanging new ideas in their organisation. Beyond following explicit rules that may be set down for a particular corporate meeting or gathering (e.g. withhold criticism, welcome unusual ideas, try to combine and improve ideas), this entails listening openly and responding with relevant, persuasive ideas, drawing on the social skills associated with 'emotional competence' as identified by Daniel Goleman (1998: 27).

The social intrapreneur is more likely to be heard and understood if they are working within an organisational culture that fosters open dialogue to stimulate the creative flow of ideas needed for truly innovative ideas to emerge—what we have referred to as 'café culture' (Grayson *et al.* 2013: 10). In other words, as

10 IBM has elevated the 'jam' into a corporate art; see https://www.collaborationjam.com/.

Danone's Cassiano Mecchi reported, there is freedom to 'think crazy stuff in any position and in any meeting'.

Through this 'ensemble' practice, many novel ideas can be generated and the best ones are refined to the point where they can be tested with a wider audience before they are implemented in pilot projects. Innovation is a collaborative activity that improves with practice.

4. 'Paying your dues' creates a licence to operate—and break rules

To make the transition from idea generation to project leadership, social intrapreneurs have to be trusted by their peers and by managers who control the investment of corporate resources, time and energy in projects. It helps if social intrapreneurs have, in the language of jazz, 'paid their dues'—invested time working and proving their abilities in an organisation, thereby earning their colleagues' trust—before asking for permission and help to develop a new project.

One of the giants of the jazz world, Charlie Parker (one of the founders of the 'bebop' movement) stepped up to play in a jam session at the Reno Club in Kansas City when he was only 16. He veered from the harmonic conventions of the day so wildly that Jo Jones, the drummer, threw a cymbal at him and drove him off the stage. Parker's immortal words were reputedly, 'I'll be back'. The *Guardian* critic John Fordham regarded this as such an important moment in jazz history that he selected it as one of the '50 key events in the history of jazz music' (Fordham 2011) and it has also been immortalised in Clint Eastwood's biographical film *Bird* (1988).[11] Only when Parker went to New York and began jamming at Minton's Playhouse in Harlem did he meet

> such like-minded young swing dissidents as drummer Kenny Clarke, former church pianist Thelonious Monk, Benny Goodman's star guitarist Charlie Christian and the harmonically advanced trumpeter John Birks 'Dizzy' Gillespie.[12] In the small hours at Minton's, bebop, or just bop, was forged (Fordham 2011).

---

11 Arnie Somogyi has noted that the young Parker's ejection from the stage may have been more the result of insufficient woodshedding at this stage of his development than the sheer unconventionality of his playing. He adds: 'A key part of Parker's musical development was transcription—he slowed down Lester Young solos and assimilated the jazz language therein. Having improved as a musician he was then able to sit in at jam sessions and develop his musicianship.'

12 Arnie Somogyi notes that although Charlie Parker may have a more prominent historical profile, Gillespie actually deserves more credit as a founder of the bebop movement: 'Parker was a mercurial genius but disorganised with a serious drug habit, whereas Dizzy incorporated all sorts of new influences into his music and managed to run the big band in which many important figures in the development of bebop flourished. Parker's compositional output was mainly restricted to written solos over 'standard' sequences, which then became 'heads'. By contrast Dizzy wrote new and innovative material. People like to think of Parker as an inventor because it fits with the myth of eccentric, tortured genius.'

Parker, in short, had been 'paying his dues' alongside other musicians, as well as developing his own musicianship skills. Only by working things out together in an organic way, over time, could the old rules be broken.

We found that aspiring social intrapreneurs were more likely to run into difficulties launching their ideas if they had not been in their companies very long. Conversely, those who have had the most long-lived intrapreneurial careers in their companies are those who have 'paid their dues'. Jo da Silva spent years developing her reputation as an engineer within Arup before making her bid to begin Arup International Development. Chris Harrop joined Marshalls UK as a marketing director and established himself successfully in that role, earning the trust of the board, before embarking on his ambitious Fairstone project. Dorje Mundle was an established PricewaterhouseCoopers (PwC) consultant working with pharmaceutical clients (and had worked at Shell and Novo Nordisk before that) before joining Novartis and getting 'permission from the top' to develop a game-changing bottom-of-the-pyramid business model.

5. Intrapreneurs 'comp' for others as well as 'soloing'

The jazz musicians in our extended team have experienced 'that thing in jazz where you have someone who does five choruses, and then everyone is lost! Usually a front-line instrumentalist'. Skilled jazz musicians are great at both 'comping' (accompanying other band members) and 'soloing' (playing their own interpretation of a jazz tune). Listening, as well as speaking clearly, are both essential skills for a great jazz 'conversation'.

Similarly, successful social intrapreneurs tend to be great communicators, unlike out-of-control 'soloists' who 'preach' about sustainability without hearing the needs of the business. Social intrapreneurs 'listen' to what others in the business say they need, 'accompanying' them as needed. Only then do they 'speak' about their ideas—always in ways that make sense to others, particularly senior decision-makers who control needed resources. They practise and refine their listening/comping and speaking/soloing skills over time.

In this vein, Arnie Somogyi cites the work of jazz trumpeter, bandleader and composer Miles Davis, considered one of the most influential musicians of the 20th century:

> Miles was great at putting 'teams' together. He employed the musicians who could move the music into new directions without it sounding contrived. All of Miles' bands were innovative but came out of a tradition with reference points to what had been done previously.

When everyone in the corporate 'band' is adept at 'soloing' and 'comping'– playing with ideas already put forward by other band members and helping new ones to emerge—the collaborative whole becomes more than the sum of its parts.

6. Intrapreneurs excel at being 'sidemen' as well as 'bandleaders'

In jazz, a 'sideman' is anyone in a band who is not the bandleader. 'Sidemen are generally required to be adaptable to many different styles of music, and so able to fit smoothly into the group in which they are currently playing.'[13]

Similarly, successful social intrapreneurism depends not just on a single individual but on a team—sometimes a small ensemble, sometimes a more highly-orchestrated 'big band'—all of whom have done their 'woodshedding', excel in their own disciplines as well as being adept at collaborating with others as 'sidemen' or 'bandleaders', to bring ideas to fruition in new products or services.

We can illustrate how these metaphors can work by applying them to a specific social intrapreneur.

Jo da Silva, Director, Arup International Development

From an early age Jo da Silva was learning the fundamental lesson of jazz music-making: life is 'not a solo act' but is lived in community with others:

Jo da Silva was born in 1967 in Washington, DC, while her father was on diplomatic assignment to the United States. From an early age she absorbed her parents' love of travel as well as what she describes as 'pre-war values', which emphasise the importance of community and contributing to society, careful use of resources and earning a living (vs. making money).

Jo did her early 'woodshedding' in the form of academic work at Cambridge. But she also travelled abroad, acquiring a working knowledge of life in developing countries that would serve her in the years ahead:

Jo's love of designing and making things led her to choose engineering as a profession. However, her parents' tales of exotic places inspired her to intersperse academic work at Cambridge with travel adventures in Turkey, the Middle East and India.

Poverty relief work enables Jo to apply her technical skills to real-world projects, improvising practical solutions with others ('jamming') in the context of practising generosity towards other human beings on a day-to-day basis. This experience would develop the social intelligence needed for being a 'sideman' or a 'bandleader' in collaborative projects:

After graduating she returned to live in India—building a clinic and a water supply as well as undertaking other projects—'living right up against nature in its raw and beautiful form ... where humanity is there in three dimensions, floodlit every day'.

---

13 http://en.wikipedia.org/wiki/Sideman.

The Indian experience proved pivotal in heightening Jo's awareness of the interdependence of human beings and their environment, shaping her desire to develop and apply her engineering skills to solving societal problems. She joined Arup as a graduate engineer, inspired by founder Ove Arup's emphasis on humanitarianism and doing rewarding, interesting work.

Next we see Jo performing as both a 'sideman' (part of the Arup Sustainable Task Force) as well as continuing to develop and apply her technical skills inside the company ('paying her dues' inside Arup as well as in poverty relief organisations) and outside the company in post-disaster relief projects:

In parallel with her engineering career, Jo began undertaking post-disaster relief projects. The psychological impact of the first—constructing refugee camps in Tanzania after the Rwandan genocide in 1994—'marked the beginning of the end of mainstream engineering' for Jo. She joined an Arup Sustainable Task Force formed by a board director who was 'looking for people to be activists, not corporate animals'.

Jo begins to perform as a project 'bandleader', recruiting her own 'sidemen' and building a small 'ensemble':

Jo co-led a building engineering group that focused on creating social infrastructure such as schools and libraries mostly for public-sector clients in deprived urban area, growing the team from 6 to 35 people in three years.

Now Jo leads a massive 'big band' and orchestrates a large-scale disaster relief 'performance' outside the firm:

Although Jo had conducted her post-disaster recovery activities separately from her work projects, the Tsunami disaster of 2004 proved a major turning point. She was invited by UNHCR, the UN Refugee Agency, to co-ordinate post-disaster shelter construction in Sri Lanka with approximately 100 NGOs, building 60,000 shelters in six months.

But she then bids to start and lead her own 'band', drawing on the full range of her technical and management skills:

Determined to create a focus within Arup to address poverty and vulnerability in developing countries, Jo wrote directly to the chairman and engaged senior directors, appealing to them to recognise a new opportunity to fulfil Arup's mission 'to shape a better world' by creating a consultancy business within the firm focused on development work.

Importantly, Jo framed this project as a business (vs. a philanthropic) venture:

> I did not ask Arup for resources. From the outset I was clear that Arup International Development would need to operate as a self-sustainable business, albeit operating on lower margins than our commercial businesses and on a not-for-profit basis.

By persuading Arup management that this would complement Arup's charitable activities and enable them to make a greater and more professional contribution to alleviating poverty, Jo was able to establish Arup International Development, which harnesses Arup's skills and networks to provide affordable strategic advice and technical expertise exclusively to organisations seeking to improve social well-being and reduce vulnerability in developing countries.

Now she is a 'bandleader' in charge of a 'crossover' ensemble that is creating an entirely new repertoire in the social intrapreneurism domain:

Starting with three months of funding, she has now grown Arup International Development into a thriving entity within the group, offering services spanning urban development, water and sanitation, disaster risk reduction, climate-change adaption, shelter and education.

I don't feel brave, I feel lucky that I've got skills that can be put to use and make a real difference ... I couldn't work for a company that's making money for third-party shareholders. [With a] social conscience, you've got to make money but making money is not the *raison d'être*.

From the single narrative of this social intrapreneur we can distil a number of parallels between jazz and social intrapreneurism (Table 1).

Table 1 Jazz activities and social intrapreneurism

Jazz activities	Social intrapreneurism activities
Woodshedding. Learning your musical craft, often through solitary practice, as a foundation for ensemble playing	**Learning the ropes.** Acquiring in-depth knowledge of your specialist 'craft' or profession as a foundation for playing a productive role in the business and wider society
Being a good sideman. Learning to 'comp' (accompany) others in your ensemble as well as 'soloing' (expressing your own musical ideas)	**Learning to be a team player.** Supporting other colleagues in your team as well as getting to lead projects
Jamming. Trying out and developing ideas with others	**Brainstorming.** Developing your own ideas with support and feedback from them in informal settings
Paying your dues. Earning the trust and respect of fellow musicians	**Building a licence to operate.** Earning the trust of colleagues in the business and others in your wider personal network
Becoming a bandleader. Recruiting musicians to a new ensemble	**Becoming a project leader.** Engaging a small team to establish proof of concept via a pilot social intrapreneurism project
Composing and performing. Creating new pieces for fellow band members to perform and others to enjoy	**Piloting a project.** Testing a new strategy to creates social and/or environmental value, as well as commercial value for the company
Launching a large-scale music project, such as a big band or a festival involving many people	**Taking a pilot project to scale.** Engaging a large number of colleagues and/or partners beyond the company

Generally, we have found that jazz metaphors have helped us to re-frame our observations of social intrapreneurism, and business activities more generally, in new and useful ways. Our Accenture colleague Lionel Bodin, a management consultant who has also led jazz bands of his own, has pointed out, for example, that while the management literature is full of sporting metaphors that focus on competitiveness, winning and the importance of individual leaders, jazz metaphors emphasise the value of cooperation and provide a more nuanced view of leadership (as in the example of sidemen who demonstrate excellence, not only in their individual instrumental disciplines but also in their capacity to listen and contribute to a greater musical 'whole').

A DEEP UNDERSTANDING OF JAZZ FORM, COMBINED WITH MASTERY OF ONE'S INSTRUMENT AND A CAPACITY FOR LISTENING TO OTHERS, CAN ENABLE THE INDIVIDUALS IN AN ENSEMBLE TO PERFORM TOGETHER IN A COMPARATIVELY SHORT TIME. THIS STUDENT COMBO, DRAWN FROM COUNTRIES AROUND THE WORLD, PERFORMED IN THE FINAL CONCERT OF THE 2013 GLOBAL MUSIC FOUNDATION LONDON JAZZ WORKSHOP IN KINGS PLACE HALL TWO AFTER HAVING BEEN TOGETHER ONLY FIVE DAYS UNDER THE GUIDANCE OF NEW YORK PIANIST BRUCE BARTH. LEFT TO RIGHT: JIN YE (PIANO), DUNCAN ALLBROOKE (GUITAR), COLE DAVIS (BASS), LUIGI VENTIMIGLIA (TRUMPET), VÍCTOR JIMÉNEZ GÓMEZ (ALTO), SCOTT HUGH DUFF (DRUMS), ACHIM KUHN (TENOR).

SIMILARLY, SOCIAL INTRAPRENEURS WITH A DEEP UNDERSTANDING OF THEIR OWN COMPANY'S PURPOSE AND VALUES, WHO HAVE MASTERED THEIR OWN 'DAY JOBS' AND HAVE 'PAID THEIR DUES' SUFFICIENTLY TO EARN THE TRUST OF OTHERS, CAN COLLABORATE WITH COLLEAGUES AND OTHER PARTNERS AROUND THE WORLD ON NEW PROJECTS.

This emphasis on collectivism also chimes well with Eastern cultural themes, particularly the emphasis in Chinese corporate responsibility on achieving a 'harmonious society' about which we have written in *Ethical Corporation* (Grayson 2013). While written from largely Western perspectives and with mainly Western examples, social intrapreneurism fits well with the increasing emphasis on the great Asian philosophical traditions in modern management theory and practice in China, India and other fast-growing global economies.

Throughout this book we will use these metaphors to bring to life the distinctive mind-sets, behaviours and skills of social intrapreneurs as well as the key features of the 'enabling environment' for social intrapreneurism that have been identified through our interviews with intrapreneurs and their colleagues as well as other experts in the field of corporate social innovation.

Our ambition: to create a new 'jazz scene' for social intrapreneurism

Like the co-founders of the bebop movement that revolutionised jazz, our aspiration is to start a business revolution by creating a new type of 'jazz scene'. We want to build a global 'community of practice' (Lave and Wenger 1991) around social intrapreneurism, enabling corporate practitioners, academics, NGOs and other interested parties to continue to develop, share and apply our collective learning to enhance the quality and scale of social intrapreneurism.

As with jazz musicians, the success of our community will depend on the commitment of our members to achieving excellence in their respective disciplines through a foundation of 'woodshedding'; a capacity for 'listening' to the ideas of others, often working in fields or sectors different from our own; a willingness to serve as 'sidemen' in collaborative 'ensembles', 'comping' for other 'soloists' who take centre stage to present new ideas; and an ongoing awareness of the ever-changing conditions that enable, or disable, intrapreneurial projects to come to fruition, working to keep the intrapreneurial spirit alive where we can.

Figure 1 A jazz social network
Source: Gleiser and Danon (2003).

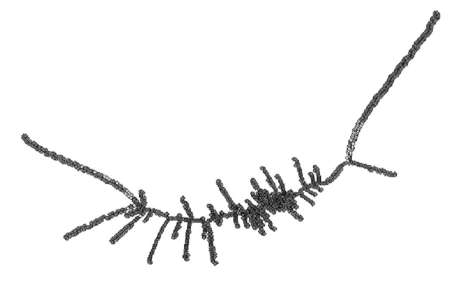

The social network diagram in Figure 1 is illustrative of how, irrespective of the merits of the work of individuals, the external 'enabling environment' can wield massive, sometimes unseen, power. Based on The Red Hot Jazz Archive, a digital database of jazz bands that performed between 1912 and 1940, this diagram depicts the shape of the jazz community during this period, based on who was collaborating with whom. While Stephen Keogh notes that successful musicians ought to 'have good listening skills, consider team work and attention to quality as indispensable', suggesting, quite sensibly, that the best musicians should be playing with each other, what emerges is that the jazz community was, in the first half of the 20th century, split along racial lines. In Figure 1, musicians on the left are black while the musicians on the right are white.

We must therefore be committed to seeking out, engaging and nurturing social intrapreneurs and other aspiring change-makers, whoever and wherever they are—hence the dedication at the beginning of this book.

To achieve this, we hope to inspire many more people already in business, as well as those who are planning to work in business, so that they can achieve significant social impact, personal satisfaction and maybe even individual success by becoming, or supporting others to become, social intrapreneurs.

We also want to convince current and future business leaders of the value of promoting an enabling environment for social intrapreneurism in their organisations, as an integral part of their innovation and new business development; the better management of their social, environmental and economic impacts; and creating a great place to work—in short, a business that 'buzzes' like a jazz club but is also built to last.

We want to persuade non-governmental organisations (NGOs) and international development agencies to think more expansively about their relationships with big business; and to challenge business schools and schools of public policy to introduce the role of social intrapreneurs into their research and teaching.

We welcome all like-minded 'cats' who want to join our virtual 'band'. The jam starts now!

How this book is organised

The model in Figure 2 gives an overview of the central argument of this book and thus explains what will follow.

Figure 2 How this book is organised

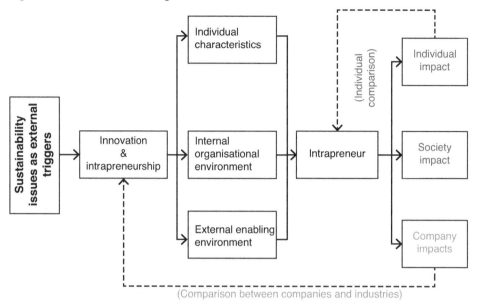

(Comparison between companies and industries)

We will start our jam session by looking at the sustainability issues that are taken as external triggers for innovation (Chapter 1). Social intrapreneurs perceive global challenges such as financial inclusion, water scarcity and regional development not as problems, but as an inspiration for innovation. This leads to innovations that on one side create value for the company and on the other create social or environmental benefits for society.

Social intrapreneurism and sustainable innovations depend, however, on a number of factors. First, the characteristics of the individual—our social intrapreneurs. Which mind-set, skills and attitudes drive their behaviour? In how far are they different from the ordinary corporate population? What are the different types of social intrapreneur? Is there something common in their journey from having an idea, to piloting, to scaling it? These questions will guide us in Chapter 2.

The second important aspect for having success with social intrapreneurism rests with the internal organisational environment. Chapter 3 looks at how corporations react once a social intrapreneur becomes active and suggests a business case for companies to support social intrapreneurism. Chapter 4 focuses on what is a truly enabling internal environment. It suggests this depends on corporate strategy, leadership, organisational culture and structures, access to resources, as well as human relations. The better the organisational support for social intrapreneurs, the higher the chances for new ideas to emerge and become successful in the marketplace. A lack of support might cause the social intrapreneur to leave the organisation and try to sell the idea elsewhere.

The third important aspect is the external enabling environment. We have seen many social intrapreneurs collaborating with NGOs, development organisations and other external partners in their innovation projects. This marks a major difference from traditional intrapreneurs, who do not or seldom collaborate with these actors in their projects. Chapter 5 explains how social intrapreneurs harvest good relationships with non-traditional stakeholders.

Once a social intrapreneur has an idea inspired by social and environmental challenges and is able to explore that idea further within an enabling internal and external environment, we can expect some results and impacts. These impacts are detailed in Chapter 6, detailing how their projects helped social intrapreneurs with their careers (or not). Of course, social intrapreneurs compare their career advancement with others in the organisation but they also have other considerations. An important aspect in business is exploring how social intrapreneurism creates value for the company (tangible and intangible), and how these projects compare to other innovation projects or other companies aiming to use sustainability issues as leverage for innovation. Finally, we explore the legacy that the innovations brought forward by social intrapreneurs leave in society.

With these first six chapters we explain the relatively new phenomenon of social intrapreneurism. Obviously, we have learned a lot during the last few years in researching the topic, talking to social intrapreneurs and their godparents, engaging with specialists and piloting programmes aiming to help social intrapreneurs to have more success with their ideas. Chapter 7 therefore gives some recommendations based on our collected insights and experiences especially to social intrapreneurs and managers.

When Muhammad Yunus founded the Grameen Bank in 1983 nobody was talking social entrepreneurship. When Grameen received the Peace Nobel Prize in 2006 *everybody* was talking social entrepreneurship. Today few people are talking social intrapreneurism. However, we feel that we are at the beginning of a new era in which people start being change-makers in their everyday jobs, leveraging their organisation's capabilities to address social and environmental issues innovatively. Therefore, Chapter 8 provides an outlook on how this future might come about. Already today we can see the formation of various networks, but much more can be done in terms of connecting people, inspiring others, developing social intrapreneurs and supporting research.

In our Conclusion, we will wrap it all up in our last song during this gig. We might have spotted the beginning of a completely new way of doing business with social intrapreneurism. A way that uses the power of business for good. However, this movement, our 'big band', needs many more gigs to happen all around the world. We look forward to seeing you on stage.

1

How social intrapreneurs are rising to global business and social challenges

Business today faces multiple 'mega-challenges'. These include:

- Difficult, on-going trading conditions in many parts of the world, in the aftermath of the 2008 global financial crisis and the Eurozone crisis

- How to reconcile the new business opportunities from the forecast three billion extra middle-consumers by 2030 with planetary constraints, so that nine billion people can live reasonably well within the constraints of one planet by 2050

- The threat to social and political stability from growing global and local inequalities, which business is seen to exacerbate with 'winner takes all' executive compensation packages

- Being persistently invited to contribute to fulfilment of the new UN Sustainable Development Goals

- A lack of trust in many institutions, including business, as illustrated by the annual Edelman Trust Barometer

- Intensifying market-place competition intensified by global connectivity and disruptive business models

- The era of the 'Naked Corporation' (see Tapscott 2003) where 'everything is for the record' and information and communications technologies, including social media, enforce greater corporate transparency and accountability
- At least for the global young talent who want to 'take their whole selves to work', a sense that their loyalty is conditional and has to be earned and re-earned by employers

Unsurprisingly, in the face of such complexity, business is often floundering and searching for new sources of innovation, insight and means of connectivity with employees and wider society. This is the global context in which social intrapreneurism and corporate social innovation is emerging.

Global challenges as opportunities for profitable social innovation

These myriad global challenges, although numerous, create opportunities for social intrapreneurs. The divides and opportunities listed in Table 1.1, set out initially by SustainAbility (2007) and enlarged from 10 to 15 by our team, describe the realities of challenges faced in many parts of the world—but they can equally be perceived as opportunities for innovation.

Table 1.1 Global divides and opportunities

Divides	Realities	Opportunities
1 **Demographics**	The world is heading to a population of 9 billion by 2050, with 95% of growth expected in developing countries. Just under 11% of the world's people are over 60. By 2050 that share will have risen to 22% (of a population of 9 billion), and in developed countries to 33%[1]	To meet the needs of billions of people affected by market failures in both developing and developed countries
2 **Financial**	40% of the world's wealth is owned by 1% of the population while the poorest 50% can claim just 1% of the wealth (Randerson 2006)	Help the have-nots become bankable, insurable and entrepreneurial

1   UN Department of Economic and Social Affairs, Population Division (2012) 'World Population Prospects: The 2012 Revision', http://esa.un.org/wpp/index.htm.

3 **Nutritional**	The world now produces enough food for everyone, but over 840 million people still face chronic hunger every day[2]	Address the needs of those with too little food—or too much
4 **Resources**	60% of ecosystem services, such as fresh water and climate regulation, are being degraded or used unsustainably[3]	Enable development that uses the earth's resources in a sustainable way
5 **Environmental**	The loss of biodiversity, droughts and the destruction of coral reefs are just some of the challenges facing the globe	Create markets that protect and enhance the environment
6 **Health**	Some 34 million people live with HIV/AIDS in the world,[4] now the sixth largest killer disease[5]	Create markets that encourage healthy lifestyles and enable equal access to healthcare
7 **Gender**	Two-thirds of the world's 1 billion illiterate people are women[6]	Enable and empower women to participate equally and fairly in society and the economy
8 **Educational**	More than 57 million children around the world do not go to primary school. At least 250 million children cannot read or count[7]	Provide the mechanisms to transfer and share knowledge and learning that empowers all levels of societies
9 **Digital**	Global internet usage up 566% 2000–12 (2.4 billion June 2012: 34% world) only 16% penetration in Africa[8]	Develop inclusive technology that enables all levels of society to tackle each of these divides more effectively

2   UN World Food Programme, 'Hunger Statistics', http://www.wfp.org/hunger/stats.

3   United Nations Environment Programme, 'Millennium Ecosystem Assessment', http://www.unep .org/maweb/en/condition.aspx, accessed 7 January 2014.

4   World Health Organization, Global Health Observatory, 'HIV/AIDS', http://www.who.int/gho/hiv/ en/, accessed 7 January 2014.

5   World Health Organization, 'The Top 10 Causes of Death', Fact sheet no. 310, updated July 2013, http://who.int/mediacentre/factsheets/fs310/en/, accessed 7 January 2014.

6   UNESCO, Education, 'Statistics on Literacy', http://www.unesco.org/new/en/education/themes/ education-building-blocks/literacy/resources/statistics/, accessed 7 January 2014.

7   DFID (Department for International Development) 'Making Sure Children in Developing Countries Get a Good Education', Gov.UK, 11 October 2013, https://www.gov.uk/government/policies/ making-sure-children-in-developing-countries-get-a-good-education, accessed 5 November 2013.

8   Internet World Stats (2012) 'Internet Usage Statistics: The Internet Big Picture', http://www.internet worldstats.com/stats.htm, accessed 5 November 2013.

10 Security	The deadliest conflicts in the world are concentrated in Central and South Asia and the Middle East and North Africa (HSRP 2012). Africa and Asia account for 8.8 million of over 10.5 million refugees and displaced people (UNHCR 2013)	Work to promote security and reduce conflict based on inequity and exclusion
11 **Local economic development and unemployment**	A record 202 million people could be unemployed across the world in 2013; nearly 13% of those under 24 were unemployed (Rushe 2013)	Creating social inclusive business models which provide jobs and support new and existing businesses
12 **Mobility**	More than 1 billion cars in world 2010 (Sousanis 2011)	Connecting and integrating mobility solutions, e.g. that allow a smart use of existing infrastructure
13 **Sustainable consumption**	McKinsey & Co (2013): Circular Economy offers materials savings in Europe that could be worth $380 billion in an initial transition period and up to $630 billion with full adoption	Innovating products and services which bring a better quality of life while minimising the use of natural resources as well as emissions and waste
14 **Urbanisation**	Urban population will almost double, increasing from approximately 3.4 billion in 2009 to 6.4 billion in 2050 when 70% world population will be urban[9]	Developing businesses and well-being in rural regions in order to reduce migration to the world's mega-cities and by providing low-cost services and facilities to urban dwellers
15 **Green energy**	World energy consumption predicted to grow 56% by 2040 (US EIA 2013)	Making better use of renewable energy sources by making renewable energy more available and, where possible, by copying nature (biomimicry)

---

9 World Health Organization, Global Health Observatory, 'Urban Population Growth', http://www .who.int/gho/urban_health/situation_trends/urban_population_growth_text/en/, accessed 7 January 2014.

Consider how social intrapreneur Vijay Sharma's Shakti initiative at Hindustan Unilever, India's largest fast moving consumer goods company, addressed the financial and gender divides outlined above. Shakti means 'power' in Sanskrit and its primary aim is to empower Indian women to become micro-entrepreneurs by distributing the company's products such as detergents, toilet soaps and shampoos in small rural villages.

Hindustan Unilever recognised that investing in the income generation of the rural poor was critical to expanding its reach and increasing sales. Starting with 17 women in one state, the programme grew to create employment opportunities for over 40,000 women entrepreneurs in 15 states in 2013, providing access to quality products across more than 100,000 villages and over 3 million households every month.

The initiative has, according to Vijay, overcome the 'barriers that strip people of dignity, and strip business of opportunity' (quoted from one of the interviewees in SustainAbility 2008) Susheela, a participant in the programme, captured the essence of its impact on women entrepreneurs: 'When the people see me, they crowd around me and call me "Shakti amma". I am someone today' (Wright 2008: 26).

Unilever have committed to increasing the number of Shakti entrepreneurs that the company recruits, trains and employs to 75,000 in 2015.[10]

Imagine how companies following Hindustan Unilever's example could contribute to bridging the divides listed in Table 1.1. How Banco Santander could narrow the financial, Danone the nutritional, Novartis the health and Microsoft the digital divides. Happily, each of these companies—and many others—is beginning to see the potential.

What is interesting about social intrapreneurs is that despite the enormous scale of these challenges, they have engaged with them in ways that are relevant to their personal experiences, skills and networks and that evolve organically over time. By 'listening' with deep awareness to the wider social and environmental context in which their companies operate, social intrapreneurs can begin to improvise solutions—working initially in small 'ensembles' on pilot projects—that can be tested to establish their viability and possibly adapted for 'big band' orchestration over time.

Shortly before his death, the 'father of modern management', Peter F. Drucker, observed: 'Every single social and global issue of our day is a business opportunity in disguise.'

Table 1.2 shows how social intrapreneurs are helping to reveal the business opportunities disguised within social and global issues.

---

10 http://www.hul.co.in/sustainable-living/casestudies/Casecategory/Project-Shakti.aspx, accessed 6 December 2013.

Table 1.2 Global challenges and social intrapreneurial response

	Issue	Social intrapreneur	Profile page nos.
Social	Digital inclusion	Arun Pande, Tata Consultancy Services	44–45
	Disease/access to medicines	Graham Simpson, GSK Dorje Mundle, Novartis	45–47
	Children/workplace human rights	Chris Harrop, Marshalls	43–44
	Homelessness	James Inglesby, Unilever	51
	Obesity/nutrition	Lucas Urbano, Danone	135
	NGO capacity building/civil society	Gib Bulloch, Accenture Development Partnerships	83–88
	Ageing and demographics	Julika Erfurt, Accenture	149–50
Environmental	Climate change	Hugh Saddington, Telstra Carrina Gaffney, *The Guardian*	39–41 42
	Water and resource depletion	Priscila Matta, Natura Emma Stewart, Autodesk	89–93 172
	Pollution and waste	Tom van den Nieuwenhuijzen, Van Nieuwpoort Group	51–52
	Green energy	Roberto Bocca, BP Stefan Koch, E.ON Mandar Apte, Shell Mark Siebert, Siemens Emma Clarke, Cavendish Nuclear	34–35 64–66 127–28 41–42 61–64
	Biodiversity loss	Marijn Wiersma, FMO	54–55
Economic	Local economic development and unemployment	Vijay Sharma, Unilever, Shakti Ian Mackintosh, SABMiller	27 35–37
	Mobility	Kenan Aksular, Athlon	66–67
	Sustainable consumption	Karl Feilder, DHL	59–61
	Poverty	Michael Anthony, Allianz Nick Hughes, Vodafone M-PESA	29–31 70–75
	Urbanisation	Jo da Silva, Arup	15–17
	Education	Paul Ellingstad, HP	37–39

Rectifying social inequalities through inclusive business solutions

Much of the work of social intrapreneurs focuses on redressing the inequalities that often arise in the developing world in terms of access to food, water and shelter as well as other basic necessities. Through the development of innovative business products and services, often in partnership with local organisations, companies can help re-engage excluded consumers at the 'bottom of the pyramid' (BoP), a concept popularised by writers such as the late C.K. Prahalad (2004).

We found that the majority of those we interviewed were engaged in 'inclusive business' (creating sustainable livelihoods and providing affordable goods and services for low-income communities), reducing resource consumption and mitigating the impacts of climate change. Social intrapreneurs do not necessarily need to scale their initiatives themselves, as the small changes they instigate inside big organisations can have an immediate impact on thousands—and in some cases, millions—of people. Let us examine some of these examples in more detail.

Michael Anthony, Allianz: providing microinsurance for the poor

Michael Anthony, who was originally a journalist reporting on social problems, wanted to do something that had a long-term impact. His personal inspiration was the work of his aunt, who lived in Sao Paulo and worked with childcare centres in a favela, Monte Azul. He was interested initially by an offer made by Allianz to found a social network. As the result of interviewing the company CEO, he established a high-level contact. Three months later, he secured a job as an Allianz project manager with a corporate social responsibility focus.

Over the next year he focused on climate change, helping to research and produce a report on how insurers could manage the associated risks (Kesting and Anthony 2007).

The social challenge: creating financial viability at the 'bottom of the pyramid'

Significant numbers of people in countries such as Egypt, India, Indonesia, Colombia and the sub-Saharan African nations of Cameroon, Senegal and Madagascar are living at the 'bottom of the pyramid', living on less than US$2 per day. They have no access to conventional financial services that would help them become bankable, insurable and entrepreneurial.

The business challenge: managing the risks of increasing natural catastrophes

The risk report that Michael produced for Allianz identified the risks of climate change for the company, as well as for the insurance industry as a whole:

For both Allianz and Dresdner Bank, earth warming has long become a matter of business. Regardless of whether it is insurance, emissions trading, asset management or project financing, many areas of activity need to take into consideration the effects of climate change (Kesting and Anthony 2007: 4).

The solution: partnership to offer microinsurance for the poor

In the wake of the 2004 Indian Ocean tsunami, a special fund was established which Michael decided should be used for more than just philanthropy. He then worked 'under the radar', outside his 'day job', with CARE, which had extensive experience with disaster relief programmes, to set up a microinsurance fund and also with Deutsche Gesellschaft für Internationale Zusammenarbeit (GIZ) (formerly GTZ) on developing public–private partnerships in Indonesia.

He developed a strong case for investing in the project, noting a range of business and socioeconomic benefits, including:

ASPIRING SOCIAL INTRAPRENEURS CAN LEARN FROM THE EXAMPLE OF GREAT JAZZ MUSICIANS WHO ACQUIRE SKILLS OUTSIDE THE NARROW BOUNDARIES OF THEIR 'DAY JOBS'. HERE, GLOBAL MUSIC FOUNDATION TUTORS SWAP INSTRUMENTS IN A 2008 JAM SESSION IN CERTALDO, ITALY: TRUMPETER KEVIN DEAN PLAYS PIANO, BASSIST ARNIE SOMOGYI PLAYS GUITAR AND PIANIST GREG BURK PLAYS DRUMS.

- Microinsurance helps the poor, low-income people and lower middle class to build up financial stability and a solid livelihood
- There is a high demand for microinsurance throughout the world
- Product communication and distribution are best done in collaboration with local partners
- Mutual product development is the best way to target the customer and create a great demand for microinsurances
- Allianz creates economically viable and cost-effective products
- Belonging to the first movers, Allianz can actively shape the microinsurance market

As a result, Michael's full-time job became managing Allianz partnerships with microfinance organisations that managed the contact between insurance and customers. Allianz and each partner would analyse what people in a particular market needed. The microfinance organisations and NGOs helped to shape a new product that could be sold via the microfinance institutions. Allianz would underwrite the insurance risks.

While it is difficult to measure social impact accurately, Allianz microinsurance commitments as of June 2013 had grown to encompass 11 markets with the number of microinsured lives totalling 23.6 million in Asia, 200,000 in Africa, 300,000 in Latin America, as well as additional microinsurance policies covering assets in these regions (Allianz 2013).

What is apparent from this account is that Michael has done his 'woodshedding'—initially as a journalist investigating social problems and then specialising in the climate change field. He did his 'jamming' to test out collaborative 'music-making' with new partners (CARE and GTZ [now GIZ]) before establishing a new 'cross-over band' within the growing microinsurance domain.

Dorje Mundle, Novartis: orchestrating a healthy business at the 'bottom of the pyramid'

Dorje Mundle attributes his interest in 'the deep questions in life' to his upbringing in a family who were interested in philosophy and belief systems, engaging him from an early age in discussions of Buddhism and Christianity.

And like other social intrapreneurs we interviewed, Dorje also developed an early interest in nature, with David Attenborough's television wildlife documentary programmes awakening an interest in zoology and biology.

Both sets of experiences were perceived as major formative influences:

> Those were the biggest things—passion around wildlife and nature—and then interest in belief systems but also questions about morality. And then, at university, understanding what is the impact of humans on biodiversity, economies, populations, weather patterns, etc. Lots of moral questions about equity, intergenerational justice and so forth.

Embedded in these experiences would have been unusual forms of conceptual 'woodshedding' and 'jamming':

- Not only being exposed to contrasting religious/spiritual belief systems (versus being exposed to only one) but also learning how to evaluate and apply them, in dialogue with others
- Not only being exposed to biological facts but also absorbing such underpinning biological principles as evolution, homeostasis and the interdependence of life forms in ecosystems

Just before university came the sort of life-changing experience that a number of social intrapreneurs have reported:

> In my gap year [1991], I spent six months in India on a social project equipping homeless women in slums with skills to sustain a livelihood. Then I travelled around India and was exposed to poverty and other social issues.

After India, Dorje went on to Reading University where he studied zoology. He then started work as an ecologist and conservation biologist, doing environmental impact assessments in a corporate environment: 'That pitched me into the sustainability stakes ... I got more interested and involved in bigger picture issues—corporate environmental policy, environmental economics, environmental law—for 3½ years.'

Next came another round of 'woodshedding'—education at a more advanced academic level: 'I then went to do the Imperial College MSc, which had a lot of these broader components in the curriculum. At that point I started working actively on climate change.'

After spells with an oil company, a consulting firm and a pharmaceutical company, in 2008 Dorje moved to Novartis in Switzerland where he became Group Head of Corporate Citizenship Management.

Novartis is a multinational healthcare products company that operates in 140 countries around the world. Its diversified portfolio includes innovative medicines, cost-saving generic pharmaceuticals, preventive vaccines, diagnostic tools and consumer health products.

The social challenge: providing products and services to people at the BoP

In *The Fortune at the Bottom of the Pyramid*, Prahalad (2004) identified the billions of people across the world who earn less than $2 a day as potential consumers and entrepreneurs at the 'bottom of the pyramid'. They had traditionally been largely ignored in global companies' business strategies because it is more difficult to operate profitable businesses targeting these groups than those on higher incomes. Prahalad called on businesses, governments and donor agencies to stop thinking of the poor as victims and instead start seeing them as resilient and creative entrepreneurs, as well as value-demanding consumers. He believed that by working with civil society organisations and local governments to create new local business models, multinationals could help reduce poverty.

The business challenge: serving the BoP sustainably

For Novartis, as for other global companies, engaging people at the BoP as producers or consumers in profitable ways has proved extremely challenging. Responses to date have included microcredit schemes; use of electronic networks to remove inefficiencies in the agricultural supply chain; new products tailored to meet the needs of the extremely poor; social and commercial venture capital funds to develop BoP products and services; and business–community partnerships to offer new services in BoP markets.

The social intrapreneur's solution: a business model that creates positive social and commercial impact

In his new role at Novartis, Dorje worked with like-minded colleagues to drive a fundamental strategic shift in the way corporate responsibility was managed in the company, with the help of a 'godparent' manager who helped prepare him for his leadership role. With his extensive 'woodshedding' experience working in different industry sectors, as well as his education, behind him, Dorje began creating an entirely new approach to corporate responsibility in Novartis—comparable to founding a new jazz genre:

> I was brought in and charged with helping drive the CR agenda in Novartis in a new direction. Built on a strong philanthropic pro bono platform around drug donations and pro bono research on neglected diseases, this was about being much more strategic and business aligned and integrated—connecting CR with broader value drivers. Be innovation-driven in that approach. Big focus on business innovation.

India has a population of 830 million people living in rural areas and 65% have no access to basic healthcare products. Most people live on less than US$3.00 a day. At the same time, 80% of all healthcare spending in India is going to the private sector, which makes the country highly attractive for healthcare providers. Confronted with this challenge, Dorje states:

> There is no magic silver bullet and no one-size-fits-all solution. We learned from our philanthropic activities that you need to work in partnership with others. It's not about simply donating medicines in a country where local doctors do not always know how to apply the medicine or where the water you drink in order to take pills is contaminated.

One of Novartis' 'Shared Value Initiatives' in India currently provides access to healthcare for 42 million people across 33,000 villages in 10 Indian states. The initiative also educates roughly 4 million rural patients on health care issues each year. According to Dorje, 'the initiative returned modest profits within 30 months—it is a high-volume, low-margin business model'. Following these positive results, Novartis is now replicating analogous models in 12 African and Asian countries.

Like a great jazz bandleader, Dorje described the key to his team's success as being 'not about me but about having bright, engaged intelligent business people'. He characterised his role as:

> something of an orchestrator. I have too many diverse responsibilities to go too deep into individual projects. This is a global role. It's about making sure the right people are involved with the right skills and capabilities, right time, right processes.

And he had ambitions to build a really big 'band' and 'compose' pieces in an entirely new style:

> It's not enough for me to have just me and an engaged CR team—if you build this into the mind-set and drive of the broader commercial organisation, you can start doing things on a fundamentally different scale.
>
> Going forward, puling this together, would like to raise our aspiration levels as an organisation ... Some what we're doing now is great but we have a couple of orders of magnitude of additional impact we can achieve if we harness this in a smart way. We're now better positioned to do that now than we ever have been.

Social intrapreneurs in the energy sector, such as Roberto Bocca, formerly at BP, have been trying to leverage the business expertise of their employers to provide micro-energy solutions to off-grid villages.

Roberto Bocca, BP: energising alternative solutions to fuel poverty

British multinational oil and gas company BP, formerly known as British Petroleum, is the world's fifth-largest energy company,[11] with operations in over 80 countries.[12]

Social challenge: tackling energy poverty at the Bottom of the Pyramid

While lack of access to affordable energy is a growing worldwide problem, it has reached crisis proportions in the developing world, with delivery of basic services such as healthcare and education impaired by its knock-on effects. According to the *Guardian* (Provost 2013, citing Practical Action' report, *Poor People's Energy Outlook 2013*), 'energy poverty has left more than 1 billion people in developing countries without access to adequate healthcare, with staff forced to treat emergency patients in the dark, and health centres lacking the power they need to store vaccines or sterilise medical supplies'. The situation is particularly acute in India, where nearly half of all healthcare facilities serving 580 million people operate without electricity, and in sub-Saharan Africa, where health centres serving a further 255 million people also operate without power.

The business challenge: developing commercially viable solutions to energy demands

Like other companies operating in the energy sector, BP faces growing worldwide demands for energy that must be met by an increasingly diverse mix of fuels and technologies across its markets. Weak economic growth coupled with concerns about the volatility of commodity and financial markets, energy security and climate change all create continuing uncertainty for BP as well as other oil and gas companies.

The social intrapreneur's solution: off-grid energy micro-generation

Beginning in 2004, Roberto Bocca, then head of Emerging Consumer Markets for BP Alternative Energy, led the development of business to provide access to cleaner, safer and affordable energy solutions to a large number of emerging consumers across the developing world.

---

11   BP ranking based on market capitalization, PFC Energy 50 (2012), https://www.pfcenergy.com/ PFC-Energy-50/PFC-Energy-50.

12   BP Annual Report and Form 20-F 2012, http://www.bp.com/content/dam/bp/pdf/investors/BP_ Annual_Report_and_Form_20F_2012.pdf.

Starting in India, Roberto and his team pioneered innovative collaborative business models and products that enabled BP to serve consumers in emerging markets profitably and sustainably. Working with NGOs to ensure quality market research, BP India managers spent time living with rural villagers to acquire an in-depth understanding of their energy needs and develop new products to meet these challenges. The team developed a distribution network of local entrepreneurs in over 3,000 villages and by the end of 2008—in only four years—the number of Indian households using BP-fuelled stoves had climbed to 400,000.

Despite this significant achievement, a change of CEO from John Browne to Tony Hayward in 2007, and a subsequent strategic shift to established markets to ensure corporate profitability, resulted in the alternative energy project being sold off to one of Roberto's subordinates who took the business forward. Roberto, who then left BP and became Senior Director, Head of Energy Industries at the World Economic Forum, was philosophical about his BP experience, noting that this enabled him to secure his new WEF job.

> What is nicer than doing business which is doing good? My approach [is that] it must be good business … but in doing business it must take into account environment and society—people, profit and planet.

Others, such as Ian Mackintosh at Nile Breweries (part of SABMiller), have worked with local farmers and indigenous communities in Uganda to source natural ingredients for their production process, giving these suppliers a stable source of income. Having set out to solve a purely commercial problem, Mackintosh subsequently discovered his innovative solution created knock-on socioeconomic benefits for local communities, and he has since become more pro-active in using business power to address social issues.

Ian Mackintosh, SABMiller: brewing up low-cost lager with a socially innovative punch

SABMiller plc is one of the world's largest brewers, with brewing interests and distribution agreements across six continents. Its subsidiary Nile Breweries is the leading provider of locally produced beer in Uganda.

The social challenge: reduce risks of alcohol consumption at the 'bottom of the pyramid'

An estimated 315 million Africans live on less than $1 a day—roughly the same cost as a bottle of beer. These 'bottom of the pyramid' consumers have traditionally manufactured home-brewed alcohol from local ingredients ranging from bananas and watermelons to root vegetables. Sometimes the ingredients are not quite so healthy: in Kenya, for instance, there were a number of fatalities after home brewers added methanol and battery acid to give their brews a kick. With no regulation of this so-called informal beer market, drinkers were 'taking their life in their hands' according to Gerry van den Houten, supply chain and enterprise development director for SABMiller Africa (Capell 2009).

The business challenge: developing competitive products for the African market

Ian Mackintosh, then Technical Director at Nile Breweries, faced the commercial challenge of enabling his company's Eagle Lager product to compete with these low-cost, albeit potentially life-threatening, beer products in Uganda. Eagle Lager's retail price was high due to the elevated cost of manufacturing, poor efficiencies, complex logistics, weak physical infrastructure and a punitive tax regime.

The social intrapreneur's solution: change the rules of the game

For Ian, these shortcomings and challenges clearly demonstrated the need to 'change the rules of the game'. This required a multi-faceted approach addressing the sources of inefficiency internally, as well as looking for opportunities to reduce costs externally.

Part of the overall response was to develop a high-quality lager beer to be produced using exclusively locally produced ingredients to replace the expensive imported material from Europe and America. The primary ingredient chosen for this product was a locally developed variety of sorghum. Sorghum is widely grown in Uganda and subsistence farmers are familiar with its cultivation. What was required was to work with local farmers to introduce the new variety and to develop more commercially viable agronomic practices to improve yields and sta-bilise quality.

The final product was in fact not significantly cheaper than the traditional lagers on offer. However, armed with a PwC feasibility study demonstrating the socioeconomic benefits of introducing a new operational model for the rural economy, Ian was able to persuade the Ministry of Finance to reduce the excise duty applicable to clear beer made exclusively with local ingredients. This in turn enabled Nile Breweries to offer the product to the market at a considerable dis-count compared to mainstream lagers and thus grow the overall market with con-comitant benefits to the company, the farmers and the government.

The social payoff: better quality of life for local farmers

Through the experience of collaborating closely with farmers across the country, Ian discovered the significant socioeconomic benefits to be gained from provid-ing a consistent, stable market for agricultural products and supporting better agricultural practices.

In recognising the 'win–win' of this collaboration model, he concluded that 'it should be a mandatory requirement of business to think about this approach'. The model developed in Uganda has now been adopted as standard best practice by SABMiller and is being successfully applied to a variety of enterprise develop-ment opportunities in many countries across Africa and around the world.

Ian Mackintosh, now Technical Director, Zambian Breweries, SABMiller, says:

> All too often, while travelling in Africa, I have been confronted by the corpses of defunct aid projects littering the landscape of poverty-stricken rural areas of the continent. I have come to believe that the international aid industry is tackling the problems of poverty relief and socioeconomic development back to front. Chequebook philanthropy is a clear contradiction in terms. I believe that the only viable approach in the long term is to identify a commercially viable business

need and then work with stakeholders to develop local capacity to fulfil that need. Anything else is simply vanity.

Paul Ellingstad, HP: transforming education through technological innovation

The social challenge: building a more inclusive world through shared knowledge

According to UK government statistics, more than 57 million children around the world do not go to primary school. At least 250 million children cannot read or count.[13] According to the UK Department for International Development (DFID):

> Without a good education, [children] will be less likely to get a job and look after their families in the future. With fewer people in work and more people in need of support, they will struggle to prosper, holding their own countries back and ultimately the global economy.
>
> High quality education can change this, helping to transform countries for the benefit of us all. Quality education helps citizens work together to create strong, open institutions and societies. An extra year of good schooling lifts a country's yearly economic growth by 1%, making poor countries richer and, in the long run, less in need of foreign aid – and more able to trade.[14]

Remedying inequalities in educational opportunity and access to knowledge is key to building a more balanced, equitable society.

The business challenge: making a difference through innovation

At HP, social and commercial purposes are intertwined through social innovation: 'We know technology can transform how people do business. To make an even bigger difference, we're devoting our people, innovative technology, and global presence to the task of improving and saving lives around the world.'[15]

HP has a long tradition of supporting innovation in education as well as health, entrepreneurship and communities. This ethos is rooted in the philosophy of the company's founders, Bill Hewlett and Dave Packard, who said:

> I think many people assume, wrongly, that a company exists simply to make money. While this is an important result of a company's existence, we have to go deeper and find the real reasons for our being.[16]

---

13 DFID, 'Policy: Making Sure Children in Developing Countries get a Good Education', latest update 11 October 2013, https://www.gov.uk/government/policies/making-sure-children-in-developing-countries-get-a-good-education.

14 Ibid.

15 HP, 'Global citizenship: Our legacy', http://www8.hp.com/us/en/hp-information/social-innovation/our-legacy.html.

16 Ibid.

The social intrapreneurial solution: using technology to transform education

Paul Ellingstad is Director of Human Progress Initiatives, leading HP's Office of Global Social Innovation, whose stated purpose is to put 'their ideals into action every day, applying HP talent and technology to make a positive difference in health, education, entrepreneurship, and communities around the world'.[17]

Over the course of his career, Paul has worked in technology companies, although not principally in technology functions. Based on the west coast of Ireland, he sees himself as a social intrapreneur and change-agent to help other change-agents pull together time, resources and connections to make a difference as HP makes the transition from corporate philanthropy to social innovation. He is a classic Malcolm Gladwell *Tipping Point* mixture of maven, connector and salesman (Gladwell 2000).

According to Paul, the essence of what the global team does is to

> set a social innovation strategy that is aligned and integrated with the overall business strategy, and then to 'lead by example'—drive programmes globally but also serve as a model for how various parts of the organisation can also drive programs within their respective area of the business. This is not an 'either or' of 'centralisation' or 'decentralisation' of strategy or execution, but rather it is a co-existence and dare I say 'shared responsibility' between our team and the stakeholders in other parts of the organisation.

HP's strategy is to focus on areas where the company can make the biggest difference:

- Assisting in the transformation of STEM+ (science, technology, engineering, math, and other 21st-century high-tech disciplines and skills) education
- Helping to drive the shift toward personalised learning
- Empowering entrepreneurs

This education work is part of a wider sustainability agenda that also encompasses health, environment and community.

Transforming STEM+ Education[18]

The **HP Catalyst initiative** 'brings together organizations from around the world that are passionate about transforming education'. The scheme 'taps into the power of collaboration through a global network of educators whose goal is to transform STEM+ teaching and learning from secondary education through the university level and to inspire students to use their technical ingenuity and creativity to address urgent social challenges'.

Education Innovation Funds provide grants to key educational institutions in China and India 'to bring to life new visions of the classroom and help teachers transform their roles from content provider and instructor to facilitator, coach and advisor ... These grants are intended to promote collaboration among educators

17   Ibid.
18   HP, 'Global citizenship: Education', http://www8.hp.com/us/en/hp-information/social-innovation/education.html, accessed 8 January 2014.

within and across classrooms, institutions and countries and to increase the visibility of personalized learning approaches.'

Personalised learning

VideoBook is a new education solution and approach to learning with an ambitious goal: to transform the way students learn in India, where only about half of all youngsters can access a primary school, and just 12.4% of India's 220 million children attend college.[19] VideoBook technology, supported by HP Sustainability & Social Innovation, transforms plain text documents into media-rich documents to bring subjects to life. VideoBook won the *Wall Street Journal* Technology Innovation Award for Education 2012.

Empowering entrepreneurs

The **HP LIFE e-Learning programme** offers aspiring entrepreneurs and small business owners valuable business skills and IT training. The **Social Innovation Relay**, a partnership with Junior Achievement Worldwide, is a worldwide competition that 'challenges young students, aged 15 through 18, to create innovative business concepts to help solve some of the world's most pressing challenges'.

Re-engineering business processes to improve resource management and mitigate environmental impacts

Many social intrapreneurs are particularly mindful of the importance and benefits of managing limited resources intelligently and have worked to promote such practices. Working in diverse sectors such as agriculture, telecommunications, logistics, health and beauty and pharmaceuticals, they have developed business processes to achieve operational cost efficiencies, as well as reduce CO_2 production and mitigate other harmful environmental impacts.

Hugh Saddington, Telstra: helping customers connect with the benefits of remote working

Telstra is Australia's leading telecommunications and information services company, providing local and long-distance telephone services, mobile services, dialup, wireless, DSL and cable Internet access to individuals, businesses and government organisations.

19 HP, 'Global citizenship: VideoBook', http://www8.hp.com/us/en/hp-information/social-innovation/learning-my-way.html, accessed 8 January 2014.

The environmental challenge: reducing energy use

For Australian organisations, the need to reduce energy use has become a press-ing social and environmental issue, with increased reporting requirements for energy consumption and greenhouse emissions and stakeholder expectations of more efficient energy and mitigation of the effects of climate change. Legislation has made CEOs legally accountable for organisations' greenhouse gas emissions and energy use.

The business challenge: sustaining operations in a carbon-priced economy

For Telstra, as well as its customers, energy use is also an economic issue. Dra-matic oil price rises and emissions trading schemes are creating both pressures and opportunities for companies to reduce and manage their energy use and associated costs intelligently.

The social intrapreneur's solution: promote the benefits of new communications technologies to reduce energy use

As a marketing specialist in the Australian information and communications tech-nology (ICT) industry, Hugh Saddington spent a lot of time thinking about mar-keting trends and campaigns. Having been 'green' since his university days, he became personally interested in raising awareness of climate change. He saw an obvious 'win–win' scenario: greater use of communications technology could help to improve Telstra's customers' productivity through video conferencing, remote and flexible working and fleet management, while also reducing greenhouse gas emissions and increasing the company's market share.

However, Hugh's initial presentation of the case for addressing climate change to a Telstra superior was met with scepticism. In response, he created his own 'sustainability calculators' and worked with WWF Australia as well as other organisations over a ten-month period to produce a White Paper (Saddington and Toni 2009) that established a more in-depth business case for action. By present-ing the calculators to enterprise and government customers in meetings, he stim-ulated interest in improving both their own and Telstra's sustainability practices.

Supported by a strong business case and an extensive web of key alliances and encompassing 'skunkworks'[20] of enthusiastic colleagues inside the organisa-tion as well as diverse allies outside (WWF Australia and friends at BT UK), Hugh amassed a 'critical mass' of resources for 'greening' the business practices of Telstra and its customers, as well as stimulating customer demand for the com-pany's ICT services.

When David Thodey, Hugh's former boss, became Telstra's CEO, Hugh engaged him as a carbon reduction champion who could promote the case for action to the company's leadership team. This move proved to be pivotal in gain-ing the commitment of senior management to take action.

---

20 A skunkworks project is one typically developed by a small and loosely structured group of people who research and develop a project primarily for the sake of radical innovation (The American Heritage Directory of the English Language, 4th edn on dictionary.com).

> My heart was always with sustainability right from beginning—[it's the] right thing to do, what society expects (Hugh Saddington, General Manager of Market Strategy and Analytic Enterprise and Government Division, Telstra).

Connecting with like-minded individuals and building networks to raise awareness of issues and instigate collective action is a salient feature of social intrapreneurs' work.

Mark Siebert, Siemens: IT for Sustainability Programme

Dr Mark Siebert worked in Siemens Business Services in several management divisions while pursuing a PhD in semantic search and knowledge creation.

A social activist, Mark was a member of the Pioneers of Change programme[21] and a member of The Impact Hub in Berlin. Like several social intrapreneurs working at the boundaries of innovation in their companies, Mark 'found things interesting which are not yet institutionalised and are implicit. Is it your job or your hobby?' Innovation was institutionalised in Siemens (e.g. innovation labs, high-potential circles) and so intrapreneurs were unlikely to be explicitly identified.

Environmental and social challenges: climate change and inequality of access to goods and services

Businesses, as well as society in general, have become increasingly concerned about the impacts and costs of climate change. While the business costs are substantial (Unilever, for example, noted in 2012 that climate change had cost the company €200 million the previous year [Business Green 2012]), the estimated societal costs are staggering: the Climate Policy Initiative[22] estimates that global investment in mitigating climate change—far short of need—plateaued at US$359 billion in 2012 (Climate Policy Initiative 2013).

Remedying inequalities in access to information technology (closing the 'digital divide') is seen as vital to ensuring economic equality, social mobility, democracy and economic growth (Internet World Stats n.d.). The 50 × 15 initiative, launched by AMD in 2004 at the World Economic Forum, is a 'collaborative ecosystem of public and private entities organized to enable affordable Internet access and computing capability to 50% of the world's population by 2015'.[23]

Social intrapreneurial idea: using IT to address climate change and deliver government services

Recognising that IT has the potential to tackle a wide range of significant social, environmental and political problems, Mark and his colleague David Murphy

21 http://pioneersofchange.net/.
22 http://climatepolicyinitiative.org/.
23 http://50×15.org.

started by building an internal Siemens network of people interested in sustainability issues.

The first wave of their engagement concentrated on 'Green IT': eco-friendly and resource-saving applications resonated with their employer as well as with clients, who were able to save costs related to their IT infrastructure. When Siemens IT Solutions and Services integrated sustainability considerations into its core strategy, a new position in 'Green IT' was created and David was appointed. This created a formal space to introduce new ideas and provided a basis to link sustainability innovations directly to the company's core strategy.

Wishing to use IT to drive social change, Mark moved into Siemens' public sector sales unit at a time when the German government incorporated IT into its constitution and promoted IT solutions to address demographic challenges.

His clients were increasingly interested in how Web 2.0 technologies such as Facebook, Twitter and LinkedIn could shape public opinion and voting behaviour. Inspired by President Obama's successful online campaigning in the United States, German parties were now looking into net dialogues and e-participation. Part of the investment programme set up by the German government to confront the economic crisis was dedicated to e-government 2.0 technologies. Siemens offered the integration of these new services into overall IT infrastructure and supported open innovation processes to generate new solutions to new challenges.

These 'Web 2.0' technology innovations have provided citizens with easier access to public services, enabled them to engage with others on topics of mutual interest and become politically active.

Social intrapreneurs working for media companies, such as Carrina Gaffney then at the *Guardian* newspaper in the UK, have recognised that a significant proportion of the population are interested in sustainability issues. Tailoring content to address this new reader segment positions sustainability issues in the mainstream media.

Other social intrapreneurs are leveraging the capabilities of consulting firms to enhance the effectiveness of civil society organisations, particularly in the developing world. Gib Bulloch established Accenture Development Partnerships as a pioneering 'corporate social enterprise' that employs an innovative, not-for-profit business model to channel the core business capabilities of Accenture to the development sector (see Chapter 2, page 83), while Jo da Silva created Arup International Development to provide 'expert technical advice and practical solutions which reduce poverty and improve human, economic and environmental health in developing countries'. Ralf Schneider, formerly Chief Learning Officer at PwC, launched the Ulysses experiential learning programme to give PwC partners the opportunity to 'develop their leadership skills, drive cultural change and promote a global perspective in difficult environments'. Chris Harrop at UK garden-paving supplier Marshalls pioneered improved environmental standards linked to ethical sourcing, and as a result of his efforts he has also now become Marshalls' Sustainability Director in addition to his marketing role.

Chris Harrop, Marshalls: paving the way for ethically sourced products

Marshalls is the UK's leading paving supplier with over 120 years' experience. The company operates quarries and factories producing natural stone and concrete hard landscaping products including bricks, slabs, tiles, paving and walling. Its customers are construction companies, builders' merchants and DIY shops.

The social challenge: addressing climate change and supply chain labour issues

In 2002, Chris Harrop, who had joined the company the previous year as Marketing Director, conducted consumer research to identify global societal trends and their impact on society and consumers. The research highlighted growing consumer concern with environmental issues, particularly climate change, and human rights issues in the supply chain.

The business challenge: developing paving products for a competitive market

Alongside identifying the environmental, social and lifestyle drivers that were shaping consumers' purchasing trends, Marshalls was trying to establish a brand advantage in an increasingly competitive market.

Chris realised that Marshalls could source sandstone in India, which was comparable in quality to, but more economical than, Yorkshire sandstone. However, he needed to find a way to address concerns about potential child labour and environmental impact issues.

The social intrapreneur's solution: ethically produced sandstone

To understand sourcing process issues in depth, Chris undertook an extended study tour of India. There he met with suppliers to gain a first-hand understanding of issues such as wages, safety and child labour—in short, 'to turn over as many stones as possible to see what was going on'.

On his return to the UK, Chris persuaded senior directors that Marshalls should become the first company in its sector to join the Ethical Trading Initiative and to commit to establishing a verifiable ethical sourcing process. Working in partnership with an Indian supplier and local NGO Hadoti Hast Shilp Sansthan, Chris developed the industry's first ethically sourced landscaping product.

Aided by reporters from the *Guardian* and the *Daily Telegraph*, whom he invited to investigate Indian supply-chain issues, Chris launched a communications campaign that persuaded the building trade, distributors and consumers to pay a premium for ethically sourced Marshalls Fairstone.

Chris is now working to replicate the ethical sourcing process in China and expand product carbon footprinting throughout the Marshalls Group.

There is no way you can be an effective environmentalist if you don't have a successful business or economy. You need the wealth to drive the improvements. You have to recognise that there are people who need jobs, pensions, heat, light and clothes (Chris Harrop, Marketing Director/Sustainability Director, Marshalls plc).

Arun Pande, TCS mKRISHI: empowering rural farmers with mobile access to business services

For Chief Scientist and Head of Innovation at Tata Consultancy Services (TCS) in Mumbai, Arun Pande, social and environmental innovation was 'about the business' and the company didn't 'do' corporate social responsibility as a separate function.

There has to be a business model, where you make money, some people get money, and other people get other benefits, so that it is sustainable ... first you look at the social problem and then you come up with a way of solving it through business.

Innovation would happen both formally and informally via corporate innovation labs and two networks: iConnect, with ideas emerging from partners and internal business groups; and CoI (CoInnovation) network, connecting TCS with small companies, technology companies, start-ups and consultancies.

Social challenge

Agriculture is a key contributor to the Indian economy but the millions of small-scale farmers face multiple challenges such as low productivity and efficiency, inadequate information and limited access to services. Economic difficulties from extreme weather conditions, disease and consequent crop and livestock failures have also led to suicides amongst farmers.

Business challenge

TCS aimed to develop integrated and personalised services for farming communities that could meet the needs of diverse customers (literate, semi-literate or illiterate), deal with the multiple languages of India and be provided at scale to millions.

Social intrapreneur's solution

Arun Pande's interest was triggered by a visit to his small home town in rural India and hearing about many farmers committing suicide. Out of curiosity, he started to investigate the causes and realised that as head of Innovation for TCS, he had access to information and communications technology solutions that might help address some of the underlying causes of rural poverty and despair. This led to the development of mKRISHI.

Using text and visual symbols, mKRISHI offers a range of services to farmers such as advice on pesticides and fertilisers, how much and when to spray, when to harvest in relation to weather to limit crop damage and making market prices available so they can choose where and when to sell based on the latest information about current global rates and futures prices, thereby enhancing income.

Banks can also use the mKRISHI programme enabling more rapid loan payments to farmers; agro-product companies can get direct access to farmers, enabling closer links to customer base; and the government is able to communicate new government policies to farmers. Among TCS's partners for mKRISHI are agro-food companies, NGOs, agricultural universities and village entrepreneurs.

The TCS mKRISHI platform garnered a wide range of national and global accolades.[24] The company's next goal is to start to measure the economic and social impact of the project, not only for the company, but also for the stakeholders. 'We want to see how it can scale up to millions and millions of farmers.'

Graham Simpson, GSK: low-cost health diagnostics for Africa

GSK (GlaxoSmithKline) is a science-led global healthcare company that researches and develops a broad range of innovative medicines and brands. According to its website, 'commercial success depends on creating innovative new products and making these accessible to as many people who need them as possible'.[25] The company has offices in more than 115 countries, major research centres in the UK, USA, Spain, Belgium and China and an extensive manufacturing network with 87 sites globally.

Social challenge: diagnosing diseases in developing countries with limited resources

Graham Simpson is an organic chemist who heads the Therapeutic Peptide Chemistry Performance Unit at GSK. Having completed the GSK PULSE skills-based volunteering programme (see description in Ch. 4, page 118), he identified the diagnosis of diseases in developing countries as an important healthcare problem that the company might address. He articulated this challenge in his League of Intrapreneurs competition entry as follows:

> Cheap and reliable diagnosis of diseases in remote, rural areas, with challenging weather conditions, lack of electricity or clean water, and inadequately trained healthcare staff are widespread problems in the less developed countries. In particular, poor maternal and child healthcare leads to significant mortality and morbidity with undiagnosed conditions being left untreated. With infectious diseases such as malaria and tuberculosis, point-of care diagnosis is not possible with the limitations in healthcare resources.[26]

24 See Tata Consultancy Services, http://www.tcs.com/offerings/technology-products/mKRISHI/awards-recognition/Pages/default.aspx, accessed 6 December 2013.

25 GSK, 'What we do', http://www.gsk.com/about-us/what-we-do.html, accessed 8 January 2014.

26 See Changemakers, 'Low-cost diagnostics for Africa', http://www.changemakers.com/intrapreneurs/entries/low-cost-diagnostics-africa, accessed 8 January 2014.

Business challenge: developing innovative healthcare solutions

According to the GSK website:

> The business is focused around the delivery of three strategic priorities which aim to increase growth, reduce risk and improve our long-term financial performance. These priorities are: grow a diversified global business, deliver more products of value, and simplify the operating model.[27]

Graham described the following 'corporate social opportunity'[28] for GSK through which the company could develop new products creating both commercial and social value:

> Tens of millions of people's lives could be saved annually with a platform solution involving an open-innovation collaboration of expert partners. In a specific example, a recent epidemiological study estimates that of the 30 million live births in Africa, more than 300,000 babies were born with sickle cell anemia in 2012. In Sub-Saharan Africa it is estimated that 50–80% of children born with sickle cell disease die by age 5 due to infectious disease, many without being diagnosed as having the disease.[29]

This is a challenge that has engaged pharmaceutical competitors in the marketplace in which GSK operates and, according to Graham, holds a distinctive position:

> The WHO [World Health Organization] supports a number of consortia who are investigating point of care diagnostics. The global expertise that GSK brings in discovery, development and distribution of novel medicines and vaccines, particularly in the developing world, bring unique strengths in the industry. GSK's expertise in diseases of the developing world, including the development of malaria vaccine Mosquirix, and extensive partnerships with NGOs, governments and institutions across the world make us the ideal partner. Johns Hopkins and Jhpiego develop innovative solutions for global healthcare issues particularly around novel devices that have been recognised by the award of several grants and awards (Gates, USAID). Other competitors in the field include PATH and FiND who have experience in developing diagnostics.[30]

The social intrapreneurial solution: collaboration to develop low-cost diagnostic tools with benefits for local healthcare workers

Graham Simpson leads a diverse team of intrapreneurial scientists collaborating closely with academia and an NGO, Jhpiego. The GSK team have experience of volunteering in Africa, with Graham and fellow team member Michelle Wobker spending six-month placements in western Kenya and Ghana in 2010. Dwight

27   GSK, 'Our mission and strategy, http://www.gsk.com/about-us/our-mission-and-strategy.html, accessed 8 January 2014.

28   See more about corporate social opportunity in Chapter 3 on 'The business case for social intrapreneurism'.

29   Changemakers, 'Low-cost diagnostics for Africa', http://www.changemakers.com/intrapreneurs/entries/low-cost-diagnostics-africa, accessed 8 January 2014.

30   Changemakers, http://www.changemakers.com/project/low-cost-diagnostics-africa?ref=related-entry accessed 8 January 2014.

Walker, another key member, has developed commercial diagnostics within the industry. The group is part of a wider team of micro-volunteers within GSK who have helped the project. With academic partners in the Biomedical Engineering Department at Johns Hopkins University and at Jhpiego, the GSK team are working together to develop innovative solutions for healthcare in developing countries.

According to Graham:

> GSK is helping to develop simple, cheap, paper-based devices capable of producing quantitative diagnostic test strips at-site. These tests can be administered by minimally trained healthcare workers in hot, humid environments common in developing countries. The ante-natal pen uses a novel design with a dropper to deliver reagents consistently with a business model generating an income for the healthcare worker. The G6PD test uses an innovative visual screen which allows quantitative assessment in difficult to detect cases.

> Both designs are part of a wider platform which will revolutionise healthcare diagnosis and companion treatment in developing countries. Systematic screening of newborns for SCD using a simple blood test is not a common practice in much of the developing world, particularly in rural areas. A simple, paper based microfluidic ELISA assay could identify infants with sickle cell disease, and distinguish them from those with sickle cell trait whom do not require intensive antibiotic therapy.[31]

Contrasting the work of social intrapreneurs and their 'close relatives'

Following on from the SustainAbility (2008) conception of the social intrapreneur as a 'species', we found many individuals working to effect positive social change who could be classified as 'close relatives' of social intrapreneurs. They differ from social intrapreneurs in that they may be working in non-commercial organisations, be working explicitly in the sustainability field (but not to achieve commercial goals) or are owners/managers of commercial businesses but are creating social or environmental benefits as a consequence of responsible management practices. Such 'close relatives' include:

Inside the company:

- Social entrepreneurs who work in enterprises created specifically to achieve social (as opposed to commercial) goals

- Corporate sustainability champions and members of corporate 'green teams' of volunteers. Some commentators also regard such champions and green team members as social intrapreneurs because they are challenging the organisational status quo. However, we classify these individuals in a separate group as they have an explicitly recognised remit to promote sustainability goals and, unlike social intrapreneurs, do not have to negotiate with managers and other colleagues to undertake their sustainability work

Outside the company:

- Public sector entrepreneurs who are instigating socially or environmentally beneficial innovations working in government departments or agencies

- Responsible entrepreneurs who are running their own for-profit businesses responsibly

- 'Sense-makers': writers, consultants and campaigners on entrepreneurship and sustainability issues

- 'Catalytic converters': people who are comfortable crossing boundaries between the public, private and NGO sectors and bringing people from different sectors together. This group encompasses individuals building public–private–community partnerships (sometimes called 'civic entrepreneurs'). Jason Clay of WWF refers to these as 'extrapreneurs': 'change agents [who] solve problems by moving between companies, organisations and sectors, spreading ideas and solutions from one to another like bees pollinating flowers' (Clay 2013)

- Corporate responsibility/sustainability directors or managers

- 'Systempreneurs' who, according to our Volans colleagues John Elkington and Charmian Love (2012),

  > focus on mobilizing resources to tackle challenges and search for innovative new solutions [but] instead of focusing on challenges of a new enterprise (as entrepreneurs do) or driving change inside big organisations (as intrapreneurs do), they have their sights set on system-level change

**'Close relative' inside the company:
James Dorling, Tesco**

James Dorling exemplifies the individual who is responsible for innovation but for whom sustainability is at the heart of his job, rather than lying outside his core remit. At the time of our 2010 interview, James was Head of Construction and the Special Projects Team at the UK supermarket retailer Tesco and had been suggested as a 'social intrapreneur' for our research by a consultant working in the sustainability field: Cranfield alumni Charles Perry, co-founder of *Second Nature*, who had worked with James to achieve '100% recyclable stores with zero waste to landfill'. However, James noted at the outset that whereas social intrapreneurs appeared to be individuals doing extraordinary things with their companies, that are relatively unrelated to their jobs, I haven't. My entire reason for being within Tesco is to come up with new ways of reducing our environmental strain; that's the job.

Rather than having to struggle to address sustainability issues within the core business, James was actively encouraged by his colleagues, including the CEO, to move as swiftly as possible:

This environment is extremely driven and, if the idea grabs people, you can go places with it. We've got enough capital to invest in priorities—we have a lot of freedom to do what we like in various stores. The company has over 1,000 stores—you're never going to get sacked for making mistakes in that. That's a great environment to be in.

This resonates well with our jazz metaphor about the value of playing in a great band to produce great music. Rolling Stones guitarist Keith Richards—a rock 'n' roll musician with an understanding of jazz—captured this idea well in his book *Life* (2010).

DRUMMER MOSES BOYD IS CAPTURED LISTENING INTENTLY TO HIS TRIO BANDMATES, PIANIST REUBEN JAMES AND BASSIST FERGUS IRELAND. ALTHOUGH ALL THREE MUSICIANS ARE ONLY IN THEIR TWENTIES, THEIR ENGAGING PERFORMANCES REFLECT A MATURE CAPACITY FOR DEEP LISTENING AND 'CONVERSATION' WELL BEYOND THEIR YEARS.

It's really teamwork, one guy supporting the others, and it's all for one purpose, and there's no flies in the ointment, for a while. And nobody conducting, it's all up to you. It's really jazz—that's the big secret. Rock and roll ain't nothing but jazz with a hard backbeat.

'Close relative' outside the company: Joseph Agoada, UNICEF

Joseph Agoada was a putative social entrepreneur who has become a public-sector social intrapreneur with the UN children's programme UNICEF. In 2009, sponsored by the International Youth Foundation, he travelled from Kampala to Cape Town to learn what young Africans wanted from the Football World Cup to be held in South Africa the following year. Joseph learnt that in the villages what they most wanted was simply the chance to see the matches since there were few TVs except in bars. This gave him the idea to erect inflatable screens in the open air and input educational content during the half-time intervals. IYF were not interested in the proposal and, as Joseph remarks, 2009, just months after the global financial crisis, was 'not a good time to find corporate sponsors for a speculative, start-up social enterprise'. A chance conversation during a 'happy hour' in a New York bar with a stranger who turned out to be a UNICEF official led to a meeting 48 hours later, resulting in an offer that Joseph found impossible to refuse: 'We will take your idea, your NGO, your network, rebrand as UNICEF and if you agree, we will provide $150,000 for you to make it happen.'

Following his success with running educational programmes on the back of the World Cup, Joseph has continued to work inside UNICEF.

Debra Meyerson has written extensively (Meyerson 2001, 2004; Meyerson and Scully 1995) about 'tempered radicals', whom she defines as:

> Individuals who identify with and are committed to their organizations, and are also committed to a cause, community, or ideology that is fundamentally different from, and possibly at odds with the dominant culture of their organization. The ambivalent stance of these individuals creates a number of special challenges and opportunities (Meyerson and Scully 1995).

Several of the subjects whose histories we reviewed appeared to occupy this category. They share the desire to achieve sustainability goals with social intrapreneurs. However, they have stopped short of developing a commercially profitable product, service or business process within the organisation that supports those goals—the defining characteristic of a social intrapreneur.

As with any extended family, social intrapreneurs and their 'close relatives' can provide each other with valuable mutual support. Richard Ellis, Group Head of Corporate Social Responsibility (CSR) at Alliance Boots, argues that social intrapreneurs need people who can, for example, guide them through the corporate innovation and approvals process. Future research could usefully examine how they work with each other to enact shared sustainability goals. To misquote Shakespeare, 'one person in his or her time, may play many different parts'[32]— sometimes being a social intrapreneur but at other phases of life being a social

---

32   Misquoted from Jaques' 'All the World's a Stage' monologue in Shakespeare's *As You Like It*.

activist or a social entrepreneur, or a responsible manager in a large corporation, for example.

James Inglesby, Unilever

James Inglesby, originally from South Africa, and a 2011 Aspen First Mover Fellow, was a project leader in the Unilever New Business Unit, working on new business models to engage 'bottom of the pyramid' consumers. He was seconded to a project to bring portable toilets to Ghana, working effectively as a social entrepreneur. He co-founded The Clean Team, a sanitation business[33] constructed as an innovative public–private partnership, which has attracted international aid donor support, and he now serves on its board. Sanitation is a major public health issue in countries such as Ghana where 80% of the population do not have access to their own toilets. While Unilever is not in the business itself of providing toilets, the intrapreneurial urge for Inglesby and his colleagues was that by causing toilets to be more widely available, they would be building the market for Unilever's sanitation products. The salesforce who are collecting money for the toilet service are also selling Unilever products. Within Unilever, Inglesby is also now Marketing Manager of Unilever Nigeria, where he is developing the personal care business with products not previously available in underserved markets.

And some may play several parts simultaneously. At one point in his career, Tom van den Nieuwenhuijzen was simultaneously Sustainability Director of a Dutch-headquartered family business, Van Nieuwpoort Group, working as a social intrapreneur championing the development of sustainable cement; an elected politician serving as a member of a ruling four-party coalition of his local Eindhoven City Council on behalf of the Dutch Left Green Party; and a social activist promoting diversity and gay rights.

Tom van den Nieuwenhuijzen, Van Nieuwpoort Group

Born in 1982, Tom van den Nieuwenhuijzen did an engineering degree at Avans Hogeschool Tilburg before joining an architectural practice as an architectural draughtsman. A year later, however, he joined a fourth-generation family business in the construction sector, Van Nieuwpoort Group.

Salvador Pozo

Tom worked initially as a project manager, then as a commercial manager and sales consultant in one of the subsidiaries of the company. Simultaneously, he was continuing his education part time, taking a Master's degree in Sustainability.

---

33 http://www.cleanteamtoilets.com/. Intriguingly for the authors, a different part of Cranfield University, the School of Applied Sciences, has provided technical advice and support for the toilet design and operation.

His thesis on The Natural Step[34] led to developing a sustainability strategy for Van Nieuwpoort Group and becoming the CSR and Sustainability manager for the group.

As part of his job crafting—changing the boundaries, design and social environment of the job (see explanatory text in the next section)—he spotted the business opportunities and societal benefits of cement-free concrete being championed by the group R&D department. Working with a range of internal and external partners, including Utrecht City Council, he successfully launched the cement-free concrete.

In parallel, and describing himself as having two full-time jobs and often working 90-hour weeks, he served as an elected councillor on the Eindhoven City Council, sitting for the Left-Green Party within a four-party ruling coalition, and part of a national talent, fast-track development programme for his party.

As he summarises his experience:

> I took a degree in Business Administration, writing my thesis about implementing CSR through the Balanced Score Card. I used The Natural Step as a change model within Van Nieuwpoort Group. Next to that I made sure that the City of Eindhoven started using The Natural Step as a system approach for all their future projects

Like other construction companies, Van Nieuwpoort Group was hard hit by the recession. Having built up a sustainability team in the group and its operating companies, Tom then had to make his team redundant; and despite enjoying the personal support of Van Nieuwpoort's CEO, who was his sponsor, Tom was also made redundant.

Today, he is a lecturer teaching Corporate Social Responsibility and International Management at the Fontys University for Applied Sciences and running his own consulting and project-management business in the field of sustainability: Avengers Way.[35]

Job crafting: what is it and why is it important for social intrapreneurs?

The concept of 'job crafting' was first defined by Wrzesniewski and Dutton (2001: 179) as 'the physical and cognitive changes individuals make in the task or relational boundaries of their work'. Berg, Dutton and Wrzesniewski (2008) added that the concept of job crafting 'captures the active changes employees make to

---

34 'The Natural Step (TNS) is a globally recognized network of offices and individual associates that share the same brand, principles and training in strategic sustainable development', http://www.naturalstep.org/.

35 Based on author's interview at Nyenrode Business School in January 2012 and subsequent exchanges; and http://www.linkedin.com/in/tomvandennieuwenhuijzen, accessed 30 October 2013.

their own job designs in ways that can bring about numerous positive outcomes, including engagement, job satisfaction, resilience, and thriving'.

Many of the individuals profiled in this book, we believe, are compelled to undertake different forms of job crafting in order to succeed as social intrapreneurs. Depending on their circumstances and working environments, social intrapreneurs negotiate with colleagues, often starting with their line managers, to acquire the time, space and resources needed to establish, as the late Anita Roddick first described it, 'business as unusual'.[36]

Applying our jazz metaphor to this concept, job crafting is a form of career improvisation that requires the aspiring social intrapreneur to first undertake a substantial amount of 'woodshedding' (to understand deeply one's job in its organisational context before beginning to alter it), 'paying one's dues' (performing the job as expected, alongside others) and 'jamming' (trying out new ideas in dialogue with managers and other colleagues). Only in this way can the intrapreneur gain the trust required for experimentation to succeed.

ALTHOUGH JAZZ IS OFTEN IDENTIFIED WITH ITS MUSICAL ROOTS IN AFRICAN-AMERICAN COMMUNITIES OF THE SOUTHERN UNITED STATES, THE APPEAL OF COLLECTIVE IMPROVISATIONAL MUSIC-MAKING HAS SPREAD WORLDWIDE, AS THIS PHOTO OF JAPANESE TRUMPETER EMI KITASAKO (PLAYING ALONGSIDE GERMAN TENOR SAXOPHONIST ROLAND HEINZ IN THE 2013 GLOBAL MUSIC FOUNDATION LONDON JAZZ WORKSHOP IN KINGS PLACE HALL TWO) ILLUSTRATES.

36 A term coined by Body Shop founder Anita Roddick to describe both the final decade of her journey with the business and a call to action by business to pursue a purpose beyond profits (see Roddick 2005).

Marijn Wiersma is a social intrapreneur who has successfully job crafted. Raised in Africa, she returned to her native Netherlands to study anthropology before returning to Africa to work for the World Food Programme of the UN in Ethiopia. She transferred to Ecuador to learn Spanish for two years and then went back again to Africa: this time Zambia. In the process, she also transferred to work for a Dutch NGO, PharmAccess Foundation, working on access to medicines for people living with HIV and AIDS. While in Zambia, Marijn also set up Zambia's first private nursing teaching school.

In 2008, she returned to the Netherlands to join the Dutch development bank FMO as a social and environmental specialist. In her own words: 'I completely lost my first year at FMO, trying to show sustainability could be something more than risk mitigation.'

A new CEO transformed Marijn's circumstances, as he put sustainability at the heart of the FMO strategy and restructured from a geographic to a sectoral focus.

Marijn changed from Latin America to finance sector. None of the other sustainability team members wanted to be in the finance sector division.

They couldn't see the Added-Value, multiplier impact you could have! First, I asked for an evaluation of our relations with each of our 200 banking clients across the world. Then I tried to create a new language. I found an American teaching at a business school in Costa Rica with 15 years experience in the finance sector. He taught me how to communicate to bankers more than sustainability specialists. On my travels, I made clear: 'I want to talk to the CEO and board more than sustainability specialists!' I also connected to my previous boss—the former manager for Latin America who also got it. By changing the conversation and the conversational partners, and developing simpler language relating to 'collateral', 'reputational risks' etc., we started to have an impact. But it took the CEO of FMO to show leadership and bless the initiative. We could offer very tangible financial rewards for banks that became sustainable banks, such as changing the credit process that will decrease margins on our loans to you if you decrease your risk profile by tackling sustainability. We are the first financial institution which has done this successfully. It is attracting huge interest worldwide in banking and in development fields—commercial banks are coming to FMO to learn about this.

Then I started itching. I'm good at start-up! So I went to the CEO and said 'I've done my current job. But I have still got added value to give to the organisation.' He then offered me the chance to create my dream job.

This was to become Head of Knowledge and Innovation to unlock people's potential and find the hidden talent in FMO.[37]

---

37 Based on author's interview at Nyenrode Business School in 2012 and subsequent exchanges, and http://www.linkedin.com/pub/marijn-wiersma/7/13b/76b, accessed 8 January 2014.

When we caught up with Marijn in November 2013, she gave us an update on her work, noting that,

as social intrapreneurs do—I have already crafted the next job.... While developing our long-term strategy (become a leading impact investor by doubling our impact and halving our footprint), early this year I transformed the knowledge part of my job into transition. Knowledge management was still too boxed in and I could not effectively manage expectations that I would contribute to the culture/competency side of knowledge [while] my colleagues kept expecting organisation/system improvements from me.

Now, her mandate is to:

(1) create so-called meaningful interventions; (2) define our 'partnership approach' and build strategic coalitions; and (3) develop organisational learning and development strategies. Overall it boils down to asking difficult questions, bringing unusual groups together and steer the passive nature of a bank into a more active and entrepreneurial direction.

2

Understanding individual social intrapreneurs

If you are an aspiring social intrapreneur, start with the short self-evaluation in Table 2.1.

Table 2.1 Self-evaluation: Am I a potential social intrapreneur?

In regard to new projects, I	Score				
	Never	Rarely	Sometimes	Often	Always
1 Try to avoid errors and mistakes at all cost	1	2	3	4	5
2 Adapt them to the existing company culture	1	2	3	4	5
3 Start thinking about project management	1	2	3	4	5
4 Am looking for social and environmental objectives	1	2	3	4	5
5 Am usually bringing in my third-sector experiences	1	2	3	4	5
6 Feel that most new projects do not really add value	1	2	3	4	5
7 Evaluate legal aspects as well as company policies	1	2	3	4	5
8 Am dedicated to planning and execution	1	2	3	4	5

9	Have difficulty explaining the business value of social and environmental indicators	1	2	3		4	5
10	Am often disguising social and environmental issues in business terms	1	2	3		4	5
11	Am often seen by others as very sceptical	1	2	3		4	5
12	Know the rules that affect the implementation of the project	1	2	3		4	5
13	Have been invited to be the manager of the project	1	2	3		4	5
14	Am bringing in social and environmental viewpoints	1	2	3		4	5
15	Am persistent in projects that I believe create value for society and the company	1	2	3		4	5
16	Am sceptical when I see social and environmental objectives	1	2	3		4	5
17	Make sure that the project uses established company processes	1	2	3		4	5
18	Oversee implementation such as delivery dates, scope and quality	1	2	3		4	5
19	Am perceived as the 'eco-guy' in the team	1	2	3		4	5
20	Lose interest in the project if I can't see how society benefits	1	2	3		4	5

Put your scores for each question into this table and add up the columns.

Scores (1)	Scores (2)	Scores (3)	Scores (4)	Scores (5)
1.	2.	3.	4.	5.
6.	7.	8.	9.	10.
11.	12.	13.	14.	15.
16.	17.	18.	19.	20.
Total	Total	Total	Total	Total

We explain the results at in Chapter 3 at page 95. First, however, we want to explore the types of social intrapreneurs, their close relatives and the social intrapreneurial journey.

Types of social intrapreneur

Based on our interview data and what we learned from previous studies, we observed the types of social intrapreneurs described in Table 2.2.

Table 2.2 Types of social intrapreneur

Type of social intrapreneur	Description
Exited	Quit their company because of a lack of support for their social intrapreneurial ideas; or the support that they once enjoyed, evaporates with a change of business leadership or business priorities
Exasperated	Remained within the company but have given up pushing for social innovation and are concentrating on their core job
Emergent	Starting out with their idea and it is still unclear how the corporate environment will respond
Empowered	The company is actively encouraging the idea, empowering the social intrapreneur

We discovered that a social intrapreneur's 'type' is not fixed but evolves over time, depending on the changing attributes of the social intrapreneur—encompassing their life experiences, behavioural tendencies, skill sets and contact networks—and the context in which they work, including organisational culture, power hierarchies and resources, business climate, as well as the wider socioeconomic and political environment.

For example, an 'empowered' social intrapreneur may grow a project to a size that requires a different sort of individual who can manage large-scale organisational processes; the social intrapreneur may then exit the organisation to launch other projects or remain within the organisation but assume a different sort of role.

By contrast, we have seen 'exasperated' social intrapreneurs who, when they do not achieve traction initially with their project ideas, subsequently shift, after 'paying their dues' in particular corporate roles, into other roles, teams or departments where they become 'empowered' to develop project ideas. Some have moved to other organisations or into completely different sectors, joining not-for-profit organisations, academic institutions or even starting their own social enterprises, often while continuing to work for companies.

For the purposes of our research, we classified our social intrapreneurs into types based on the 'snapshot' of their circumstances we obtained at the time of interview. However, we have continued tracking them and have been struck by the diversity and fluidity of their paths—see the next section on 'The social intrapreneur's journey'.

Here are some examples of the different types of social intrapreneurs we encountered.

Exited: Karl Feilder, DHL Neutral

Karl Feilder's entrepreneurial drive is rooted in the difficult early years of his childhood. His father left home when he was four years old, forcing him and his mother and sister to move into a caravan where a dining table doubled as a bed and there was no inside toilet. A key memory is that his father took his toys away to give to his new stepchildren and, as a consequence, he 'spent quite some time in life metaphorically trying to get my toys back!' He won a scholarship to a fee-paying boarding school, the first in his family to do so, and then earned an B.Eng. honours degree in Engineering and German at the University of Hertfordshire in 1987).

Karl became a software engineer but, craving more human interaction, he moved into sales in the late 1980s. In 1990, he and six colleagues started their own company (Network Managers), aided by a bank loan for a new car, which he used to finance the business. It was a 'classic garden shed start-up' and Karl drew no salary for a year. After flirting with venture capitalists, the business was eventually sold to Microsoft in 1995.

Moving to South Africa, Karl started a second software company (Greenwich Mean Time Holdings) with his wife-to-be Sarah, hiring a dozen top students from the University of Cape Town and paying off their start-up loan within six months. Within a few years, he had 'made piles of money, even more than I could spend—and I could spend'. In 2000 the company was sold to Sempres Holdings and Karl returned with Sarah to the UK, where their first daughter was born.

Karl then embarked on a series of company turnarounds for venture capitalists, 'fixing dot-coms that had not had the good grace to go bust', but found the work as a 'gun-for-hire' demotivating. 'You would put heart and soul into fixing a company, hire and motivate great people, and then the VC [venture capitalist] would simply sell the business on a whim—often at a crazy price'.

During this time, in some ways proving his ability to do more than seemed possible, he and Sarah had another two daughters, he turned around three companies, and he returned to studying at Henley, graduating with an MBA in 2006. Karl later said 'with the benefit of hindsight, I think entrepreneurs should be barred from taking an MBA—it slows you down and makes you think twice about things you just instinctively "know" to be right.'

The social intrapreneurial project: building a business to tackle climate change

Next, urged to do something 'useful' by Sarah, a keen biodynamic gardener ('Why don't you solve the carbon crisis and save the planet?') he turned his attention to climate change, although he had not been interested previously in sustainability issues. Through a serendipitous reunion with a friend from boarding school who had become Strategy Director for DHL, Karl started The Neutral Group with an initial focus on helping DHL reduce its carbon footprint. However, as a successful commercial entrepreneur, he recognised the importance of having a viable business model to do it.

There have been CSR, green, sustainability people in companies for the past 20–30 years but boards and senior management don't take them seriously because they cannot put their agenda in language that the board cares about. Carbon footprinting and carbon reduction needs to be numerate, disciplined, objective and expressed in monetary terms. Too many people with sustainability titles are not numerate and are uncomfortable talking about kWh.

Feilder acquired enthusiastic backing from a 'godparent'—DHL CEO John Allan, who subsequently became CFO of DHL's parent company Deutsche Post. When Allan moved to Bonn, Feilder did the same. While there, he was able to influence the parent company to support DHL in undertaking company-wide carbon footprinting and a number of pioneering energy and carbon saving projects. In this context, having 'paid his dues' as a commercial 'entrepreneur with very good patronage, [I was] given freedom and flexibility to go for it.'

LIKE THESE YOUNG MUSICIANS FROM THE JUGEND JAZZ ORCHESTER SAAR PERFORMING IN A 2013 CONCERT IN SAARWELLINGEN, GERMANY, 'PAYING YOUR DUES' IN A LARGE ORGANISATION DEVELOPS ONE'S 'SOLOING' AND 'COMPING' SKILLS AND EARNS THE TRUST OF MANAGERS AND OTHER COLLEAGUES.

Exiting to a new entrepreneurial life

Feilder's 'air cover' vanished when Allan left Deutsche Post to become Chairman of DSG (formerly Dixons). Karl negotiated his departure from DHL by selling one of his subsidiary companies to them, and now chairs The Neutral Group, based in Dubai,[1] which offers 'a range of managed services and solutions including carbon supply chain consulting, software, emission reduction plans and carbon reduction implementation programs'. Key milestones include the first carbon abatement consultancy in Masdar City, the emerging global clean technology cluster in Abu Dhabi, and a biofuels business.

1   www.tng.ae.

Never one to sit still, Karl spent the next few years with The Neutral Group, working on global projects with British American Tobacco and Lockheed Martin, before finally finding his latest success as a social intrapreneur working in conjunction with McDonald's restaurants.

After Neutral Consulting had helped write and commence execution of a new ten-year sustainability strategy for McDonald's across the 38-country Asia Pacific/Middle East/Africa region, Karl proposed to McDonald's senior leadership team a bold plan to make the company's delivery fleet independent of the global oil price. He set up Neutral Fuels, achieving the seemingly impossible task of becoming the first licensed biofuels-producer in the Middle East. Today, Neutral Fuels operates a profit-sharing biorefinery with McDonald's in Dubai, with a second dedicated McDonald's biorefinery in Melbourne, Australia, and he plans many more.

Reflecting on his three-year DHL experience, Karl observes that, 'I had a fantastic time. I feel I made a real difference—influenced the sixth largest employer in world—they have more than half a million employees.' However, noting his intense, entrepreneurial working style, Karl concludes that 'I don't think my blood pressure would have taken much more of them—or theirs of me!'[2]

Exasperated: Emma Clarke, Cavendish Nuclear

Emma Clarke was born in 1985 in London. When she was eight, her family moved to the rural town of Frome. Spending time in Wales at her grandparents' farm, Emma experienced a dual urban and rural upbringing that fostered a love of the countryside and sustainability. She absorbed her parents' interests in gardening, self-sufficiency and a desire to minimise waste.

Travelling and camping with the Woodcraft Folk—a progressive educational movement that fosters understanding of the environment, world debt and global conflict—heightened Emma's awareness of the countryside. As a result of these experiences, she developed an enduring ambition to create a retreat location where people could experience sustainability practices first hand.

To develop the skills needed to create such a project, Emma opted to follow her philosophy degree with a Master's degree in Sustainable Development at Exeter University via distance learning.

Meanwhile, an initial placement at engineering company Cavendish Nuclear (a wholly-owned subsidiary of Babcock International Group) led to subsequent administration and marketing work stints during summers and holidays and finally a contract. Although she started as a Business Improvement Coordinator, she aspired to a more sustainability-focused role, harbouring ambitions to set up a company-wide sustainability network. Here she set out her ambition at the time of her first interview in April 2010:

> I am involved in reducing [the company's] carbon footprint for the CRC Energy Efficiency Scheme soon coming into force, and as part of this hope to raise awareness among employees of the importance of sustainability...[as the company is] such a large organisation (17,000 employees in 6 divisions) I also hope to create a sustainability network for employees working to improve sustainability.

2 Based on interviews 28 April 2010 and 18 November 2013.

Phase 1: Exasperation

In April 2010, when she had been working for her then boss for six months, Emma was experiencing a fair amount of frustration. While she perceived sustainability as having value in its own right, her remit was to improve efficiency and cost savings. Like many social intrapreneurs or other sustainability activists, she was told that she would be required to demonstrate a robust business case for sustainability initiatives before she would be allowed to implement any of them.

Emma was also experiencing difficulty connecting with like-minded peers who were progressing sustainability projects, either inside or outside the company. She had made contact with a like-minded colleague in the Infrastructure division. She had also connected with the Facilities Manager at her site who understood the value of reducing the company's carbon footprint. However, he was finding his own attempts to make sustainability improvements on site difficult. So it was going to be extremely challenging to set up a company-wide sustainability network.

When asked to predict where the next three to five years might lead, she said:

> It all depends on whether I'm successful in managing to make these changes. If I can make a small breakthrough or if I get my contract renewed and become permanent, I can see myself being happy here. After my Master's, I don't want to become full time but may have to. I see myself progressing as far as possible in a sustainability role, but I might have to move to another organisation.

Phase 2: The road to emancipation

When we caught up again with Emma in November 2013, a lot had changed: she had completed her MSc in Sustainable Development, which she said 'gave me more credibility', and she was now working as an Environmental and Sustainability Advisor in the company, splitting her time between Cavendish Nuclear and the Infrastructure Business Unit. How, we wanted to know, had she been able to gain this role, which was so much more closely aligned with her sustainability interests?

After our previous interview, Emma had done a project management stint as a project assistant in another part of the business and her line manager had subsequently sent her on some project management training. While she described it as a 'good experience', she added that, 'The whole time I was still wanting to get involved with sustainability and environmental work'.

Then a series of events led to a significant change in her work. In February 2012, one of the company's principal customers organised an exhibition with a focus on sustainability. She organised a stand for the exhibition, gathering some case studies linked to sustainability.

Next, Emma joined the team preparing a bid for Hinkley Point C power station. 'Because EDF are hot on sustainability, sustainability was a key part of the bid. It was an amazing opportunity.' She 'got really involved' with the project, working on it from April to September 2012. The bid team 'were really open-minded. I ran a workshop to make sure everyone was aware of sustainability requirements—came up with ideas we could do... [these] went down really well.' It was 'quite a challenge' getting sustainability integrated into all the bid documents. While Cavendish Nuclear is still waiting for the outcome of the bid process, if they win the work, Emma would have an opportunity 'to work on site as part of the project team in a sustainability/environmental role. That's a really positive thing.'

As the result of a maternity leave in the Infrastructure Business Unit, which was more advanced than Cavendish Nuclear in managing its environmental/sustainability performance, Emma was able to be seconded to Infrastructure part time to gain valuable experience working with the environmental/sustainability team. She was able to hand over her document control and project management responsibilities to other people.

While Emma has to balance her workload between her Infrastructure and Cavendish Nuclear commitments, which can sometimes be quite challenging, she notes: 'I've been really lucky with my managers, they've always been really good. Some are not involved in the environment at all but are happy to let me do that stuff on the side. They're always very understanding.'

Cavendish Nuclear's progress on sustainability has also been accelerated by the establishment of an environmental working group to ensure the company works towards environmental objectives and targets to achieve the ISO 14001 standard. This has been a challenge because, through acquisitions, Cavendish Nuclear now comprises five different businesses having to work as one. According to Emma, at the outset 'none of our management procedures or processes were aligned'. She wrote the over-arching manual and put together some of the documents required for the environmental management system so that it could be standardised across the business. The working group also established a standard requiring an environmental coordinator at every site in the business and instituted monitoring energy usage measures to help reduce the company's carbon footprint.

However, challenges remain, as Emma notes: 'I still haven't managed to get a consistent approach and policy in place and senior management buy-in.' In the meantime, the company's Director of Assurance, with whom her line manager arranged an initial meeting, has given her licence to come up with a sustainability policy and process to be presented to the Managing Director.

We asked whether there was anyone on the horizon who could help her with this. She mentioned a couple of senior managers who were engaged with EDF and mentioned that the company had been asked to report on sustainability progress. She had also been approved to do a course to become an associate member of the Institute of Environmental Management and Assessment, an institution for environmental practitioners.

Looking back on her transition, Emma admits that:

> I have definitely been frustrated ...I felt I'd been in the company such a long time; I thought I should move on ... not just for sustainability but was thinking, I've been here too long. But things started to pick up. I thought, I *am* happy, things are moving along ... I need to get training finished, a good step forward ... I am much happier.'

Key critical elements that enabled Emma to remain within the company and transition from 'exasperation' to 'emancipation' appear to be:

- **Gaining credibility**, both through completing the Master's degree in Sustainability and **paying her dues** in key projects
- An internal secondment that enabled Emma to learn more about the business (**woodshedding**), discover like-minded peers interested in environmental and sustainability issues
- **Pressure from a client** (EDF) to improve sustainability performance in order to gain a major contract

- **Support from a line manager 'godparent'** who, despite not necessarily being conversant with the detail of environmental/sustainability issues, recognised Emma's commitment to these issues and their importance to the success of the business
- **The establishment of a network** committed to improving environmental performance

Emma is still awaiting, and preparing for, a critical 'gig' with the senior management team to take the sustainability agenda forward in a coherent way.

Several paths are now open to Emma, depending on future events and the 'enabling environment' within Cavendish Nuclear:

- She could pursue the path of a 'tempered radical', helping to create and implement a coherent company-wide sustainability strategy and policy that becomes adopted by senior management
- She could become a 'social intrapreneur', developing genuinely new products, services or processes that are adopted by the company
- She could, further in the future, turn social *entrepreneur*—as Michael Anthony (Allianz) or Nick Hughes (Vodafone) have done—returning to her original dream of creating a retreat where people can experience sustainability practices first hand

Meanwhile, however, she is proof that, by building a foundation of technical 'woodshedding', improvisational 'job crafting' and the support of others in one's working 'ensemble', it is possible to transcend 'exasperation' and carve out a sustainability-focused role within a company.

Emergent: Stefan Koch, E.ON

Stefan Koch grew up in a small German village and learnt to appreciate the people and nature surrounding him. When starting his career, he was disappointed to learn how little business organisations recognise their potential for societal value generation. Stefan is convinced that mainstream business can create societal as well as financial benefits simultaneously. However, companies—especially multinational firms—still need to learn how to integrate both aspects.

His confidence in helping organisations to improve their social and commercial performance grew during his studies at Lund University (Sweden) and the University of Cologne. While there he organised a lecture series on 'Ethics and Economics' that attracted many of his fellow students. Together they approached the Dean to integrate ethical issues into the business curriculum. His Master's thesis aimed to prove that sound CR practices and double-bottom-line approaches are attractive to potential employees.

Equipped with confidence as well as sound CR knowledge and CSR experiences gained at Deutsche Bank AG, he joined E.ON Energy as a CR manager in January 2009, attracted by the huge potential that energy could have on sustainable development.

With an expected population of 9 billion people by 2050, with the majority of the growth coming from developing countries, there is a growing need for energy while at the same time resources are becoming more limited. Developing convenient energy solutions (solar, wind, anaerobic digestion, energy from waste, energy-efficiency-increasing end-product models) that are affordable to people in these regions could potentially create a market of US$500 billion (Aron, Kayser, Liautaud and Nowlan 2009). Any company finding feasible solutions might transform into an international leader in energy over the next 30–40 years while at the same time helping to address global challenges such as climate change and environmental degradation.

The social intrapreneurial idea: MicroEnergy for the 'bottom of the pyramid' market

Fascinated by Muhammad Yunus's microcredit idea, but at the same time maintaining a critical perspective, Stefan decided to test whether the concept could be translated to the energy sector. Inspired by a presentation by MicroEnergy International, he designed a plan through which E.ON Energy could use its experience in energy production and distribution to provide affordable access to energy in developing countries, especially in regions where local businesses are energy intensive. Traditional forms of energy production by fuel engines or burning wood generate high costs for local consumers and also imply serious environmental and healthy impacts. If E.ON Energy could use its experience in the energy sector to provide access to energy in developing countries, this would represent a clear business opportunity as well as addressing environmental and social issues around energy.

Project development

Stefan's initial success came with the presentation of the MicroEnergy idea to the E.ON Energy CEO who reacted positively to the proposal. He and colleagues from different departments such as Climate & Renewables, Energy Policy, Research & Development, Energy Projects and Finance & Risk teamed up to generate a feasibility study and to develop a pilot project. He also worked on opportunities for know-how transfer. Sending senior managers or experts into existing micro-energy projects would provide an alternative approach to personal development and would broaden the horizons of decision-makers. In his very low-key manner, Stefan said: 'I would consider my efforts a success if we have the first direct or indirect pilot working and we can prove first the societal benefits and estimate potential financial outcomes in the long run.'

To progress the project to pilot stage, Stefan and his team would have to overcome a number of obstacles. One would be to convince a senior sponsor to invest in the project (commitment, time, resources). Another would be to overcome the dichotomy of philanthropy versus business development as others classify his idea as one or the other. However, Stefan was convinced that both needed to be aligned:

> You will not be able to scale up the societal impact if there is no long-term market approach and profitability, as profit is one of the main drivers of business especially in developing countries. At the same time, a pure focus on profits would destroy the potential for realisation and also the trust in the stakeholder network which makes this initiative feasible in the first place.

A third major obstacle would be the incentive systems, which were based mainly on short-term results. For the MicroEnergy pilot, Stefan was expecting a pay-off period of at least three years, if not longer, from the financial point of view. The improvement for the people and regions would hopefully generate significant outputs before then.

His advice to other social intrapreneurs: 'Be courageous, hold on to your idea even if this is difficult at times. If you can't find the business case for your project—think again and create it. But don't leave the social one behind!'[3]

Empowered: Kenan Aksular, Athlon

Kenan Aksular is an empowered social intrapreneur. He works for the Dutch-headquartered car-leasing firm Athlon, which is owned by Rabobank. Athlon leases 240,000 vehicles across ten countries. Kenan, the son of a Yugoslav immigrant father and a Dutch mother, had dreamt as a youngster of starting his own business. However, school studies disrupted by family difficulties led him to join Athlon instead, initially as a salesman, where he has had a career of nearly two decades.

After five months' enforced time off as a result of 'burn-out' he asked to transfer to a new role, and in 2005 he became Athlon's first Innovation Manager, reporting to the company president. Shortly thereafter, he was approached by a student from the Technical University of Delft who was seeking an internship in which to develop his Master's thesis on 'Mobility 2020'. The student's work led Kenan to start questioning the existing Athlon business model.

The business challenge: creating new sustainable services

The business rationale for Kenan is clear: On average, Athlon's corporate customers lease vehicles for around 20% of their employees. The other 80% are, crudely speaking, left to make their own way by bus, train, bike or, possibly, their own car. If Athlon could give these remaining employees 'mobility solutions', as Kenan likes to put it, the company could potentially shift its customer base from 20% to 100% of employees. His personal motivation? 'I have two young kids and I would love to tell them "your dad was in the movement which changed things". I want to do something meaningful!'[4]

The social intrapreneurial idea: a sustainable mobility plan

As a first step, he developed a website showing where fuel prices were cheapest within a 5 km radius of the user's location. His rationale was that the total cost of lease-ownership included a substantial element for fuel and 'save-lease' would reward drivers who reduced their fuel consumption and used cheaper gasoline stations. He found variations between the lowest and highest price per litre of fuel of €0.15. In its first three days the website drew 4 million hits. When Kenan sought the endorsement of the NGO WWF for the website, he was introduced to

---

3 Sources for this profile include author interview with Stefan Koch, 10 March 2010; websites www.eon-energie.com; www.microenergy-international.de/; and the following references: Morris, Winiecki, Chowdhary and Cortiglia 2007; Navajas and Tejerina 2006.

4 Based on author interview in Amsterdam, 2012, subsequent exchanges and Balch 2013.

the European Insulation Manufacturers Association (EURIMA) Trias Energetica model for energy-saving buildings.[5] This in turn, stimulated him to develop a five-step mobility plan, based on the following questions:

- Do you need to travel? Compare with working from home, video-conferencing etc.
- If yes, what is the most sustainable transport, for example, public transport, car-pooling etc.?
- If car, what is the most environmentally friendly vehicle that Athlon can offer?
- How can we change the behaviours of drivers? For example, employer gives the travel budget to employees to manage themselves.
- Can we re-invest savings in CO_2 reduction with more costly options or if necessary use savings for carbon offset?

Project development

Progressively, Kenan has been developing intrapreneurial solutions for the different steps.

Athlon has invested in more than 1,500 electric vehicles. The company is now participating in the **A15 Energy Highway initiative**, a €4.5m cross-sector project that aims to get 3,500 electric vehicles on the streets of the Netherlands by 2015. In addition, Kenan has negotiated a deal with the US-based luxury EV manufacturer Tesla to lease the new Model S in Athlon's European markets.

Car-sharing is another business area Kenan is developing. On average, a leased car is used for less than 2.5 hours a day. For most of the day, it is sitting in the office car park. In 2012, Athlon took a minority share in peer-to-peer Dutch car-sharing firm SnappCar and is now encouraging its corporate lessees to share their car during the day with colleagues— 'B2E' (business to employee). The 'ideal situation' would ultimately be to open the sharing scheme to all-comers.

Another of Kenan's non-leasing ventures is an **independent advisory service** that focuses on reducing companies' transport-related footprint. Athlon Mobility Scan Consultancy works on everything from introducing corporate bike schemes to developing car-pooling options. 'The technology is there. The products are there. But now it's a matter of helping our customers drive change', he states. One way of facilitating that is through a mobility card, which enables employees to bundle together taxis, parking, bike hire and other non-leasing mobility services through a single billing system.

What started as a unit specifically for the Dutch operations has, since 2009, become a cross-European innovation team for sustainability and mobility.

Let us now look at the social intrapreneur's journey in more detail.

---

5 http://www.eurima.org/energy-efficiency-in-buildings/trias-energetica, accessed 6 December 2013.

The social intrapreneur's journey

The notion of the social intrapreneur's journey was described initially by innovator and entrepreneur Maggie De Pree[6]—then with the consulting firm Imaginals[7]—in a model focusing on the development of a social intrapreneur's project. The social intrapreneurs may pass through several stages described as:

Inspire → Design → Lift → Launch → Scale

1. **Inspire.** 'Aha' moment–get ideas

2. **Design.** Research the idea

3. **Lift.** Find finance, mentors, allies, momentum

4. **Launch.** Test and perhaps go to scale

5. **Scale.** Take the intrapreneurial idea from test-market to broad scale

Figure 2.1 The social intrapreneur's journey

Source: © Imaginals: www.imaginals.net–Maggie De Pree.

Based on our interviews, we believe that the developmental journey of the social intrapreneur may contain cycles of project/enterprise development but in the context of a larger life journey, often with multiple threads running in parallel along the way.

Depending on the conditions present in the 'enabling environment' for social intrapreneurism—and the amount of 'woodshedding' and 'jamming' the social intrapreneur has undertaken—opportunities for transformation from one 'type' to another will arise.

As we suggested at the beginning of this chapter, here are some examples of individuals we encountered whose 'types' changed over the course of their journeys:

---

6 Maggie De Pree (née Brenneke) is an innovator, entrepreneur and co-founder of the League of Intrapreneurs. See her profile at http://www.thehumanagency.net/about-us.html.

7 www.imaginals.net.

Empowered social intrapreneurs have subsequently become **exasperated** or **exited** from their organisations as the result of a change of senior management or other conditions in the corporate environment.

An **empowered** social intrapreneur may have grown a project to a size that requires a different sort of individual who can manage large-scale organisational processes; the social intrapreneur has then **exited** the organisation to launch other projects or remained within the organisation but assumed a different sort of role.

Successful business **entrepreneurs** may have belatedly recognised the positive social impacts of their operations and become sustainability activists.

Israeli entrepreneur Naty Arp was a member of Kibbutz Hatzerim in 1965 when he and his fellow kibbutz members co-founded Netafim, the drip irrigation company, based on innovative technology developed originally to ensure the group's survival in the Negev Desert. Although the company grew into a global corporation, it retained the positive social values of the kibbutz, which were closely intertwined with its business purpose. Naty, now Chief Sustainability Officer and a member of the steering committee of the UN Global Compact CEO Water Mandate, observes:

> People care. They don't have to be socialists to care for their society and community. When we did it in the past, when we introduced drip irrigation, we thought it was the right thing to do. At that time we didn't know the meaning of the word 'sustainability'. We did know that drip irrigation can help farmers around the world to grow more with less.
>
> Today, when we do it, we realise that it is a tool for sustainable productivity. We know that it gives an answer to the core issues of sustainability: food security, water scarcity, arable land availability, and climate and energy issues. We do it for the society and for the company—we are doing good things for the company—to improve the spirit of our employees so they are part of it. Volunteering together to help unprivileged farmers in the nearby town or helping poor farmers in Africa to grow more with less is helping the company, not only the society.

Exasperated social intrapreneurs may have moved within an organisation to a team with whom they are more ideologically aligned or they may have **exited** from their organisations and gone on to become **empowered** social intrapreneurs in other companies.

Some sustainability practitioners have become **social entrepreneurs** running their own enterprises in parallel with their corporate 'day jobs'. One social intrapreneur, a serial entrepreneur who had been headhunted by a global business to create an intrapreneurial unit, had **exited** the company and gone back to being an independent commercial entrepreneur.

Empowered social intrapreneurs may stay with the projects that they have initiated and continue to manage them. Other social intrapreneurs may remain with their multinational employers but move jobs, replicating their idea in another market or move on to other sustainability initiatives.

Let's examine some aspects of the journey in more detail.

Vodafone's social intrapreneurial journey with M-PESA in Kenya

Social intrapreneurism and M-PESA

Vodafone's M-PESA illustrates this social intrapreneurial journey. The brainchild of Nick Hughes, a senior executive, and Susie Lonie, an m-commerce expert at Vodafone, M-PESA ('Mobile Money': *pesa* means money in Swahili) helps swift and secure transfer of money from one person to another through mobile phones—thus meeting a socioeconomic need of making cash readily available to people dependent on liquid money to sustain their livelihoods, while significantly expanding Vodafone's local subscriber base. The service was developed in Kenya through a partnership between Vodafone Group Services, Safaricom (its Kenyan network provider), Faulu Kenya (a microfinance organisation) and Commercial Bank of Africa. M-PESA—which would give an economy made up of numerous small traders rapid and secure access to funds—attracted 20,000 subscribers in the month of its launch, growing to over 10 million users in three years. The service, which now accesses over 80% of the country's adult population and handles funds worth around a third of the country's GDP, has clearly met a pressing socioeconomic need.

Background: why was M-PESA so successful in Kenya?

M-PESA uncovered a new market for Vodafone in Kenya—one where the population needed to be able to move money across distances safely and quickly, often to places and people with no access to banks or financial services. The migratory nature of Kenyan working population—with part of the family working in urban areas (e.g. Nairobi) and part of it based in villages—stimulated the need for domestic remittances and M-PESA provided a user-friendly solution. What began during a trial phase as a means of repaying microfinance credit loans, grew popular when launched and marketed as a person-to-person payment system and has since evolved into a comprehensive m-commerce platform. Using their M-PESA accounts, people can now pay for a range of services from electricity bills to school fees. The Bridge International Academy, which runs low-cost private schools in the poorest parts of Kenya, for example, accepts payments only through its bank account or through M-PESA. Not only does this avoid security risks involved in handling cash at the school premises, it also relieves parents of the need to be present while making payments.

How it works

M-PESA works simply. Customers can register for an account at one of Safaricom's outlets, where cash can be converted to e-money. By following instructions on their phone, payments can be made into their accounts and transferred to another M-PESA account holder; for example, for city-dwellers to send money home to their families still living in rural areas. Recipients can encash the amount at an M-PESA outlet or ATM machine. Accounts are secured by pin numbers, supported by round-the-clock customer service and subject to nominal transactional charges. Most importantly, Safaricom's vast network of M-PESA dealerships across the country and highly visible brand ensures that customers have easy access to mobile money. M-PESA's success in Kenya demonstrates how mobile technology can facilitate financial inclusion and improve the quality of life for developing economies. To understand how mobile phones can plug the developmental gap caused by financial exclusion, an overview of its role in connecting people to essential services is given below.

Mobile phones and financial inclusion

In 2010, a study conducted by the International Finance Corporation and the Harvard Kennedy School estimated that were over 5 billion mobile phone connections globally and that, by 2012, 1.7 billion people in developing economies would have access to mobile phones but not formal banking services. If banks, mobile network operators, technology support services and financial regulators proactively came together to overcome this development deficit, potentially 364 million 'unbanked' people could have accessed mobile financial services by the same year.

Mobile money's power lies in its convergence between two key industries: telecommunications and banking. Partnerships between several other players (such as public sector bodies, regulators, technology applications providers and retailers) formed the external framework of an ecosystem that helped M-PESA take off in Kenya. The other components of this ecosystem were the internal collaborations within Vodafone that brought the product to life. In Kenya, the combined impact meant that access to financial services had increased significantly in a short span of time as highlighted below.

M-PESA's impact on Kenya

In 2007 only 2.5 million out of a population of 39 million had bank accounts in Kenya. By April 2013 Safaricom enjoyed a 70% market share in Kenya with 19 million subscribers, of which approximately 15 million were active M-PESA users transacting over $50 million daily (Cheballah 2013). M-PESA now contributes 18% of Safaricom's total revenue and is serviced by 65,547 agents, 26,000 being added in the last financial year (Mwangi 2013). In March 2013, its revenue was found to have increased by 29.5% since the last financial year to KSh21.84 billion (US$253 million) (Safaricom Ltd 2013).

The high levels of financial exclusion combined with Safaricom's market share had thus given M-PESA access to a vast untapped market. In addition to the well-developed mobile network in Kenya, what worked in its favour was that the Central Bank of Kenya allowed Safaricom to operate M-PESA outside the banking law framework because the funds held in M-PESA accounts earn no interest and are held in a trust account with a licensed bank, meaning that neither Vodafone or Safaricom can use these funds and put them at risk. Technically, at launch the Central Bank did not give Safaricom or Vodafone a licence: it simply issued a letter stating that the Bank had no objections to the company offering M-PESA as a payment services.

M-PESA paved the way for more mobile financial products for a hitherto unbanked population. In 2010, M-KESHO, a microsavings account (which earned interest), was launched by Safaricom in partnership with Equity Bank and offered to M-PESA clients. M-PESA also partnered with Syngenta to provide crop insurance—accessing almost 11,000 farmers in 2010. In 2013, M-Shwari was introduced, allowing Safaricom subscribers access to savings accounts, to earn interest on deposits and to borrow through their mobile phones. It now has 1.2 million active customers (Cheballah 2013; Mwangi 2013). Other financial products introduced in the past year, include m-health, e-learning, m-agriculture services and M-Kopa solar lighting on a pay-as-you-go basis (Safaricom Ltd 2013).

Social intrapreneurism: journey within Vodafone

As shown in Figure 2.1, the social intrapreneur's journey, according Maggie De Pree, follows five key stages: inspire (when the idea is born), design (studying the idea), lift (finding resources, champions, mentors and drivers), launch (pilot and start scaling) and scale (market to a broad scale). Figure 2.2 traces developments at Vodafone in each of the five stages.

Figure 2.2 Vodafone's social intrapreneurial journey

Source: Developed from © Maggie De Pree.

Stage 1: Inspire

Vodafone grew dramatically from 1999 to 2001 with the acquisition of Mannes-mann. This created the need to upscale corporate functions quickly, and the company headhunted teams from other companies including a three-person corporate affairs and corporate responsibility team from BP that included Nick Hughes.

The stage where ideas are born, the 'Aha' moment at Vodafone occurred when Nick, then responsible for helping the company address the Millennium

Development Goals of reducing poverty by 50% by 2015, heard during an international conference on microfinance in Johannesburg that the UK's Department of International Development (DFID)'s Challenge Fund might be interested in supporting a pilot project to use mobile telephony to support microfinance. Created to pilot public–private partnership projects to tackle poverty, this fund would help Vodafone research and test a product that would bring financial inclusion to Kenya through mobile technology.

Despite being encouraged to submit a proposal to the Challenge Fund, Nick's proposal nearly fell through because some evaluation panel members questioned the appropriateness of giving taxpayers' funds committed to international development to a major multinational. It was approved, however, and the £1 million from the Challenge Fund, which Vodafone matched with resources and technical expertise, enabled Nick to 'go off radar' and enjoy a degree of autonomy during the crucial early phase. As Susie Lonie, one of the key people in the development of M-PESA, put it in an interview after receiving *The Economist*'s Social and Economic Innovation Award 2010 jointly with Nick for the M-PESA project: 'Money ... was the real determining factor for us ... M-PESA would have never existed had it not been for DFID's Challenge Fund.'[8]

Armed with the DFID money, Nick embarked on the work leading to the 'design' stage, including establishing links with potential partners, such as banks and microfinance agencies, technology service suppliers, NGOs and banking and telecom regulators to identify key barriers to accessing financial services in Kenya. A partnership between Vodafone, Faulu Kenya, a microfinance organisation, and Commercial Bank of Africa, was formed to pool competences required to test the product. Initially, the focus was on supporting people to repay microfinance loans in a mutually advantageous way. By using Safaricom's vast airtime sellers' distribution network, customers could make loan repayments while topping up their airtime. Not only would this allow repayments to be made quickly and efficiently, it would also give Faulu speedier access to remote areas.

Stage 2: Design

Nick initially tried to design the project by monthly visits to Kenya from the UK. Little happened between visits, however, and instead Nick persuaded Susie Lonie to accept a three-month secondment to Kenya to understand the practical realities of meeting user need. This was to end up being a two-year assignment in Kenya. The need to customise m-commerce products soon became apparent, as they were more tailored for mature Western economies. Some of the factors she had to consider while developing M-PESA included: developing tools to support Safaricom as it would be delivering the project locally; determining how money would be stored, given that the target audience was unbanked; partnering with a commercial bank to provide conventional banking services, as e-money issued needed to match real money in the bank; using basic mobile phones to access larger numbers; finding customers to participate in the pilot; and identifying retail outlets that would act as M-PESA agents, making a start with Safaricom airtime dealer network.

8 Interview of Nick Hughes and Susie Lonie following the receipt of the Social and Economic Innovation Award 2010, available at http://www.economistconferences.co.uk/video/economists-innovation-award-winners-2010/4500, accessed 8 January 2014.

This phase saw Susie augmenting infrastructural and operational details such as: identifying a software developer to customise the product, determining where servers should be located (Safaricom was found to be most suitable), finalising the brand name of M-PESA, recruiting and supporting agents, and trialling the system at Faulu. Nick and the team at Safaricom also initiated early discussions with the financial regulator (the Central Bank of Kenya) keeping it informed of progress and key developments.

Safaricom's support in managing consumer queries and cash-flow transactions through its customer care and finance departments significantly helped progress the project onto its launch phase. Ongoing training and guidance for employees on the workings of the system, from its business model to the use of the handset, ensured that staff were engaged and trained. Their belief in it propelled it forward, according to Susie—evident from the fact that staff across functions supported it over and above their existing roles. M-PESA had clearly been a hearts-and-minds project, although there was initial scepticism among the Safaricom country management.

Training sessions also had to be held with Faulu's employees to build their confidence in the security of electronic transactions, which were different from the paper-based systems they were accustomed to. Susie found she was not only introducing a new technology but also having to overcome mind-sets wary of the robustness of the new technology.

Stage 3: Lift

This phase saw Vodafone piloting M-PESA through eight agent stores and 500 clients in October 2005 in the Thika region of Kenya (Joseph 2013). Provided with mobile phones and an understanding of how to make cash transactions and loan repayments respectively, agents and customers began testing the product that was to soon to change the economic profile of Kenya. Operational hitches were found along the way, from basic issues such as getting people accustomed to using mobile phones to make payments, to building agent confidence in paying out cash withdrawals on receiving a text message. Other usage-related problems included customers having to swap sim cards to make payments, and some even losing them!

Lonie improvised the product as the pilot progressed, rolling out training for consumers and customising the technology to expand business. Improvisations included the SIMEX, which combined mobile phone numbers with M-PESA accounts onto a single sim, enabling consumers to purchase airtime with M-PESA e-money. The Lift phase also highlighted that M-PESA was proving even more usable for clients than for the microfinance institution. Clients were using it not just to repay microfinance loans but for a range of other payments, especially the quick transfer of funds between individuals (person-to-person payments). The microfinance partner (Faulu) on the other hand struggled with reconciling its traditional accounting systems with those of the M-PESA's e-commerce model. Thus the project evolved from the initial perceived need to the actual need.

Stage 4: Launch

At Vodafone, this stage saw the M-PESA team and supporting consultants making a series of technical improvements to make the service as user-focused as possible, based on the findings of the pilot, which concluded in October 2006. The pilot demonstrated that the product was technically sound, commercially viable and had a market not just in Kenya, but in other emerging economies as well—reason enough for Vodafone and Safaricom to consider launching it. For the latter it meant not only a new revenue stream as a payment service provider but also an opportunity to increase its customer base. For Vodafone its value was apparent as a low-cost payment remittance service, relevant due to its presence in areas witnessing significant international remittances such as from Germany to Turkey and from Europe to India. Other lessons learned during the pilot included: keeping the service simple, ensuring agents had the means of transacting between real money and e-money and, most importantly, that a microfinance institution may not have the infrastructure to run the service—mobile dealerships had more reach to scale up. M-PESA's launch offer thus included three basic functions: ability to withdraw and deposit cash at agent stores, make person-to-person payments and buy pre-paid airtime. This was done in keeping with Vodafone and Safaricom's procedural norms and succeeded because of their administrative infrastructure.

Stage 5 Scale

To prepare for scaling up, Safaricom and Vodafone with strong legal counsel and support worked with financial regulators to ensure there were no objections. Susie started recruiting a team to run the service and set up a training agency to support dealers. The service took off rapidly, bringing other challenges, notably the need to redevelop the platform to allow for very high numbers of transactions, building in tools to support the 'cash-in/cash-out' network across a hierarchy of agents and dealers. By 2013, there were over 15 million subscribers (Cheballah 2013).

Support from the leadership and in-house buy-in to start testing the product were also critical enablers that helped the project off the ground. While Vodafone's leadership backing helped secure the Challenge Fund and initiate the project, it was Safaricom's willingness to test it despite risks that lent it vigour. As Michael Joseph, Managing Director for Vodafone's Mobile Money, then head of Safaricom, subsequently explained in a film for USAID: 'We launched this (M-PESA) in 2007 not knowing how successful or unsuccessful it would be, but I had an inkling it would be a fantastic product, but I really didn't know' (Joseph 2013). Indeed, he had initially been sceptical but prepared to see the pilot evolve.

M-PESA's spread

The success of M-PESA lies not just in the fact that it increased access to financial services for millions in Kenya, while building Safaricom's customer loyalty, but also that the project has been replicated in other countries as well, such as Tanzania, South Africa, Philippines, Afghanistan and, more recently, India (Standard Digital 2013), after earlier attempts stalled because of regulatory hurdles. Vittorio Colao, Vodafone's CEO, persuaded Michael Joseph to come out of retirement to become Managing Director Mobile Money at Vodafone—to help the company roll out M-PESA-type services. Colao has also said that Vodafone will use some of the proceeds from the 2013 sale of its stake in Verizon to finance further roll-out.

Thus, our interviews suggest that social intrapreneurs may be some (or indeed all) of these types at different stages during the development of their ideas. While the interaction between the social intrapreneur and the corporate environment varies, we observed some stable sets of mind-sets, behaviours and skills.

Mind-sets, behaviours and skills of social intrapreneurs

> There's a way of playing safe, there's a way of using tricks and there's the way I like to play, which is dangerously, where you're going to take a chance on making mistakes in order to create something you haven't created before (Dave Brubeck, jazz pianist)[9]

One of the distinguishing characteristics of outstanding jazz musicians, particularly the ones who change the fundamental conventions of musical form, is their ability, and even predilection, to take artistic risks. This is not rooted in recklessness but rather a natural desire—even a requirement—to push musical boundaries beyond the current repertoire that musicians have already invested considerable 'woodshedding' time to master.

Risk is, in fact, at the very heart of all jazz music-making by virtue of its improvisational nature. Whether it's a jam session with a handful of musicians or a concert with an audience of thousands, no two performances of a tune by any ensemble are alike, no matter how many times they have played a composition together.

SOCIAL INTRAPRENEURS EXPERIMENTING WITH NEW PRODUCTS AND SERVICES CAN LEARN FROM THE EXAMPLE OF JAZZ MUSICIANS WHO COMPOSE GROUND-BREAKING NEW PIECES REQUIRING UNUSUAL ENSEMBLES TO PERFORM THEM. HERE, THE GLOBAL ARTS ENSEMBLE COMBINED A CLASSICAL STRING QUARTET (DARRAGH MORGAN (VIOLIN), NICKY SWEENEY (VIOLIN), GUSTAV CLARKSON (VIOLIN), ROBIN MICHAEL (CELLO)) AND A JAZZ QUARTET (PETER KING (ALTO), BRUCE BARTH (PIANO), JEREMY BROWN (BASS), STEPHEN KEOGH (DRUMS)). TOGETHER THEY REPRISED PETER KING'S *JANUS*, A SPECIALLY COMMISSIONED SUITE FIRST PERFORMED AT THE 1997 LONDON JAZZ FESTIVAL, AT THIS GLOBAL MUSIC FOUNDATION CONCERT AT KINGS PLACE HALL ONE, LONDON IN 2011.

---

9 Quoted in 'All About Jazz', http://www.allaboutjazz.com/php/jazzquotes.php.

There is already significant historical documentation of what great jazz musicians think, learn and do. But less is known about the distinguishing characteristics of social intrapreneurs.

Once we began to interview and classify different types of social intrapreneurs and the wide range of journeys they were experiencing—exasperated, exited, emergent and empowered—the next questions we wanted answered were: What are the characteristics of social intrapreneurs that make them different from their 'close relatives' and other colleagues in their companies? And how can we distinguish different types of social intrapreneurs from each other?

We therefore began to look at:

- **Mind-sets.** How social intrapreneurs *think*; particularly their strongly-held beliefs about their own lives and careers, about the companies where they work and about the world at large

- **Behaviours.** How social intrapreneurs act, inside and outside their companies, and the principles that guide them

- **Skills.** What social intrapreneurs have learned how to do that makes them different from others

Only with the right mind-set, appropriate behaviours and skills will individuals be able to deal with current sustainability challenges. We therefore took as our unit of analysis the personal history of the social intrapreneurs themselves to better understand how these attributes emerge. We were particularly interested in discovering through our interviews whether there are specific life circumstances (e.g. early exposure to social issues or entrepreneurism, opportunities for skills development) or personality traits (e.g. a consistent tendency to persist in the face of adversity, openness to new experiences) that are common to social intrapreneurs.

We were also interested in discovering whether any of these environmental factors or personal characteristics enhance or diminish a social intrapreneur's chances of guiding a project to a successful conclusion (i.e. producing both positive commercial and social impacts).

Mind-sets

A mind-set is defined by the principles and values that shape individual decision-making. The principles and values of the majority of social intrapreneurs we interviewed centre on societal value creation, such as preserving nature and serving others.

> 'I've been brought up not to waste anything … my mum's a cook and my dad's a social worker but they've always had the same interests as me—they like gardening and they've got a book on self-sufficiency I found interesting.'

'I always liked to be involved in projects and wanted to see the fruits. I was inspired by an aunty who was in Sao Paulo and worked in a favela in Monte Azul with childcare centres.'

'I think I have a different mind-set, possibly because I have had such a varied career.'

Early experiences build awareness of the interdependence of people and their environment

Several of our subjects reported having early experiences of nature, whether by the sea, in the countryside or on farms, which kindled an interest in, and often a desire to preserve, the natural environment.

'Although I was born in London, we then moved to Frome when I was aged 8—quite a rural town. I spent time in Wales at my grandparents' farm so had a dual urban and countryside upbringing. I've always loved the countryside. I've always been attracted to the idea of being self-sufficient, which has evolved into sustainability.'

'There was my immediate family and my half-sister's family on a smallholding in Cornwall ... On a smallholding you see where your food comes from. There were influences from there.'

Even later experiences can awaken a similar awareness:

'Apart from a two-week exchange in France, I hadn't travelled at all. Then I was living in the jungle in India, living right up against nature in its raw and beautiful form ... humanity is there in three dimensions, floodlit every day. It was huge and—realising we are all human beings—different from home—realising dependency and balance with the environment. My thinking about society and the environment goes back to that year.'

As one of our Doughty Centre Visiting Fellows, Ron Ainsbury has observed, what seems to distinguish social intrapreneurs from others who develop an awareness of social and environmental issues—for example, social entrepreneurs—is that they also recognise the potential for large companies, with their significant scale and breadth of resources, to play an important role in addressing those issues.

Transcending 'either/or' thinking about business and society

Social intrapreneurs have overcome the traditional dichotomy of thinking either in business or in societal terms. Many of our interviewees struggled with a corporate environment that either placed their ideas in a philanthropy or business field. They, however, were able to articulate how their ideas can integrate both business and societal goals to a business audience.

'There was a long-term relationship. I could present that in a business framework. This isn't about making money but it's not about philanthropy, either. This debate went on for months. People presumed this was philanthropy—I said, no, this is about doing good business.'

'Key lesson? Almost disguise social aspects and present [the project idea] as helping business to grow revenue. You can still talk about sustainability but emphasise business—then people are happier to talk.'

Our interviewees clearly exhibited principles and values oriented around social and environmental care and preservation. One intermediary in the social intrapreneurship environment remarked: 'The loyalty of social intrapreneurs is bigger regarding the societal value than to the company.' Therefore, we describe their mind-set as oriented towards societal value creation. However, in contrast to many people working in the non-profit sector, social intrapreneurs are able to understand the business value of addressing societal issues and have overcome the dichotomy of either profit or societal value.

Behaviours

Social intrapreneurs demonstrated some dominant behaviours in the process of becoming aware of societal challenges and in their approach to resolving them. Three behaviours were most common: persistency and self-belief, learning, and outreach.

All our interviewees referred to being persistent in following through their ideas, especially when asked what advice they would give to others.

'Perseverance—there were times when it felt like I was fighting a guerrilla war inside the organisation. Be determined to make happen where you think it right for organisation.'

'Be resilient and thick-skinned about the cynicism and doubt you will get.'

'Don't give up—this is where dogged determination comes in. In the early days, I was accused of all sorts by competitors, trade associations, the media. It would have been easy to sweep it [labour issues] under the carpet. [Q: What kept you going?] I was right and they were wrong. I'd seen it and they hadn't.'

'Be courageous, hold on to your idea even if this is difficult at times. If you can't find the business case for your project think again and create it.'

Be pleasantly persistent

Gib Bulloch, founder of Accenture Development Partnerships, elaborates further:
Many years ago (when I had a 'normal' job), a client told me that I was 'pleasantly persistent'. At the time, I saw this as being shorthand for 'pain in the backside', which no doubt I can often be. But the learning for me was really around the need for resilience. Striving for change and battling corporate inertia can be very

tiring and it's very tempting to give up hope. Numerous barriers, obstacles and small-minded thinking can get in your way. A degree of unrelenting optimism and resilience is required. The prize is too great to give up easily!

Furthermore, social intrapreneurs exhibited a strong learning orientation mostly expressing an experiential learning experience that involved trial and error.

> 'I loved engineering—I'm a learning junkie——you learn new stuff every day.'

> 'It was one of those environments where if you tried something, you could do more of it if you succeeded. From that I decided to do Economics at A level and Maths, decided I wanted to go to university and do business. But I wanted to do a sandwich degree: two years' study, one year working, and another year's study.'

A significant learning opportunity for social intrapreneurs can emerge from the experience of reaching out to the communities or environments where they want to make a difference.

> 'I went out there [India], got a good tour of all of the areas, tried to turn over as many stones as possible to see what was going on. If you look at social issues, it's easy to be taken round by someone with a vested interest. I had been to places people had never been before—people there said they'd never seen anybody like me before ... You've got to really understand the issues. It's really easy to say bonded labour is a problem. You've got to visit, understand, deeply analyse what's going on.'

> 'I had spent a year travelling into very remote, poor areas, where a dollar a day seems like a lot of money, and I saw then the impact when I started to pay the farmers for their first crop. I saw the wonderment and relief on the faces of farmers—I realised we did not understand poverty. I felt then that it should be a mandatory requirement of business to think about this approach—it allowed families to create income. I felt proud. [The company] is a pioneer—we should now be promoting this to other companies on the international stage.'

> 'In Rwanda I watched the forest walk backwards day by day, watching water in the lake drop inch by inch as water was taken for drinking. It goes back to my time in India, the whole business of mankind's balance with nature. Part of the world, the developed world, has produced amazing things and is obsessed by consumerism, yet there are billions of people without. We have one global society floating on one shining blue planet floating in the cosmos. That was the beginning of the end of mainstream engineering for me.'

Some of the social intrapreneurs were also sent to a local environment for business reasons and experienced their epiphany during such a visit, realising the potential for societal value creation. This is an important insight for anyone wanting to create an enabling environment for social intrapreneurs inside their company.

The key learning outcome is to understand deeply the social or environmental issues social intrapreneurs want to address. This often results from visiting the areas and communities where they want to make a difference.

In conclusion, social intrapreneurs' behaviour can be characterised as being persistent and having a learning orientation. As we have seen, however, persistence in pursuit of a social intrapreneurial goal can have different outcomes: they can become 'emergent', 'empowered', 'exasperated' or 'exited', depending on the qualities of the 'enabling' (or 'disabling') environment in which they find themselves.

Skills

Skills are also called talents and describe learned capacity to perform a task with a minimum outlay of time and energy. The common skills we recognised among social intrapreneurs were entrepreneurship and communications—both together created the necessary trust that social intrapreneurs need to earn in order to pursue their ideas internally.

Many of our interviewees honed their entrepreneurial skills at an early age, learning how to sell goods and services and to address client needs.

> 'From age 15, we all had jobs: greengrocer, gas station, started making dresses for friends. So quite young we learned you could earn money and use it to do what you wanted to do.'

> 'While I was in school, I had a part-time job on a market stall—sold pots and pans, M&S seconds, fabric—that whole commerce side of things really. I enjoyed it and it attracted me. So from an early age—12, 13, 14—I was learning about making money and being entrepreneurial.'

Marketing and communication skills appeared to help several of our subjects build a business case for their project and engage the support of others.

> 'While I was there I got more interested in marketing—really understanding what consumers needs and wants were, understanding customer/consumer dynamics.'

Other specialist technical skills in fields such as IT and engineering appear to have aided a number of our subjects in preparing an in-depth business case for action, designing or implementing a project.

Social intrapreneurs also appear skilled at working in partnership with other organisations; this can be the key to establishing credibility and gaining the expertise needed for building the business case for action on social/environment issues and to implement, or provide external validation for, social innovation programmes.

Our interviewees reported numerous collaborative relationships with other parts of their business but also with NGOs, governing bodies, educational institutions and even commercial organisations, all benefiting their projects in various ways.

'Work with NGOs ensured quality market research, probably the most extensive quality market research done into that business segment in India. Indian management went to stay with villagers to understand them.'

'Everything I do is checked by an accredited third party. If you get caught through greenwash, the damage is massive.'

These entrepreneurial as well as communication skills, combined with a deep knowledge of their business, helped them to gain the trust of their employer. This trust then was considered essential for the necessary leeway to experiment with new ideas and to gain the support of key corporate decision-makers who determine strategy and have the power to invest resources in social innovation projects. Social intrapreneurs have an ability to find and inspire champions to give 'air cover' and sponsors to sanction resources.

Athlon's Kenan Aksular persuaded the company president to give him organisational freedom. The president who is chair of the board gave air-cover, which was crucial in the early days when there was scepticism on the board. Asked to explain why the president gave this early backing before the momentum of Kenan's work became obvious, he says: 'the president is a visionary, thinks the same way as me. He's a non-conformist too, not a traditionalist!'

Kenan bubbles with new ideas such as linking personal mobility with real estate; or linking his personal passion for old classic cars to his work with the idea that as part of an overall package of leasing sustainably, Athlon might offer classic cars for a sporty weekend treat—not per se sustainable but if it encourages more sustainable practices overall, he reckons it could be worth it.

'I was lucky—I had two or three senior directors who believed in me. One I'd worked for for ten years knew me as a character, knew [this person] doesn't set herself up for failure.'

'In the early days it was fair to say that they just let me get on with it. The trust I'd built up with the other directors meant they trusted my judgement. It takes a lot of personal passion and commitment and convincing.'

'Managers have always given me leeway because they know I deliver.'

Trust is linked to a general tolerance of experiments that has been cited as a feature of long-lived companies (De Geus 1997) and those that are generally innovative.

Gib Bulloch, Director of Accenture Development Partnerships, has elevated collaborative partnerships to an art.

Gib Bulloch, Accenture Development Partnerships[10]

Gib Bulloch was educated at the University of Strathclyde (MBA, 1992) and the University of Cambridge (Post-Grad Certificate, Cross Sectoral Partnerships, 2004). He spent the first phase of his career in professional roles at large private-sector companies (Petroleum Engineer, BP; Business Analyst, Mars) before joining Accenture's strategy team in 1996 where he worked as a management consultant to multinationals for several years.

This represents a significant amount of 'woodshedding'—gaining a top-quality education and then acquiring a range of in-depth technical, analytical, consultancy and managerial skills in different industrial sectors.

He describes a 'Eureka moment' that occurred while he was travelling on the London Underground and came across an article in the *Financial Times* on Voluntary Service Overseas (VSO) looking for individuals with business skills to volunteer in developing countries.

> The article was about VSO's new corporate volunteering programme called 'VSO Business Partnerships'. Instead of seeking cash from business, VSO wanted business skills. There was no shortage of doctors, nurses and teachers applying to do a two-year VSO placement—but there were very few accountants, MBAs and business managers. VSO wanted companies to supply them with people with these skills for about 6–12 months at a time, on a loan basis, with their jobs held open for their return.

He adds: 'I'd thought development was only for doctors, nurses and teachers. Not business people like me.'

This is the catalytic event that triggered a dramatic change of mind-set: realising that people in business could play an important role in the field of development. Gib persuaded Accenture to second him and he went to western Macedonia to work in a small business support centre for small and medium enterprises (SMEs) seeking to build the business skills of local staff.

This change, in both mind-set and subsequent behaviour, is somewhat analogous to a musician in the pre-bebop era—who would have been accustomed to hearing major, minor, seventh, sixth, augmented and diminished chords—suddenly being exposed to, and then learning to incorporate into their playing, 9ths, 11ths and 13ths. These chords contained the 'colour tones' that became more prevalent during the bebop era of Charlie Parker, Miles Davis and Dizzy Gillespie, along with the fast tempos, instrumental virtuosity and improvisation built on harmonic structure and melody that characterised this genre as it emerged.

10 This account is based on the following sources: Bulloch 2012; SustainAbility 2008; interview conducted in March 2010; Net Impact: http://london.netimpact.org.uk/gib-bulloch/, accessed 8 January 2014; LinkedIn profile for Gib Bulloch: http://www.linkedin.com/in/gibbulloch, accessed 8 January 2014.

He spent a year in Macedonia as part of VSO's Business Partnerships Scheme. During this time, Gib provided business planning to a local non-profit business support centre for SMEs.

This was a very important preparatory phase of Gib's career. He had to apply his management consultancy skills in an entirely new context, learning how to 'jam' (improvise) in the cultural context of a foreign country, with colleagues in a new sector (not-for-profit). The 'harmonies' and 'rhythms' would have been different from anything Gib had done before. It is like a 'trad' (traditional) jazz musician learning to become fluent in a 'bebop' jazz idiom.

JAZZ MUSICIANS MAY FORM ALLIANCES WITH CREATIVE ARTISTS OUTSIDE THE MUSIC DOMAIN TO PRODUCE INNOVATIVE MULTIMEDIA PERFORMANCES. HERE, THE KIT DOWNES QUINTET (WITH LUCY RAILTON, CELLO, AND JAMES ALLSOPP, BASS CLARINET) WORKED WITH ANIMATOR LESLEY BARNES TO CREATE A NEW FORM OF STORYTELLING FUSING ORIGINAL NEW MUSIC WITH SHORT ANIMATED FILMS.

SIMILARLY, SUCCESSFUL SOCIAL INTRAPRENEURISM PROJECTS CAN EXTEND THE RANGE OF PRODUCTS, SERVICES AND PROCESSES THAT COMPANIES CREATE. AS ADP FOUNDER GIB BULLOCH HAS NOTED, INNOVATIVE COMPANIES THAT FOCUS ON SOLVING SOCIAL PROBLEMS MAY FIND THEMSELVES WORKING WITH NGO PARTNERS IN ENTIRELY NEW BUSINESS DOMAINS.

The social intrapreneurial idea: Accenture Development Partnerships

His stint abroad fostered an ambition to combine

> Accenture's convening power in the corporate sector with ADP's in the develop-
> ment sector to help broker and integrate cross-sectoral coalitions to help tackle
> major social, economic and environmental challenges.
>
>   On the way home from Macedonia, I tasked myself with putting this thinking
> into a form my colleagues at Accenture couldn't ignore. Instead of producing
> a thick deck of PowerPoint presentation slides, I wrote a faux press article pro-
> jecting six months into the future. It was set at the World Economic Forum in
> Davos where Accenture's Chairman had just announced the launch of an inno-
> vative new not-for-profit to great acclaim. This faux article got the attention of
> the Chairman who agreed to discuss it over breakfast. He wanted to hear more
> about the idea. The journey to create Accenture Development Partnerships had
> begun.

By telling a compelling story in the form of a 'press article from the future',
Gib created a novel 'composition' that caught the attention and support of the
Chairman:

> We had a mandate to do more. First step: put some flesh on the bones of the
> idea to create a new hybrid business that would effectively turn the classical
> management consultancy model upside down. A business model that was
> based around a three-way contribution: Accenture provides access to its high
> performers free of profit and corporate overhead; these employees voluntar-
> ily give up a substantial percentage of their salary; and non-profits would cut
> a check to Accenture for consulting and technology services at significantly
> reduced rates, with no reduction in quality for those services.

Figure 2.3 illustrates these three contributions from Accenture (ACN in the diagram), employee participants and clients.

Figure 2.3 The Accenture Development Partnerships business model
Source: Accenture.

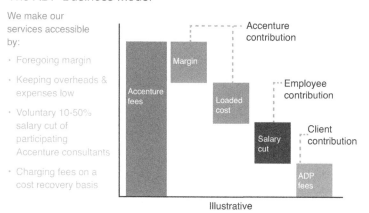

At this point Gib was transformed from a 'soloist' to being a 'bandleader' in an 'ensemble':

This is where the concept went from an individual dream, to a pioneering team; it's where 'I' became 'we' in the evolution of the story. At this stage we were a 'guerrilla movement'—a small group of supportive friends and colleagues who worked in their spare time, evenings, weekends, coffee breaks, whenever. We set out to gather data on the latent needs of the development sector, what our competition were or weren't doing, sizing the market opportunity, and so on. Jointly, we took our findings to Accenture's UK leadership team, seeking their buy in. Our ask? We wanted each unit head to lend us a body to be part of a feasibility study, for three months.

A significant amount of 'jamming'—collecting, exchanging and developing ideas (in dialogue and surveys)—then followed to create a viable business model for the project.

From extensive interviews with non-profit leaders, it became clear that there was a genuine interest and need for our services. The finance team showed that if overhead and profit were waived by the firm we could take very significant costs out of the business model. Yes, the numbers could add up!

But perhaps the most significant finding came from a survey of thousands of our staff. We not only asked about their interest levels but also how well they were rated within Accenture. The results showed a strong correlation between interest and performance—the bell curves were skewed to the right, meaning that the people we wanted to attract, retain and develop in the business were exactly the people to whom the proposition most appealed.

This certainly captured the attention of leadership and the feasibility study soon morphed into a pilot in the middle of 2002 and then full-scale launch in 2003 initially focused on working with NGOs.

Here Gib was developing an entirely new 'form' of collaboration for Accenture. But his early years of technical, analytical and managerial skills development, followed by his VSO 'woodshedding' and 'jamming' practice would have helped him develop and refine the critical skills that would enable him to orchestrate a new form of 'ensemble working'—across national borders and sectors—in ADP.

A particular feature of the programme was the manner in which Accenture employees were released from their corporate 'band' to serve in a cross-sector partnership ensemble overseas, where a significantly greater amount of improvisation would be required, and then returned home, where a completely different form of improvisation would be required.

The key principles were the 'three Rs': Release, Reintegration and Recognition.

Release. Individuals who satisfy our performance criteria (you must be in the upper bands) can apply to do an Accenture Development Partnerships project and then seek approvals from HR and the entity in Accenture they are deployed to. Once a project has been found that matches their skills and availability (and personal preferences as much as possible), they attend two days of training which most love.

Reintegration and Recognition. These two go hand in hand—something we perhaps didn't pay enough attention to in the early days. Employees will have had an exciting, demanding and sometimes life changing experience which will have tested their resourcefulness to the limit. They will usually come back better, happier and more engaged ... However, some will struggle to adjust to coming back to a 'day job' where they may have less responsibility or client exposure. Some of this is inevitable but we've worked very hard to mitigate these downsides. Recognizing the contribution of the individual through the formal performance management process, as well as informally in the likes of community meetings, goes a long way to making the returning participant feel valued. We also seek to ensure that the new skills, development knowledge and confidence can be harnessed back in the commercial business, often on commercial project which have elements of sustainability or emerging markets to them.

After a period of rapid growth, the business had by 2009 reached something of a plateau. ADP's 'playing style' needed to be refreshed by bringing new, different players into the 'band':

We were at an inflexion point and the team thought hard about how to take Accenture Development Partnerships to the next level.

This was to focus on cross-sector convergence—where business, government and civil society are converging to create markets and innovative solutions that tackle development challenges.

Cross-sector convergence goes beyond the current discussions around shared valued and inclusive business models to talk about a more profound change that will challenge the roles, structures and actors within the broader development landscape. While we would continue to provide business and technology advice to NGOs and foundations and support their programmes in the field, the most exciting and innovative work started to emerge as commercial clients leveraged Accenture's convening power to act as a broker, or more often an integrator, for a new breed of partnerships and increasingly complex coalitions.

This meant we could, for example, work at the interface between Unilever and Oxfam to get more smallholder farmers in Tanzania into the corporate value chain; and with Barclays, CARE and Plan to take the bank's microfinance offerings to village level where their NGO partners had the reach, the trust of the community, and an understanding of local needs. This saw us work increasingly side by side with Accenture's Sustainability Services group, which led to commercial pull through—i.e. we won work that we wouldn't have on the back of Accenture Development Partnerships.

The impacts of this new 'genre' of ensemble have been significant:

By 2013, ADP had completed more than 640 separate projects; was working with more than 140 clients including international NGOs such as Oxfam and World Vision, foundations such as Gates and Rockefeller, donor agencies, businesses and governments (see Figure 2.4); and staff had contributed in excess of $28 million in salary foregone.

Figure 2.4 ADP client base

Source: Accenture Development Partnerships.[11]

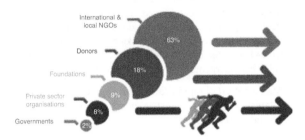

We collaborate with
140+
organisations

International & local NGOs
63%
Donors
Foundations 18%
Private sector organisations 9%
Governments 8%
2%

According to Gib,

> There is a demonstrable effect on our recruitment and retention, but ADP is having a positive effect on our brand and our reputation. We are also gaining useful first-hand experience of the emerging markets where our clients are going.

While his job title has not changed in several years, Gib's role 'changes every six months'. He now spends more time talking to Accenture commercial clients and is working with partners to expand the ADP offer and develop it into a self-sufficient, cost-neutral 'corporate social enterprise'.

Like the bebop movement, Gib has established an entirely new genre of social intrapreneurial 'music-making'. And he has developed ADP from a small ensemble into a 'big band'.

> Don't run [a social innovation project] out of CSR—run it out of business and with people who know the business ... Know which policies you can bend/break—how close to the wind you can sail without getting sacked!

11 http://www.accenture.com/SiteCollectionDocuments/PDF/Accenture-FINAL-10-Year-Infographic-May-2013-FINAL.pdf, accessed 8 January 2014.

3

How companies react

The following case on the Brazilian cosmetics company Natura gives a good impression of how even companies regarded as sustainability champions can react to social intrapreneurs. While reading, we suggest you note which aspects of the company's culture foster and hinder the work of the social intrapreneur.

Priscila Matta, Natura: the social intrapreneur's challenge

Natura was born as a sustainable company when economist Luiz Seabra fell in love with the world of formulas and aromas while working in a little laboratory in the 1960s and decided to found his own business in 1969.

In the beginning, Natura was only a small laboratory and a tiny store at Oscar Freire Street, in the elitist neighbourhood of Jardins, São Paulo. The day it opened, Seabra gave away white roses to passers-by, with a message explaining what he wanted to do there: talk to his clients (*Gazeta Mercantil* 2000). In 1974, Natura changed to a direct sales system, which would become one of the main reasons for its enormous success. Seabra himself inaugurated a door-to-door engagement method, being the first Natura 'consultant', a term used by the company to describe its sellers. He says:

> The first Natura consultants were our own clients, women aged 40–45 years who thought they could not do anything else in life, who thought they could not sell anything. And I said that they should not sell anything; instead, they should stimulate people to take care of their hair, their skin, and enhance their self-esteem.[1]

---

1 http://www.youtube.com/watch?v=cJ03jf7eJ3Q&feature=related, downloaded 11 July 2009, accessed 7 January 2014.

Integrating health and beauty and creating a sensation of well-being were at the heart of Seabra's intentions. Throughout the years, the therapeutic cosmetics appeal evolved to the widespread motto of the company: Well Being Well (in Portuguese: *Bem Estar Bem*). In the metamorphosis from entrepreneurial endeavour to successful business, Guilherme Leal and Pedro Passos joined Seabra, creating an effective management formula: Leal is the man of social causes, while Passos is the man of numbers, and Seabra the philosopher, according to their own descriptions. This combination shaped the company's vision, mission and values:

Reason for being.[2] Our Reason for Being is to create and sell products and services that promote well-being/being well.

Well-being is the harmonious, pleasant relationship of a person with oneself, with one's body.

Being well is the empathetic, successful and gratifying relationship of a person with others, with nature and with the whole.

Vision

Because of its corporate behaviour, the quality of the relationships it establishes and the quality of its products and services, Natura will be an international brand, identified with the community of people who are committed to building a better world, based on better relationships among themselves, with others, with nature of which they are part, with the whole.

Beliefs

- Life is a chain of relationships. Nothing in the universe exists alone
- Everything is interdependent
- We believe that valuing relationships is the foundation of an enormous human revolution in the search for peace, solidarity, and life in all of its manifestations
- Continuously striving for improvement develops individuals, organisations, and society
- Commitment to the truth is the route to perfecting the quality of relationships. The greater the diversity, the greater the wealth and vitality of the whole system
- The search for beauty, which is the genuine aspiration of every human being, must be free of preconceived ideas and manipulation
- The company, a living organism, is a dynamic set of relationships. Its value and longevity are connected to its ability to contribute to the evolution of society and its sustainable development[3]

Natura's strategy

Marcelo Cardoso, Natura's VP for Innovation and Sustainability in 2012 says: 'Today, Natura considers sustainability as a source for innovation.' This is reflected in its innovation strategy and its best example is the Natura Ekos product line. Launched in 2000, Natura Ekos is a pioneer line of cosmetics and fragrances based on the sustainable use of resources from Brazilian biodiversity,

2   Natura, que valia um Fusca usado, é empresa do ano do 'Valor 1000', ibid.
3   Translation from corporate website.

which are sourced from different traditional extractivist communities and small groups of family farms.

> In Greek, Ekos is ôikos, our home. In the Brazilian indigenous language Tupi-Guarani, ekó is synonymous with life. In Latin, echo corresponds to everything that has resonance, or reverberates, and is therefore heard. We are the echo of all those peoples who have obtained their living from, and lived with Nature before us.[4]

Considered to be the company's top market-based initiative in its quest for sustainability, Ekos is built around the idea of appreciating the knowledge of local communities, recognising their work, collaborating to build a supply chain that allows self-sufficiency, and conserving the natural environment. This means, for instance, that, if sustainability considerations limit the supply of a certain ingredient, the company will stop production of related products or switch to alternatives. To mediate and facilitate the complex processes required by these relationships, partnerships with NGOs, research centres and government agencies have been established. In 2013 Natura launched a new open innovation platform called 'Cocriando Natura' (co-creating Natura) to further stimulate innovation by entering in dialogue with everyone interested in contributing new ideas.

In the last ten years, the unusual business model proved to be a success and became the main platform of innovation and growth for the company. Natura Ekos contributed with 10%–15% of Natura's business volume,[5] having generated from 2008–2010 more than US$11.9 million for 2,301 families in 25 communities.[6] The company invests approximately 3% of its revenues in R&D, with an increasing focus in biodiversity since the establishment of the Ekos line (*Estado de Sao Paulo* 2009). Initially, the research on new ingredients from communities was subcontracted, but from 2004 Natura started changing its approach. First, the company internalised the work of discovering new ingredients as well as the traditional knowledge on how to use them, and finally it set up its own team to manage relationships with supplier communities.

The Brazilian law on genetic heritage and associated traditional knowledge

Since 2001, the Brazilian Management Council of Genetic Heritage (CGEN) requires companies profiting from the access to genetic heritage to share the benefits obtained with suppliers (landholders), through the Brazilian 'Biodiversity Law' (MP 2.186-16).[7] Also, the law states that suppliers, including indigenous and local communities, need to formally authorise companies to use their ingredients and their associated traditional knowledge. Natura had started its innovation and research on Brazilian biodiversity inputs before the enactment of the law (*Valor Econômico* 2003). This meant that the company needed to start a series of regulatory processes to legalise its relationships—a complex task considering the diversity of the supplier communities involved, the lack of experience in dealing with

4 http://www.natura.net/port/cosmoprof/ing/portfolio/corpo.asp.
5 http://www.natura.net/port/cosmoprof/ing/portfolio/corpo.asp.
6 Natura Annual Report 2010.
7 http://www.planalto.gov.br/ccivil_03/mpv/2186-16.htm, accessed 7 January 2014.

local communities on the business side, and a legislation full of grey areas (*Valor Econômico* 2008).

In 2000, before the Biodiversity Law was enacted, the company had purchased a 73 kg sample of the rich buriti oil produced by the community of Palmeira do Piauí in order to initiate the development of a range of products such as soaps and body oils. As Natura had no experience in buying ingredients from Brazilian biodiversity, and no team to manage the relationships with communities at that time, access to the buriti oil was made through a subcontractor, who in turn had acquired it from a local trader in Palmeira do Piauí. In doing that, the company was accessing the result of the traditional knowledge accumulated in that community over many years. Although the Brazilian Biodiversity law had not been enacted in 2000, Natura freely decided to apply the corresponding norms to that past relationship. Therefore, in 2006, the company went to Palmeira do Piauí to legitimise the access to the buriti oil and share the benefits of associated product development.

The first step was to contact the local trader who sold the initial sample to identify the buriti oil producers. As benefit sharing was not required by law at that time, there was no need to register sellers' information, and he remembered only some of the names involved. Then, Natura decided to hold meetings open to all the community in order to clarify the advantages of following the law and discuss a proposal to share the corresponding benefits.

However, when the company started to discuss how benefits could be shared with the people of Palmeira do Piauí, several issues emerged. First, buriti oil producers did not know anything about the legislation. Second, they were not organised into any type of association. Third, participants of those meetings said they preferred to receive the benefits in cash. And last, many who had nothing to do with the initial purchase wanted to profit personally from the benefits to be distributed. Lists of people had been set up, and it was hard to distinguish who were the producers from those who only wanted the money. Also, despite the company's excellent reputation, a few articles appeared in the media suggesting that Natura was being unfair in its relations with local communities.

For Natura there was an important relationship at stake, as well as the results of this initiative for both the community and the company. Lacking experience in understanding the conflicting needs and interests of the community, Natura had failed in its initial approach to communicate and establish the benefit-sharing process locally, and created a hot potato nobody in the company really dared to touch.

Priscila Matta is an anthropologist and joined Natura in 2007. Her baptism of fire was to develop a strategy on how to resolve the distressed relationship with the community of Palmeira do Piauí. In order to do so, it seemed natural to her to visit the community, but due to the conflicting issues that resulted from Natura's past visit, her immediate supervisors wanted her to build a solid internal strategy first. The difficulty of trying to solve such a complex issue from a distance worried her. Priscila says:

> I wanted to get to this community to find out what happened and how people were socially and politically organised, but my direct boss said that I could only go there if there was a strategy on how to act. I said that it would be impossible to come up with a strategy without going there, but he would not let me go.

It had been 13 months since Priscila joined Natura. Without direct access to the community, she delved into the case as much as she could. Supported by a cross-functional team, she had outlined potential scenarios, being prepared for whatever outcome the negotiations with the community might present. Gradually, her efforts allowed her to design a consistent and detailed strategy, which could be presented to the executive committee.

Priscila clearly had the potential to act as a social intrapreneur in this case creating value for the company (re-establishing relationships, keeping the innovation process flowing and safeguarding reputation) as well as for the communities (sharing benefits).

For what happened next see pages 150–55. First, however, we want to explore how companies react to social intrapreneurs and why they should consider aiming for mature empowerment of the potential social intrapreneurs in their midst.

How companies react depends very much on their maturity in issues on corporate responsibility and sustainability. Simon Zadek (2004) tracked the changes in the child labour crisis Nike faced in the 1990s. He distinguished the stages described in Table 3.1, to which we add how this impacts on the social intrapreneur.

Table 3.1 Obstacles encountered by social intrapreneurs

Stage	Description	Impact on social intrapreneurs
Defensive	The company neglects any responsibility for social and environmental impacts, irresponsible practices and outcomes	A defensive company might actively reject ideas of social intrapreneurs and thus provides a hostile environment
Compliance	The organisation adopts a law- and policy-based approach and accepts social responsibilities as a cost of doing business	Social intrapreneurs can expect ignorance, lack of awareness, indifference or even bemusement on this level
Managerial	At this stage the company defines social and environmental performance indicators and inserts them in their management processes	At this stage social intrapreneurs are often tolerated, but closely observed. Ideas are accidentally smothered, not intentionally but because the company has difficulty understanding the idea's strategic value

Strategic	On a strategic level the company integrates social and environmental issues in their business strategies in order to differentiate from competitors and to offer more responsible choices to consumers	On a strategic and civil level social intrapreneurs are actively empowered to create shared value by new business ideas
Civil	As the social and/or environmental issue is relevant for everyone in the industry, the company engages in corporate activism in order to deal with the issue on an industry or even cross-industry level	

Table 3.2 shows how these very same categories can be applied on an individual level.

Table 3.2 Corporate responsibility maturity level of employees

Employee type	Characteristics
1. Blocker	This type is afraid of anything new happening within the company. He or she tries to avoid risks at all costs and is particularly sceptical towards social and environmental initiatives as 'we have not done this in the last 20 years, so why should we now?' This person will definitely not support a social intrapreneur realising his project.
2. Complier	This type of employee knows all about company rules and procedures in order to cover his back. If approached with a new project proposal he will carefully evaluate if this is in line with company procedures—which it is most likely not. Therefore this person is also an unlikely ally of a social intrapreneur because challenged to work around the rules he will ask you either to talk to Human Resources to change his job description or to his boss in order to tell him to help you.
3. Implementer	This type is best described as project manager. She knows what a social intrapreneur is talking about and already starts planning project timelines, deliveries and quality criteria. However, this person does not fit well in the role of a motivator, much less inspiring other people.

4. Champion	Debra Meyerson describes these people as 'tempered radicals'. They have good ideas for social and environmental projects, but lack the business acumen to sell them in business language to senior management. They are good to have on board on a social intrapreneurial project but you need to complement the team with the people who speak business language and have the confidence of senior business leaders.
5. Social intrapreneur	These are the employees who are able to think business and sustainability together in order to create what Porter and Kramer termed 'shared value'. If they don't feel they create some good for society, they do not get involved.

Is there an alignment between company and social intrapreneur?

Remember the self-evaluation at the beginning of Chapter 2 on 'Understanding individual social intrapreneurs' (Table 2.1)? The sum of the columns refers to the five individual maturity levels in Table 3.2. So the sum in column (1) tells you how far you are a blocker as questions 1, 6, 11 and 16 aim to see how far a person is opposed to new projects. The sum of column (5) represents the social intrapreneur as questions 5, 10, 15 and 20 summarise behaviours of social intrapreneurs when it comes to new projects.

The five maturity levels on the organisational side can now be crossed with the five maturity levels on the individual characteristics, which provides us with a 5×5 matrix shown in Table 3.3.

Table 3.3 Company/social intrapreneur corporate responsibility maturity matrix

	Blocker	Complier	Implementer	Champion	Social intrapreneur
Civil					▨
Strategic				▨	
Managerial			▨		
Compliant		▨			
Defensive	▨				

Why are some cells shaded and what does this mean?

The matrix maps individual and organisational maturity levels. The shaded areas are the ones where the individual maturity is on an equal footing with organisational maturity. We call this the area of 'zero change'. A blocker is happy in a defensive company and a defensive company is happy with the blocker so there is no need for change. The same is true for a complier in a compliance-oriented company and so forth. At the final stage we have an empowered social intrapreneur in a civic company that aims to collect all ideas for shared value creation. This is where today Priscila Matta and Natura meet—a social intrapreneur in a civil company—and which explains why Priscila did not change jobs recently.

ANTONIO DIANGELO (FLUTE), ALEX ZAPHIROPOULOS (TENOR SAX), TOM NEALE (ALTO SAX) PERFORM A 'FREE JAZZ' PIECE IN THE FINAL CONCERT OF THE 2011 PAROS JAZZ ACADEMY IN PAROS, GREECE. ALTHOUGH 'FREE JAZZ' MAY APPEAR TO BE FORMLESS, IT DOES DRAW ON ESTABLISHED JAZZ IDIOMS BUT IT 'PLACES AN AESTHETIC PREMIUM ON EXPRESSING THE 'VOICE' OR 'SOUND' OF THE MUSICIAN, AS OPPOSED TO THE CLASSICAL TRADITION IN WHICH THE PERFORMER IS SEEN MORE AS EXPRESSING THE THOUGHTS OF THE COMPOSER' (SOURCE: en.wikipedia.org/wiki/free_jazz).

SIMILARLY, WHILE A CORPORATE 'BRAINSTORM' OR 'JAM SESSION' MAY EMPHASISE THE FREEDOM TO 'THINK CRAZY STUFF IN ANY POSITION AND IN ANY MEETING', THIS TAKES PLACE WITHIN THE CONSTRAINTS OF THE ORGANISATION'S SHARED CULTURE AND VALUES.

What happens in the cells above the shaded area?

Above the shaded area the individual maturity is lower than the organisational maturity. This creates a problem for HR, as the employee needs either to be trained or let go.

What happens in the cells below the shaded areas?

The cells below the shaded area are fields in which the individual is more mature than the organisation he or she works for. And this can create various consequences:

- **Changing the company.** This is a social intrapreneur's first choice. Through the social innovation project you make the company aware that sustainability can create value for business and society

- **Quitting the job.** The second option might be to change jobs and to look for an organisation that provides a better environment for social innovation. This is the exited social intrapreneur mentioned earlier

- **Blending in.** This is the exasperated social intrapreneur who has given up pushing for social innovation. Sometimes you hear them moaning in the coffee area about the culture of the company

How much resistance can you expect?

Figure 3.1 shows you how much resistance you can expect. In the worst case scenario we have a social intrapreneur working in a defensive company. If there are no signs for change, quitting the job might be the only option. Even if the company is on a managerial level there is significant distance to be covered, so prepare for years of engagement as convincing leadership and changing company culture takes time.

Social intrapreneurs clearly have entrepreneurial and marketing skills. They know what people want and how to address their demands profitably. At the same time, these skills help them to generate the trust necessary to embark on new ideas with the support of senior executives.

There appears to be a spectrum of corporate reactions to social intrapreneurship:

Hostility—active rejection

Ignorance—lack of awareness

Indifference

Bemusement

Guarded tolerance

Smother accidentally—do not intend to suppress, but do

Mature empowerment

The challenges

Social intrapreneurs encounter a wide range of obstacles to developing their projects. Table 3.4 illustrates the types of key obstacles and specific examples mentioned in interviews.

Table 3.4 Obstacles encountered by social intrapreneurs

Obstacles	Examples
Limitations of middle and senior management mind-sets	Don't 'get' social intrapreneurs 'Either/or' thinking Sustainability seen as 'left-wing' Short-term thinking Resistance to criticism of consumerism within the advertising industry
Internal political climate	No senior sponsor Other business priorities seen as more important Change in success criteria (profitability more important) linked to loss of sponsoring CEO Internal scepticism as to how ideas would work Difficulty in releasing corporate assets Silo thinking Inappropriate scale of key performance indicators (KPI) (focus on business vs. group)
External socioeconomic climate	Recession
Stakeholder conflict	Prioritising clients over NGOs
Social intrapreneur personality issues	Need to keep developing new projects or become restlessness
Corporate bureaucracy	Many internal procedures and approvals necessary to be overcome
Lack of processes to engage employees in innovation	The company does not have an innovation pipeline into which employees can feed their ideas
Leaders without vision	The executive committee does not see the business value of sustainability and therefore there is no 'godparent' providing support
No criticism please	Corporate culture treats criticism as an offence to the current leadership style

The business case for social intrapreneurism

STIR: the opportunities

To understand the business case for encouraging and empowering social intrapreneurs, companies need to grasp the ways in which social intrapreneurs can contribute to value creation. We have called this 'STIR': Sustainability, Talent, Innovation and Reputation (see Fig. 3.1). Table 3.5 sets out the business case for STIR,

Figure 3.1 STIR: Sustainability, Talent, Innovation and Reputation

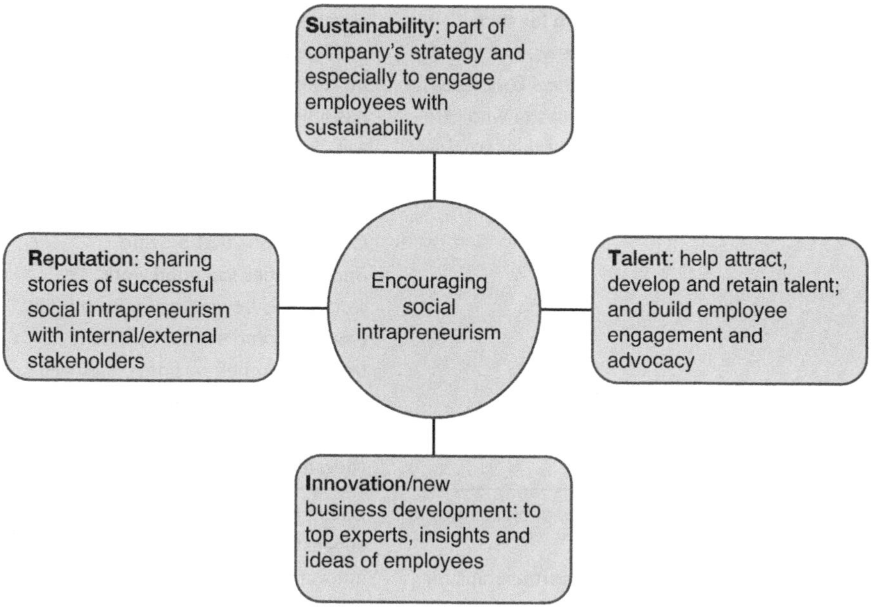

Table 3.5 Business case for STIR (Sustainability, Talent, Innovation, Reputation)

Categories of business benefit	Actual/potential business benefits	Supporting facts
Sustainability	New insights into issue of sustainability (may not be very aware of implications for their business) May save or make money Could help business to participate fully in the implementation of the proposed Sustainable Development Goals post-2015	93% of CEOs interviewed for the UNGC Accenture 2013 CEOs survey say that sustainability issues will be critical to the future success of their business 78% see sustainability as an opportunity for growth and innovation

Talent	Enhances employee motivation and morale—both for social intrapreneurs themselves but also potentially for others concerned by sustainability issues or who care about the values of their employer	Organisations that foster employee engagement enjoy a wide range of positive business outcomes: research by Towers Perrin (now Towers Watson) has linked engagement with employee well-being and positive financial outcomes (operating margins) (Towers Watson 2012) Organisations that provide opportunities for 'good work', i.e. work that is 'rewarding for employees, employers and society', create benefits for their businesses as well as their employees, according to research by The Work Foundation (Bevan 2012)
Innovation	Additional source of creativity and innovation May create new partnerships for business to create new business opportunities	Gallup research from 2010–12 suggests that engagement and innovation are linked; 'engaged employees come up with most of the innovative ideas, create most of a company's new customers, and have the most entrepreneurial energy' (Gallup 2013) 'We believe that the innovations required to create the future won't come from a single source. Not from science. Not from technology. Not from governments. Not from business. But from all of us. We must harness the collective power of unconventional partnerships to dramatically redefine the way we thrive in the future' (Hannah Jones, Nike's global head of sustainability and innovation)
Reputation	Possible reputational benefits as an international company that empowers its employees; but also for resultant products and services that the social intrapreneurs generate	Vodafone and Accenture, for example, have increased their international profile and received positive publicity as a result of creations by their social intrapreneurs to help demonstrate to governments and civil society that the business is a potential partner

The societal case for social intrapreneurs is derived from having more people working on solutions to the challenges of sustainable development, which can be taken to scale as part of large successful corporations. These examples can then inspire copycat initiatives and further social intrapreneurs.

The challenges *and* the opportunities: corporate social innovation

Corporate innovations can be predominantly for business benefit, for societal benefit or—best of all—for both. This last category is defined as 'corporate social opportunities' (CSOs).

> We see individual corporate social opportunities as commercially viable activities which also advance environmental and social sustainability. These tend to be based on one or more of the following: innovations in developing new or improved products and services; serving under-served or creating new markets; or organising the business differently in a new business model: for example, in how it conceives and develops the new products and services, or how they are financed, marketed and distributed. The goal is to be able to create an environment where numerous CSOs are possible. When that starts to happen, you might also then use corporate social opportunity to describe the corporate culture, the mindset, 'the way we do business round here' (Grayson and Hodges 2004: 11).

How do companies create a regular, high-volume, quality deal-flow of CSOs? Besides being developed by social intrapreneurs, CSOs may come from:

- Brand management and new product development teams

- Formal innovation or brainstorming process

- Suggestions schemes and ad hoc suggestions from staff

- 'Traditional' sources of external innovation, such as customers, academics and trade associations

- Green teams etc.

- The CR function translating employees' suggestions into reality

- NGOs willing to propose ideas to companies that they consider open to CSO proposals and able to grasp the potential and to run with the ideas (see Grayson and Hodges 2008)

- Business–NGO partnerships, for example, company charity of the year scheme etc. These CSOs could be an intended or accidental result of the partnership and, of course, a social intrapreneur may have got their idea as a result of being aware of or even been actively involved in the business–NGO partnership

Successful companies will want to encourage social intrapreneurship as part of a wider drive to engage all employees on sustainability, and as part of wider efforts to encourage more innovation from within and from outside. Companies need a culture that stimulates innovation and engages employees generally. The successful approach will be to establish an enabling environment for social intrapreneurship as an integral part of this.

Nick Hughes of Vodafone felt innovation often resulted from 'having an openness to ideas ... any idea ... whether from a customer or competitor ... and testing it with real customers'. The approach, according to colleague Susie Lonie, should be to identify 'a problem that needs to be solved—not a particular way of solving it'.

In his description of the TCS mKRISHI project to support rural farmers (see Ch. 1, pages 44–45), Arun Pande identified the following business benefits:
New market for the company
Direct contribution to existing business
Enhanced TCS brand as a pioneer and innovative company
Enhanced corporate reputation
Positive perception of the company by stakeholders

4
Enabling environment inside companies

Towards the end of our initial phase of research with individual social intrapreneurs, it became evident that in order to explain the wide variation in their individual journeys and outcomes, it would be necessary to better understand the 'enabling environment', both inside and outside their companies, that helped or hindered them along the way.

Companies can create an enabling environment for social intrapreneurship or, at the opposite extreme, a disabling environment. Harnessing the talents and commitment of all employees to achieve sustainability goals is part of the mind-set, behaviours and skills of managers in companies at the more advanced stages of CR maturity (Dunphy, Griffiths and Benn 2007; Mirvis and Googins 2006; Porritt and Tuppen 2003; Zadek 2004).

Managers need to consider the creation of the 'enabling environment' for social intrapreneurship as a key milestone on the journey to embedding sustainability and empowering all employees to treat sustainability as part of their day jobs. One leading company characterises this as an evolution from corporate social responsibility (CSR) to today's 'way we do business' to (tomorrow's) 'the business we do'.

How do companies create an enabling environment for social intrapreneurship? What follows is a discussion of the major factors that we identified in the literature review and in our interviews as the enablers and disablers of social intrapreneurism: culture, human resources, management and leadership, resources, organisational processes and infrastructure, strategy, and the external environment.

Culture that D.A.R.E.S. to foster social innovation

Organisational culture has been identified as an important influence on social intrapreneurism in both our literature review and by our interview subjects. But what is 'culture'? It has been defined variously as:

> The way things get done around here (Deal and Kennedy 1982).

> The specific collection of values and norms that are shared by people and groups in an organisation and that control the way they interact with each other and with stakeholders outside the organisation (Hill and Jones 2001).

> A pattern of shared basic assumptions that the group learned as it solved its problems of external adaptation and internal integration, that has worked well enough to be considered valid and, therefore, to be taught to new members as the correct way to perceive, think, and feel in relation to those problems (Schein 2004).

Which cultural elements support social intrapreneurism? The result of our empirical research largely converged with the factors identified in our literature review (Antoncic 2007; Antoncic and Hisrich 2003; Christensen 2005; Kuratko and Goldsby 2004; Mantere 2005; Narayanan, Yang and Zahra 2009; Stopford and Baden-Fuller 1994). The following factors were particularly salient:

Dialogue

Autonomy

Risk-taking

Experimentation

Sustainability

Dialogue

> The way to get good ideas is to get lots of ideas, and throw the bad ones away (Linus Pauling, double Nobel laureate).

A culture of open dialogue is a distinctive attribute of organisations in which social intrapreneurism succeeds. Creating time and space for a wide range of voices to be heard—face to face, not just online—enables people in organisations to open up to what is happening in the wider world (vs. remaining immersed in their own immediate individual or team environments). Such dialogue also facilitates the creative flow of ideas needed for truly innovative ideas to emerge.

Our interviewees often described qualities of their organisational environments that appeared to promote (or inhibit) what could be described as ideational fluency—a term usually reserved for describing intelligence or creativity in individuals (Guilford 1959)—in *teams* or *organisations*.

Csikszentmihalyi' (1990) defined 'flow' as 'a mental state of operation in which a person performing an activity is fully immersed in a feeling of energized focus, full involvement, and enjoyment'. Sawyer (2006) built on this concept, examining a wide variety of creative activities—not only highly valued activities such as production of art masterpieces and scientific endeavours but also films, music videos, cartoons, video games, hypertext fiction, stage performance, business innovation and advances in computer technology. He proposed that 'creativity isn't just a property of individuals, it is also a property of social groups'.

One specific activity cited by Sawyer—with which one of our research team has had direct experience—is jazz improvisation. Sawyer notes that, 'although each musician is individually creative during a performance, the novelty and inventiveness of each performer's playing is clearly influenced, and often enhanced, by "social and interactional processes" among the musicians'.

These 'social and interactional processes' also shaped the experiences, both positive and negative, of the social intrapreneurs we interviewed. The success of their efforts to develop innovative products or services producing both commercial and social benefits depended not just on their own personal attributes, such as persistence and the ability to communicate effectively with others, but also on the degree of like-mindedness and engagement of colleagues who worked with them to bring projects to fruition.

DIALOGUE IS AN INTEGRAL PART OF BOTH JAZZ MUSIC-MAKING AND SOCIAL INTRAPRENEURISM. HERE, BASSIST ARNIE SOMOGYI AND TROMBONIST JEREMY PRICE ENGAGE IN A LIVELY MUSICAL DIALOGUE DURING THEIR 'SCENES IN THE CITY' TRIBUTE TO THE MUSIC OF CHARLES MINGUS.

ASPIRING SOCIAL INTRAPRENEURS ALSO NEED SPACE TO ENGAGE IN DIALOGUE WHEN DEVELOPING SOCIAL INNOVATION PROJECTS. THIS CAN BE SUPPORTED BY COMPANIES THAT CULTIVATE 'CAFÉ CULTURE' AS PART OF AN 'ENABLING ENVIRONMENT' FOR SOCIAL INTRAPRENEURISM.

The organisational capacity to create time and space for creativity and learning has been labelled as 'café culture' (Business in the Community 2010) and is a feature of organisations where learning is part of everyday life. In these vibrant environments, time and space are set aside regularly for people to relax, converse, learn something new and connect with others. Innovative ideas flow naturally in settings where learning of all types is intrinsically valued.

> '[There is a] culture of openness to new ideas.'

> 'You need a culture of dialogue, people able and willing to listen and discuss ideas. Interest to know how things are seen from the outside … There is a genuine interest to talk, debate listen, consult with externals.'

> 'We have brought a lot of resources to help people to get out of a debate mode and into a dialogue mode.'

> 'Good communication/storytelling is needed to create impact with Boards—can be better than indicators.'

> '[We have a] habit of "yes but" mentality, even though [we are an] innovation company. Made a rule—can't say "yes but"; it must be "yes and"'

Conversely, culture can be a disabler if it induces fear of expressing views openly:

> '[I am] interested in [sustainability] topic, but careful because I feared ridicule by colleagues.'

> '[Company] lost a potential intrapreneur because of corporate culture, not valuing open discussions and not providing an enabling environment.'

> 'The people fear to do things differently as if there is an error I might be fired. If there are good results one doesn't get recognition.'

Autonomy

Intrapreneurs need to be empowered to develop their ideas by providing them with autonomy (Antoncic 2007; Christensen 2005; Kuratko, Ireland, Covin and Hornsby 2005; Narayanan *et al.* 2009; Roberts and Hirsch 2005). The freedom to experiment and take risks that was granted to some social intrapreneurs was cited as a key factor for their accomplishments.

> 'Here I was able to make my own decisions and I'm driving what I need to do.'

> 'Her immediate boss in [the bank] was in London, [she was in] Amsterdam. He gave her plenty of discretion and autonomy.'

A specific challenge for social intrapreneurs is that sustainability may be perceived merely as a bolt-on to the business or purely as a form of risk mitigation (vs. as a business opportunity). While they may be able to carve out time and space for their projects, they are often operating 'against the grain' of their company's pre-vailing culture, where sustainability is considered, at best, only partially relevant to the core business.

> '[The company is] two years into transition from corporate philan-thropy to social innovation ... looking to create new markets, new cus-tomers and new products and services through better social innovation.'

> 'Company was 'market-driven' regarding the social intrapreneur's project, [so he] had to pursue his microfinance interest in his spare time ... had to deliver on day job.'

Some social intrapreneurs were prepared to go 'against the grain' of conserva-tive organisations to develop new projects:

> 'Organisational culture was deeply conservative but innovation comes from "naughty" people who go to the edge.'

Risk-taking

The culture needs to encourage intrapreneurs to take risks (Anderson, de Drew and Nijstad 2004; Christensen 2005) and provide time to solve problems with co-workers (Hisrich 1990; Kuratko, Montagno and Hornsby 1990). As intrap-reneurial experiments might well fail, the organisational culture needs to display a tolerance for failure, recognising the value of learning through failed experi-ments (Anderson *et al.* 2004; Christensen 2005; Kuratko *et al.* 1990; Stopford and Baden-Fuller 1994).

Our interviewees also cited the importance of being encouraged to take man-aged risks and being rewarded for doing so, even when failure occurs:

> 'We have a very risk oriented culture ... we have the culture where we can think crazy stuff in any position and in any meeting.'

> 'Culture is very entrepreneurial, as if you have a good idea you are chal-lenged to implement it ... a major challenge is [achieving] scale [with a social intrapreneurism project].'

Culture can be disabling if people fear they will not be recognised or rewarded for taking risks. This occurred, for example, in an environment that was perceived by one interviewee as 'highly political, rigid ...survivors interested in their career [were] most likely to succeed'.

Experimentation

Social intrapreneurs also need encouragement, room and resources for experi-mentation (Anderson *et al.* 2004; Christensen 2005; Hostager, Neil, Decker and Lorentz 1998; Stopford and Baden-Fuller 1994).

'In an environment where the target is to reduce carbon footprint by half by 2020, and the CEO is frustrated you're not moving faster, you've got a great experimental playground, freedom to spend money, a load of push from elsewhere, that's a fantastic environment.'

'High tolerance for experiments, applying flexible criteria for defining and measuring success.'

One interesting suggestion was that innovation is a naturally-occurring phenomenon in organisations and the imperative for companies is not to promote or create such innovation but simply not to interfere with it:

'Now in this moment we have thousands of [consultants] doing something innovative, something they developed to have new experiences with clients and with [the company] ... What we need to achieve ... is avoid interfering with the natural flux of innovation which exists ... Our innovation culture is in this sense bringing to life the experience of well-being to the consumer and to society.'

'[There is an] ethos of "innovation for companies and nations"—doing things on a large scale; freedom to do interesting experiments but in a disciplined way.'

Sustainability at the heart of business

In contrast with companies that focus purely on commercial innovation, companies that promote social innovation incorporate sustainability and ethics explicitly into their business strategy, vision and values. Communicating clearly how sustainability is integrated with the success of the business provides useful direction for social intrapreneurs (Antoncic 2007; Antoncic and Hisrich 2003; Christensen 2005; Kuratko and Goldsby 2004; Mantere 2005; Narayanan et al. 2009; Stopford and Baden-Fuller 1994).

Our interviews demonstrated that the strength of companies' social and environmental paradigms (Andersson and Bateman 2000) determines the extent to which social intrapreneurs can 'live according to their values ... and to harmonize corporate conduct with societal expectations' (Spitzeck 2009: 169). The more that responsible, sustainable business practice is perceived as integral to, and enhancing opportunities for, business success (Grayson and Hodges 2001, 2004), the better the chances of developing and sustaining social intrapreneurism in the organisation.

'We are looking for products and services which will impact on our customers' sustainability issues ... drive in the organisation is seeing sustainability as a business opportunity and a necessary part of the innovation cycle.'

'Our roots are entrepreneurial and innovative ... look at [company's] CSR Award winners who [have] not got CSR responsibility.'

'They don't do "CSR": here we are talking about the business.'

How the traditional corporate responsibility specialist can disable social intrapreneurism

In contrast with organisations where sustainability lies at the heart of business strategy, more traditional companies may conceive of sustainability as a 'bolt-on' to the core business. A number of social intrapreneurs described how the presence of a corporate responsibility specialist or function in such a company could hinder, rather than enable, social intrapreneurism.

In traditional business contexts, corporate responsibility is often equated with philanthropic activity and can be perceived only as a cost or risk, not as a business opportunity. Potential social intrapreneurs might therefore refrain from undertaking any activity that counters prevailing views about CR, especially if it could impede their career progression in the organisation.

> '"Either/or" mind-set about CR—CR costs money—is a challenge.'

> 'Although [the company] had external corporate reputation for sustainability, [there was] little internal awareness—compliance mentality.'

> 'CR criteria for supplier selection may exclude engagement with some smaller suppliers [who could be partners in social intrapreneurial activity].'

> 'In the fast track I am in [it] is not really good to be seen as interested in what might be thought of as leftie.'

> 'Perception from the grapevine [was] don't rock the boat on sustainability or else.'

> 'Values are not innovation, culture is more compliance, and risk-averse ... not seeing sustainability being perceived opportunity.'

These observations support the fact that the company is still on a compliance level and struggles to see how sustainability can go beyond that and add value to business strategy. Occasionally the relationship between social intrapreneurism and CSR specialists can be competitive (for example, for resources):

> 'The CSR department had some competition from [the company's] corporate foundation.'

> 'Some [CSR managers] tend to be very defensive turf protectors.'

Some social intrapreneurs, however, work to change perceptions of CR/sustainability in their organisations, despite the risks:

> '[Company] was 'only on risk-mitigation and not opportunity ... Therefore I changed debate and conversation ... starting from risk and transferring to opportunity ... now 'entrepreneurial development bank [has been established].'

Some have previously suggested that the CR department may become obsolete as more companies embed CR within their business purpose and strategy.

However, we expect that CR departments will continue to evolve and take on different roles and become more of an internal consultancy, centre of expertise and provocation for action, rather than disappear. The analogy would be with the evolution of the HR function from being the repository of all personnel-related matters to the situation today where it provides specialist advice and expertise, but where all managers are expected to be able to handle general HR issues. The promotion and support of social intrapreneurs could be among these new roles for the specialist CR function of the future.

A positive role for CR can be driven emphatically by a social intrapreneur who finds himself or herself in a CR specialist role:

> 'I joined the staff four years ago as CR Global Director reporting quarterly to CEO and to chairman; and to excom and board. I see myself as being hired in as a licensed social intrapreneur i.e. with a brief to be a change-agent.'

CR departments usually develop along with the maturity stages of the company (see Table 4.1).

Table 4.1 Maturity stages of CR department

Stage	Company CR maturity	Role of the CR department
Defensive	The company neglects any responsibility for social and environmental impacts, irresponsible practices and outcomes	Some companies engage in philanthropic projects at this stage that are in no way related to business. So the CR department gives the money earned to NGOs and social institutions and have little interaction with business
Compliance	The organisation adopts a law- and policy-based approach and accepts social responsibilities as a cost of doing business	The CR department starts to have a role in order to map social and environmental risks
Managerial	At this stage the company defines social and environmental performance indicators and inserts them in their management processes	The CR department starts to collect environmental and social data from business departments. However, most of this data is seen as a nuisance by business as they do not understand how this links to profits and investments

Strategic	On a strategic level the company integrates social and environmental issues in their business strategies in order to differentiate from competitors and to offer more responsible choices to consumers	The CR department acts as internal sustainability consultants and corporate venture capitalists investing in social and environmental innovation projects
Civil	As the social and/or environmental issue is relevant for everyone in the industry, the company engages in corporate activism in order to deal with the issue on an industry or even cross-industry level	Members of the CR department represent the company in industry initiatives and help capacity-build the company value chain

What happens to social intrapreneurs acting 'against the grain' of their organisations?

One question that arose from our interviews was whether social intrapreneurs actually *need* cultural opposition against which they can act. If a company has made a strong strategic commitment to sustainability and set out specific goals and policies, does this discourage social intrapreneurs because they and their managers feel they are given less discretion, given there is already much to do in order to achieve agreed corporate sustainability goals?

There does not appear to be a simple answer to this question. Some social intrapreneurs—like commercial entrepreneurs—appear to thrive in the start-up phase of new projects when they have a licence to act independently and have opportunities to create social, commercial or organisational change. This is consistent with Ryan and Deci's self-determination theory (2000) in which competence, autonomy and relatedness are key to self-motivation and mental health. One of the expert panel members who reviewed our second Occasional Paper highlighted Ryan and Deci's work in suggesting that prospective opportunities for social (vs. purely commercial) intrapreneurism would, in particular, 'stimulate a sense of purpose [relatedness] with employees'.

> '[I] wouldn't say [I was] most popular but could get people to do things. Manipulator characteristic came out repeatedly.' [Self-described key personality attributes]: 'Tenacity, sheer bloody-minded[ness], wouldn't surrender.'

> 'No salary for year. Free office in University ... Science Park—when exhausted, slept in sleeping bags in office. Loved it. Classic garden shed start-up.'

But not all social intrapreneurs described the experience of working alone in inhospitable cultural climates positively. Resilience and political navigation were cited as critical qualities for surviving opposition but social intrapreneurs did not necessarily relish such experiences:

> 'It's quite lonely, you live on self-belief and determination.'

> 'Don't give up—this is where dogged determination comes in. In the early days, I was accused of all sorts by competitors, trade associations, the media. It would have been easy to sweep it under the carpet.'

> 'Know which policies you can bend or break—how close to wind you can sail without getting sacked!'

All three of the individuals quoted above are still working in their organisations, suggesting that perhaps what matters most is not whether the sustainability mind-set of the social intrapreneur is aligned with organisational culture but whether the social intrapreneur is able to recognise fully the cultural challenges they face in developing their new projects and have the skills and emotional intelligence required to overcome these. Social intrapreneurs who are unable to overcome such cultural challenges might be at risk of becoming cynical and exasperated, believing that 'this organisation is not living up to its values'.

What kind of innovation culture does your company have?

Knowing the key elements of an organisational culture that D.A.R.E.S. to foster social innovation, to what extent would you agree or disagree with the following statements about your own company's culture?

Table 4.2 What kind of innovation culture does your company have?

	Strongly disagree	Somewhat disagree	Neither agree nor disagree	Somewhat agree	Strongly agree
We practise open dialogue					
People have autonomy					
Culture encourages Risk-taking					
Intrapreneurs are allowed to experiment					
Sustainability is linked to core business					

Odebrecht: a Latin American company culture that D.A.R.E.S to be different[1]

Odebrecht is a diversified Brazilian business holding company headquartered in Salvador de Bahia (Brazil) and active in construction, engineering, infrastructure, real estate development, biofuels, oil and gas, environmental engineering and petrochemicals, employing 87,000 people, and reporting revenues of US$23.34 billion in 2009. 54% of revenue was generated in Brazil, 24% in other Latin-American countries, 10% in Africa and the remainder in North America, the Middle East and Europe.

The company's mission is to 'generate increased wealth for Clients, Shareholders, Members and Communities, aiming to Survive, Grow and Perpetuate'. A core part of Odebrecht's sustainability approach is institutionalised in the so-called Tecnologia Empresarial Odebrecht (TEO). This policy, originally formulated by the company's founder (see Odebrecht (1983), describes the company's values and principles, which govern the achievement of results, client satisfaction and sustainability in all operations. It values human beings' strengths, particularly the willingness to serve others, the ability and desire to progress and the drive to surpass previous results.

As Odebrecht is a very entrepreneurial organisation, a rules and compliance approach would limit the creativity and engagement of the firm's leaders, who have contributed to the creation of the highly diversified business portfolio. Therefore Odebrecht opted for a principle-based approach, based on 'trust in people' and their development through work. Accordingly, Odebrecht employees are entrusted with a lot of autonomy and are able to take risks in the execution of projects, as the following example demonstrates.

Because of its values and vision, Odebrecht does not see itself as a construction firm but as a service provider to the government and society wherever the firm is present, as well as an inductor of local development. Sustainability is core within the company's long-term strategy for 2020 as well as in the discourse of senior leaders such as Marcelo Bahia Odebrecht, President and CEO:

> Linked to the Growth projected for 2020 are two basic commitments: to social development ... and to environmental protection ... By 2020 we will be bigger, but we will still be ourselves: knowledgeable people who can make things happen and create businesses that induce sustainable development wherever we are present.

In Peru, Odebrecht has a 70% share in the CONIRSA consortium for the construction of a 700 km road connecting Iñapari with San Juan de Mancona, Matarani and other cities. CONIRSA will hold a 25-year licence for the operation and maintenance of the road. The project began in 2005 and the value of the contract adds up to US$1 billion.

Right from the beginning the project was conceived as an opportunity for social inclusion and environmental protection. Before construction began

---

1 The information on Odebrecht is based on a case published in Spitzeck, Boechat and Leão 2013.

Odebrecht ran a diagnostic of social and environmental indicators and discovered that 70% of the population lived in rural areas; 91.4% of those lived in poverty, nearly 50% of the children suffered from malnutrition, 25% were illiterate, and 35% of the population were without access to energy, clean drinking water and sanitation. The mapping of communities and their interest in being connected to the highway as well as avoiding environmentally sensitive areas facilitated the planning of the road.

In 2007 the consortium started to invest in local development for the communities affected by this work and developed initiatives that aimed to improve health and education as well as to develop sustainable forms of tourism that would enable the communities to benefit from the new highway. Total investment was expected to reach US$12.5 million over a five-year period, with US$3 million coming from Odebrecht and the rest from other partners. These funds financed pilot projects in responsible tourism and handicrafts, eco-business such as sales of local fruits, conservation of biodiversity and strengthening of local governance structures. Responsible tourism centres have been created in Tinque and Ausangate; these include trekking routes, camp sites and accommodation facilities.[2] In the eco-business section one project focused on training 120 families of guinea pig farmers, increasing their production ten-fold and increasing prices by 300%. More than 230 handicraft producers have been trained in order to improve management and profitability. As a result of initial progress Odebrecht was able to attract co-funding from various banks and development institutions. These initiatives experimented with different business models that had a good chance to create shared value for the company and for Peruvian society.

The implementation and funding depended on the support of local citizen groups; handicraft associations; NGOs such as Conservation International, Instituto Machu Picchu, Acción Sin Fronteras; banks such as Corporación Andina del Fomento, Fondo de las Américas, Inter-American Development Bank; government institutions such as the Ministry of Tourism and the Regional Government of Cusco; industry associations such as the Asociación Peruana de Turismo de Aventura y Ecoturismo; as well as other partners.

Aligning and mobilising all these partners behind a common goal demonstrates that Odebrecht is open to dialogue not only internally, but also with external partners.

Estimates from the Peruvian government overseeing the construction calculated that the highway had generated approximately US$3 billion in benefits for the country by 2011 due to the creation of 10,000 direct and 30,000 indirect jobs as well as the economic development of the region now connected to the road network of Peru and Brazil.

2 For these and more examples see www.isur.org.pe/proyectos, accessed 6 December 2013.

Human resources management

Our literature review found that human resource (HR) practices can contribute to an enabling intrapreneurial environment, mainly by developing personnel and offering recognition. Personnel development starts by recognising the value of employees' skills and knowledge (Antoncic 2007; Christensen 2005; Hayton and Kelly 2006), as well as their future potential (Kuratko and Goldsby 2004; Mantere 2005). Employees' potential can be developed by providing training and clear career paths (Mantere 2005; Parker 2011). Intrapreneurial behaviour should be rewarded (Antoncic 2007; Hornsby, Naffziger, Kuratko and Montagno 1993; Kuratko *et al.* 2005) not only financially but also by other means such as recognition, promotion, broader responsibilities and autonomy (Christensen 2005; Morris and Kuratko 2002; Sathe 2003; Stopford and Baden-Fuller 1994).

Consistent with the literature, our social intrapreneurs and their colleagues identified a broad spectrum of management tools supporting social innovation. These include the following.

Personal innovation time

Google allows employees to spend a designated percentage of their work time pursuing their own ideas for projects that could benefit the company and is explicit that this includes environmental and social performance.

Perhaps less ambitiously, but more acceptable to senior management teams, would be to build on the trend for companies committed to sustainability and CR actively seeking their employees' engagement in this commitment (e.g. Wal-Mart's drive to get all their two million employees to have personal sustainability projects).

Group brainstorming and innovation sessions

> '[There are] regular "big picture" presentations of the business, the marketplace, the technological developments taking place and ARM [Holdings plc] developments; periodic [group sessions on] where do we want to be in ten years' time exercises; innovation days: typically within offices or divisions, to step back from immediate tasks and brainstorm.'

Knowledge management

> 'Knowledge management system connects people/skills/know-how (Now/New/Next) but also encourages a wider, future-oriented global perspective on what matters to the organisation.'

> 'An important part is our knowledge management. We want to increase the significance of nutrition. So we have forums of synergies involving different units.'

'Any employee can suggest projects and innovations are not only coming out of the R&D dept. In meeting with the innovation team they usually ask all participants if they have any idea for new products. They then bring that to marketing and if the idea is interesting the initiator is challenged to develop a more detailed proposal.'

Innovation at TCS is encouraged through an employee portal. Employees of all Tata companies are encouraged to share their ideas through the portal and once a year there is a request for ideas on specific topics. Some ideas are then selected for experimentation. The social interaction in the platform is a way to encourage people to share their ideas.

Education, training and personal development

'[Company] is now developing a top management education programme, based around the core values, to develop a common language and understanding of how to lead with values and with corporate social intelligence ... ESADE provide training, and [company] provide mentors for each of the social entrepreneurs the company is supporting from among senior managers.

'[HR Manager] uses sustainability to enhance recruitment/retention; sustainability activities are part of trainee development. The background is that HR (as a corporate function and field) is not innovative.

'[Company] is ranked 43rd among the world's 500 greenest firms in the 2011 *Newsweek* Green Ranking. Making significant investments in ... values-led management education.'

'[New head of Knowledge and Innovation aims] to unlock people's potential and hidden talent of [company] ... Aim now to uncover social intrapreneurs—to introduce the idea of social intrapreneurism.'

'People rotated around the world across developing markets to get different cultural experiences.'

'Global Growth Group: not mentors specifically for innovation but do have mentoring.'

Several companies have had experiential learning programmes designed to increase awareness of societal challenges and opportunities. For example: PwC's **Ulysses initiative** was a global leadership development programme for future leaders of PwC, which ran for several years. The Ulysses programme was designed to build a global network of responsible leaders who were committed to developing quality, trust-based relationships with a diverse range of stakeholders. The programme comprised five learning modules with an eight-week project assignment where multi-cultural teams worked in developing countries in collaboration with social organisations.

Companies can also proactively encourage their social intrapreneurs to join external networks, online mutual support groups and developmental programmes, such as the Aspen First Movers programme (see Chapter 5 'External Enabling Environment').

IBM Corporate Service Corps

IBM Corporate Service Corps was launched in 2008 to 'help provide IBMers with high quality leadership development while delivering high quality problem solving for communities and organizations in emerging markets'. The programme 'empowers IBM employees as global citizens' by sending groups of 10–15 individuals from different countries with a range of skills to an emerging market for four-week community-based assignments. During the assignment, participants perform community-driven economic development projects working at the intersection of business, technology and society.

Corporate Service Corps was developed by social intrapreneur Kevin Thompson, a Senior Programme Manager for Corporate Citizenship and Corporate Affairs at IBM and an Aspen Institute First Mover Fellow. In this role he supports IBM leadership as a specialist on the policies, trends and status of corporate citizenship worldwide among other corporations, NGOs, governments and multinational organisations.

According to IBM, this initiative 'offers a triple benefit: leadership development for the IBMers, leadership training and development for the communities, and greater knowledge and enhanced reputation in the growth markets for IBM'.

Since its launch in 2008, the Corporate Service Corps

has had a positive impact of the lives of more than 140,000 people through skills transfer and capacity building. Many thousands more have been positively impacted through the services of the organizations the Corporate Service Corps has supported. The Corporate Service Corps program has sent over 2,400 participants in over 200 teams to more than 30 countries around the world. The participants come from over 50 countries and have served communities in Argentina, Brazil, Cambodia, Chile, China, Colombia, Egypt, Ethiopia, Ghana, India, Indonesia, Kazakhstan, Kenya, Malaysia, Mexico, Morocco, Nigeria, Peru, The Philippines, Poland, Romania, Russia, Senegal, South Africa, Sri Lanka, Taiwan, Tanzania, Thailand, Tunisia, Turkey, Vietnam, UAE and Ukraine . The program continues to expand to new locations each year.[3]

---

3 IBM Corporate Service Corps Overview, http://www.ibm.com/ibm/responsibility/corporateservicecorps/, accessed 13 December 2013.

PULSE: The GSK Volunteer Partnership[4]

The PULSE Volunteer Partnership is GSK's skills-based volunteering initiative. Through PULSE, motivated employees like Graham Simpson (see page 45) are matched to a non-profit organisation for three or six months full-time, contributing their skills to solve healthcare challenges at home and abroad. When PULSE Volunteers return to GSK, they act as catalysts to change the company for the better.

The PULSE Volunteer Partnership contributes to the GSK mission to **do more, feel better and live longer** by acting as a catalyst for change.

Change communities

Using our professional skills to create positive, sustainable change for non-profit organisations and the communities they serve.

Change yourself

Challenging employees to think differently about the world, facilitating leadership development and personal growth.

Change GSK

Bringing fresh ideas and new energy back to GSK to activate change in step with global health needs.

Since its launch in 2009, PULSE has empowered nearly 300 employees from 33 countries to partner with 70 NGOs in 49 countries, impacting hundreds of communities.

High-impact employee development

Each year, PULSE invites motivated employees to apply for a PULSE volunteering assignment, empowering them to develop their leadership skills while working for a partner organisation. Committed employees who believe they can make a sustainable change and have been with the company for three years or more go through a rigorous selection process.

Volunteering support

'Employees are encouraged to be non-executives on for-profit boards, social enterprises, charities to cross-fertilise; Sustainability director is looking to promote a programme like GSK's PULSE where high-flyers have opportunity of circa three-month secondment to NGO partners.'

---

4   PULSE Information, http://www.gsk.com/content/dam/gsk/globals/documents/pdf/PULSEInformation_PDF.pdf; www.gsk.com/content/dam/gsk/globals/documents/pdf/2012%20PULSE%20Impact%20Report%20-%20Final%20Version.pdf.

'Working with Street Football helps to identify "the adaptable leaders of the future" … when he brought the partnership into leadership development, leaders saw the potential for the company … for every employee survey completed, donate 1 Euro for Street Football.'

Reward and recognition

'Employees are recruited, inducted, trained in, appraised against and rewarded for performance versus the [company] values.'

'[Company] spends × bn Euros on its research and development … we reward the individual for feeding in new ideas … with more emphasis on sustainability you see people feed in more of that kind of idea.'

Reward and recognition may not only be financial: in TCS, employees' non-financial recognition comes, for example, in the form of publishing papers, travelling to present a paper at a conference in Europe or America.

Blended methods

Organisations could blend HR management tools to provide a range of support for innovative activities, particularly when the workforce is a mix of cultures and generations and innovation proceeds through several stages.

Establishing green teams and similar initiatives, for example, can create opportunities for employees to 'test the waters' as would-be social intrapreneurs. More sophisticated approaches integrate social intrapreneurship into talent development and innovation.

'You need a couple of HR instruments such as suggestion management, knowledge management. (1) CR Academy focuses on capability development—enabling execs to be "capable to generate a culture of innovation". (2) you need to "provide room for innovation"'

'The company was composed of many grey-haired people. Now we have six generations living here at the 'nerve centre' of [Company] in Brazil, which have different visions and values … Managers need to make use of our Recognition Programme and stimulate the teams to participate. Also they need to tolerate more errors.'

'Have annual awards for each of the company values … have mentoring programme with Ashoka where staff can mentor young social entrepreneurs plus countless different volunteer programmes … do see business by-products.'

'In general, innovation at [company] is encouraged through an employee portal. Employees of all [group] companies are encouraged to share their ideas through the portal, and once a year there is a request for ideas on specific topics. Some ideas are then selected for experimentation … [head of innovation lab] got personal recognition for his role in developing [new service] for farmers.'

We would like to see New Business Development and CR functions meeting regularly to brainstorm the potential for CSOs (corporate social opportunities— new products and services, access to new or under-served markets, new business models that have positive environmental and social impacts (Grayson and Hodges 2004); and publicising these ideas internally. Part of the job description of the volunteer sustainability champions in KPMG Canada is to find and encourage social intrapreneurs. Supporting social intrapreneurs could become one way for line managers to fulfil a KPI around innovation, talent, new business development and sustainability.

HR as disablers

Our literature review found that HR management practices may also act as *disablers* for intrapreneurship, mainly when failing to address change-resistant employees who are less able to cope with challenges and setbacks, and thus do not collaborate (Jones, Jimmieson and Griffiths 2005; Kuratko and Goldsby 2004; Lombriser and Ansoff, 1995), and when employees have difficulties in getting to know co-workers (Mantere 2005).

The reports of our social intrapreneurs focused more on obstacles to their individual action. In quite a few cases, there was no official support for social innovation initiatives and therefore budding social intrapreneur's projects had to be initiated and developed in employees' spare time and with no designated budgets or other resources. However, this had the effect of disciplining social intrapreneurs into using their spare time effectively as well as developing projects with a strong business case that would appeal to managers.

'There is no institutional support for such initiatives. But I do not see this as a disadvantage—engagement relies on the principle of entrepreneurial activity.'

'[Support?] We don't. One of my big challenges. No special bonuses etc. I've been trying to give people a belief in the future in a harsh market.'

'You don't get official time to do this. [Godparent] helped [social intrapreneur] to get my back covered until we got approval from the top to do this full time. There is some slack to use time and there was no resistance from management to explore.'

Management and leadership

A key feature of an enabling environment for social intrapreneurship is 'tone at the top': corporate leadership giving employees permission and genuinely empowering them to take the initiative; regularly emphasising the importance of sustainability to the business; and telling stories that positively highlight examples of social intrapreneurs both inside and outside the company, in order to encourage other employees.

Our literature review found that top managers need to guide and sponsor intrapreneurs, which in turn requires that they develop essential managerial skills. First, they need to communicate a clear corporate vision (Christensen 2005; Kuratko and Goldsby 2004; Kuratko *et al.* 2005; Mantere 2005) as well as the importance of intrapreneurship and innovation (Antoncic 2007; Dess and Lumpkin 2005; Kuratko *et al.* 2005; Narayanan *et al.* 2009). In line with corporate culture requirements, they need to encourage risk-taking (Hornsby *et al.* 1993; Kuratko *et al.* 2005) and demonstrate tolerance for failure (Kuratko, Montagno, and Hornsby 1990). As top managers have access to slack resources, an important role is to champion innovation projects by providing resources (Christensen 2005; Kuratko *et al.* 2005; Kuratko *et al.* 1990), and delegating authority and responsibility (Kuratko *et al.* 2005).

In addition, providing clear direction and acting as a sponsor require good communication (Mantere 2005), long-term thinking (Christensen 2005; Kuratko and Goldsby 2004) and having experience with innovation (Kuratko *et al.* 1990).

Generally, these findings also resonated with the experiences of our interviewees:

> 'Central is leadership and the leader ... central aspects are for me culture, structures and how to form teams.'

> '[Innovation culture] depends a lot on management ... [like an] orchestra—depends on how conducted, [determines] what kind of music you get.'

[Manager] 'creates space', 'ring-fences' project, 'changes rules' and also has high awareness of sustainability issues.

> 'New CEO strategically put sustainability at core of business ... CEO showed "leadership and bless initiative", "extremely supportive".'

Bottom-up push needs top-down pull

Gib Bulloch of Accenture Development Partnerships says:
I learned very quickly that if I wanted to try to drive change from the bottom up, I'd need to have support top down from leadership. I think that applies to change in any organisation, however big or small.

The role of leadership evolved over time. In the early days we needed air cover—we had to ensure that the idea would not be snuffed out by someone blindly following inappropriate policy or procedure. But over time I realised that the rules had to change: this idea would actually need oxygen if it was to avoid withering on the vine. In the beginning it was the Chairman, Sir Vernon Ellis, who provided the air cover and protection. When he retired, he made sure that a new emerging senior leader (Mark Foster, former Group Chief Executive of Global Markets and Management Consulting) would take over. We were lucky that this leadership transition was handled smoothly. We're now onto our third executive sponsor, Sander van't Noordende, Group Chief Executive of Accenture Management Consulting, replaced Mark in 2011 and is thankfully proving to be every bit as supportive.

Managers also have a role in framing the business context clearly for social intrapreneurs, setting standards and opening doors to ensure the long-term viability of a project:

> '[There is a] genuine open-door policy involving all senior people including the CEO and executive vice presidents as I saw for myself—but also emphasised that [there are] tough gateways to get ideas through.'

> 'Message from top was don't do too much in order not to raise expectations. He thinks it's important to lower expectations and to be open about limitations, struggles, problems as it is an experimentation process ... Management saw that this is not a bad thing, we can explore, test and learn. They also saw that this area has a potential significance.'

The magic of dynamic duos: social intrapreneurs and 'godparents'

Duos are the smallest of the jazz ensemble forms but they can be extremely powerful music-making combinations. Saxophonist Branford Marsalis and pianist Joey Calderazzo, a well-known 'dynamic duo' in the jazz world who performed at Newport Jazz Festival in 2009 and subsequently released their own duo album in 2011,[5] named their own top five duos from jazz history: Don Byas (tenor sax) and Slim Stewart (bass); Bill Evans (piano) and Tony Bennett (vocals); Duke Ellington (piano) and Ray Brown (bass); Frank Sinatra (vocals) and Count Basie (piano); Thelonious Monk (piano) and John Coltrane (tenor sax).

Writing on the All About Jazz website, jazz critic Mark Corroto (2011) commented on jazz duos:

> The defining characteristic of all great partnerships in cinema, from the male-bonding buddy movie to the classic Katherine Hepburn and Spencer Tracy films, is the tension created between two self-assertive characters, before their eventual collaboration. The same can be said of jazz and improvisational duos. By matching two authoritative players, sparks fly and, if the two cooperate for sympathetic ends, the session produces a worthy result.

5 Branford Marsalis and Joey Calderazzo, *Songs of Mirth and Melancholy*, Marsalis Music (2011).

Social intrapreneurs, working in tandem with their 'godparents' (see Introduction, pages 8–9), can also be powerful 'dynamic duos'. In the duos that work best, the attributes of these two 'players', identified through our research, complement each other (see Table 4.3).

THIS VOCAL DUET BETWEEN AMERICAN JAZZ VOCALIST DEBORAH BROWN AND HER GREEK PUPIL GINA ATHANASIOU AT PIZZA EXPRESS DEAN STREET, LONDON ILLUSTRATES HOW AN EXPERIENCED 'GODPARENT' AND AN ASPIRING SOCIAL INTRAPRENEUR CAN BEGIN TO GENERATE NEW IDEAS IN A 'DYNAMIC DUO'. THIS DIALOGUE CAN THEN EXPAND TO ENGAGE OTHERS IN A MORE EXTENDED ORGANISATIONAL 'CONVERSATION' ABOUT CORPORATE ACTIVITIES THAT PROMOTE SOCIAL, AS WELL AS COMMERCIAL, INNOVATION.

Table 4.3 Godparents and social intrapreneurs

Godparent	Social intrapreneur
Power broker	Desire for agency/competency
Networker	Networker/NGO engagement
Translator (ideas => corporate purpose)	Business case creator/seeking sponsor
Coach/Listener	Communicator
Sustainability advocate	Sustainability/nature/health advocate
Openness to challenge	Openness to experience
Risk-taker	Entrepreneurism/persistence in face of opposition
Diplomat ('Channelling' intrapreneur)	Restlessness/impatience
Talent spotter/nurturer	Learning/personal development motive Seeking meaningful work Seeking recognition/reward

The godparent who has the courage to join the social intrapreneur in forming a 'dynamic duo' not only provides support for the social intrapreneur but can also be the key to sparking a wider 'movement' in the organisation.

Our friend and Doughty Centre Visiting Fellow Ron Ainsbury made us aware of a TED Talk, 'How to Start a Movement', by Derek Sivers (2010) in which he explains in just three minutes the importance, not of the leader—in this case the social intrapreneur—but of the 'first follower'. The godparents we interviewed might in some respects, be characterised as the first followers, 'crazy' enough to embrace the social intrapreneurs and transform them from an 'eco-warrior' or 'tree-hugger' to a social innovator within the company.

Sivers notes that

> the first follower is an underestimated form of leadership in itself. It takes guts to stand out like that. The first follower is the one that trans-forms a lone nut into a leader ... if you really care about starting a move-ment, have the courage to follow and show others how to follow. And when you find a lone nut doing something great, have the guts to be the one to stand up and join in.

This duo can begin to change corporate culture by working together to influence its key attributes: skills and competencies, mind sets, organisational structures, control systems, power structures, group behaviours and norms. The corporate 'eco-system', as Maggie De Pree calls it—or the 'big band' in our jazz metaphor—starts to evolve, with champions, funders, technical experts and others working together to catalyse change on a larger scale.

Tables 4.4 and 4.5 provide some excerpts of interviews with our social intrapre-neur/godparent duos. These illustrate how each individual played complementary roles in crafting projects within the challenging corporate environments where they worked. Although the godparent has more formal power than the social intrapreneur, the excerpts from our interviews suggest that their relationship is actually symbiotic: each provides benefits for the other.

Table 4.4 Dynamic duo (1): Jo da Silva and Justin Evans at Arup

Jo da Silva Director, Arup International Development	Justin Evans Leader, UK-MEA Social Infrastructure Market, Arup
I started working for Arup as a graduate engineer. And that was great because I was designing buildings and working with some of the top architects in the world and earning money, sharing a flat with friends—that was quite exciting, I loved it—those were great days, with no responsibility. I loved engineering—I'm a learning junkie—you learn new stuff every day.	Jo and I intersect: when she was younger, a graduate engineer out of Cambridge, she worked for me. I maintained a link to Jo through the Arup broader network.
I started with a feeling that this [creating Arup International Development to deploy engineering skills where most needed] was the right thing to do. To substantiate that with an evidence base. Create a viable business out of it. It required a lot of self-conviction. Initially, I was very much on my own— I carved out the space in Arup. I wrote a paper for the chairman, that was the beginning of an unsolicited conversation ... I said I'm a start-up business, here's the plan, want to grow it to this size in 2–3 years. You're the banker; I'm asking you for somewhere to sit ...	When she came back from Sri Lanka, she was keen to establish a group doing things to alleviate poverty but also engage in the broader sustainability agenda, particularly in the developing world.
There was lots of talking—some people didn't think it was relevant to the firm. Other people thought it was hugely relevant. It was about persuading key directors, carving out the space to do it. I was lucky—I had two or three senior directors who believed in me. One I'd worked with for ten years—he knew me as a character, knew Jo doesn't set herself up for failure.	I would say, as her sponsor, I started 18 months ago. Just by a series of conversations—Jo was finding it difficult to make her great idea happen. There was a lot of organisational 'treacle' that prevented her getting off the starting blocks effectively. I would say my role ... I persuaded the Board I should take an interest in her and the international development business.

This isn't about making money but it's not about philanthropy, either. This debate went on for months. People presumed this was philanthropy. I said, no, this is about doing good business.

The link between our international development work and philanthropic cause work—Jo was in the middle.

It was a dialogue—not a negotiation with a predetermined endpoint. I drew a diagram that explained the spectrum running from philanthropy to major business opportunity. I was asked to present at the Annual Group Meeting. That's where I got the endorsement because people could see this was not just about spending the firm's money but about investing in a new business area that would have long-term business benefits.

What I did with her was to establish international development, ring fence and set it up as a non-profit business in the firm. Passed on her responsibilities for Arup Cause to other people.

I was keen to get the business model right which properly chimes with the international development community: NGOs and a series of other organisations from the UN to International Federation of the Red Cross, Rockefeller Foundation and so on. We could provide access to Arup's expertise and specific services on disaster risk reduction, poverty alleviation. Some of it is expertise.

Arup International Development started as a sub profit centre, but I then negotiated being my own profit-and-loss centre and got made a director as well—important for credibility. Year by year—I recognise you have to climb through the system—Arup International Development is a declared not-for-profit entity in the firm.

Rather than doing it as a normal part of our business, Jo and I developed this new model for the way the business should be operated. Overheads that are applied are appropriate. Arup International Development is a non-profit and has a reduced set of overheads—it is given space in the global Arup world to address international development projects with clients—in Bangkok, South America—Jo and her team can move across.

I gave her space—I facilitated all that—her natural entrepreneurial side.

Shell EMPOWER programme: fostering innovation culture

Chemical engineer Mandar Apte is part of Shell's GameChanger[6] programme, an initiative designed to invest and take 'novel, early stage' ideas about energy to proof of concept. With the support of his 'godparent' manager Russ Conser (see Table 4.5) and other colleagues at Shell, Mandar developed the EMPOWER programme, which uses meditation techniques to help participants identify and overcome their blockers to innovative thinking and thereby unleash their creativity.[7]

Social challenge: meet rising global energy demands

As Shell has framed this challenge:

> More than 9 billion people are expected to live on Earth by 2050, up from 7 billion today. Asia's fast-growing cities will absorb much of this growth, with three in four people living in urban centres. Billions of people will rise out of energy poverty. As living standards improve for many across the world and more people buy their first refrigerators, computers or cars, energy use will rise. Total global energy demand could rise by up to 80% by mid-century from its level in 2000.

Business challenge: shaping the energy future through innovation

To keep up with worldwide energy demands, Shell is required to 'enter more challenging environments to unlock new resources and boosting production from existing fields'. At the same time, the company is required to develop 'new technologies and an innovative approach to limit our impact on the environment and find effective ways to engage with communities near to our operations'.

The social intrapreneur's solution: EMPOWERing innovation culture

As Mandar (Apte 2013) describes his idea:

> In early 2011, Shell CEO Peter Voser shared his vision, both internally and externally, for Shell to be the most innovative energy company to address the global energy challenges. A few of us brainstormed on how we can play a role in achieving the CEO's vision. Since Shell has over 100,000 staff spread in over 100+ countries, we would need to change individual attitudes as well as the overall organisational culture that would support creativity and innovation.

Over two years, Mandar and his team interviewed over 1,000 Shell staff, asking them: 'What are your personal blockers to being more creative and innovative?' The answers indicated that the blockers were less a lack of 'technical or professional' skills and more a reflection of a 'lack of mental and social' skills. These results resonated with Mandar's own experience; he had discovered first

---

6 http://www.shell.com/gamechanger.

7 'Can Meditation Lead to Innovation?', http://www.shell.com/global/future-energy/innovation/inspiring-stories/ashoka-changemakers-award.html. accessed 6 December 2013.

hand that 'an absence of mental and interpersonal skills [is] what kills an innovation' before it reaches the experimentation stage. This knowledge provided him with important guidance in designing the content of the EMPOWER programme.

Mandar then collaborated with the Transformational Leadership for Excellence programme (www.tlexprogram.com) offered by the International Association for Human Values (www.iahv.org), and designed a unique two-hour intervention called 'Introduction to EMPOWER' to help participants identify their personal blockers to innovation and foster innovation-friendly habits. Tasters of breathing and meditation techniques were also provided to nurture 'inner' resilience and creativity. Participants could then choose to attend a two-day EMPOWER workshop designed to provide a deep dive in innovation learning, identifying various roles in the innovation process that they could choose to play (beyond idea generation only) and nurturing resilience using meditation practice.

Benefits and impacts

In two years, over 400 staff have attended the full two-day EMPOWER training programme and over 1,000 staff have undertaken the 'Introduction to EMPOWER' module. These events were organised in bottom-up manner by enthusiastic staff who participated in the programmes and saw personal and organisational benefits to sustain the momentum. Some of the benefits reported by participants from the full EMPOWER workshop are:

- 96% of respondents highlight how they now have better understanding of their own blockers to innovation
- 82% of respondents indicate they have better understanding of what role they can play in the innovation culture
- 88% of respondents rate that workshops help one to accept multiple perspectives—a key enabler for innovation
- 90% 'would recommend the workshop to their colleagues'
- 82% of respondents rated very highly that the training was a good use of their time
- 82% of respondents said that their self-awareness had increased for a substantial part of the day due to the meditation practices learnt in EMPOWER training

Mandar's EMPOWER programme has been profiled by Wharton Business School (Knowledge@Wharton 2012). Mandar was also named one of four winners in the inaugural League of Intrapreneurs (Building Better Business from Inside Out) competition in April 2013 (Schwartz 2013).

THE IMPORTANCE OF SILENCE—IN MUSIC-MAKING AND INNOVATION—IS OFTEN OVERLOOKED. BRITISH PIANIST FRANK HARRISON, SHOWN PERFORMING WITH HIS TRIO AT ST MICHAEL AT THE NORTH GATE CHURCH, OXFORD IN 2012, BECAME KNOWN FOR THE SPACIOUSNESS OF HIS MUSIC, INFLUENCED PARTLY BY GREAT JAZZ PIANISTS SUCH AS BILL EVANS AND KEITH JARRETT.

SOCIAL INTRAPRENEUR MANDAR APTE, WHO DEVELOPED SHELL'S EMPOWER PROGRAMME EMPLOYING MEDITATION TECHNIQUES, NOTES THAT 'SILENCE IS THE MOTHER OF CREATIVITY'.

Table 4.5 Dynamic duo (2) Mandar Apte and Russ Conser at Shell

Mandar Apte GameChanger, Shell International	Russ Conser Manager GameChanger, Shell International
After ten years of working at Shell, I applied for the role in GameChanger as the job description 'resonated' with my personality. The job involved investing in early stage novel ideas in energy to create proof of concept	Innovation is fundamentally a people challenge. I had learned that in the business as well … you get the people part right, then put in good business structures, create winning teams. This is especially true in innovation. When you are doing something truly new—when people say it's not possible—I learned early that passion, belief against the odds, the rebel makes that work.
I was not a venture capitalist but a chemical engineer by training. I soon realised that GameChanger, more than anything else, was a 'safe' place where change-makers/innovators could bring their creative ideas and get the 'permission' to try out the idea if it met certain investment criteria. During my job interview, my manager, Russ Conser, one of the most empowering managers I have known in Shell, had asked me about my volunteer life outside of Shell where, for over a decade, I had taught meditation practice to thousands of people including returning war veterans, high school teachers and students. In response, I had said that if we empower people with tools to handle negative emotions then naturally they will become change agents to spread positivity around them. He had said that innovation is all about your mind-set, especially early stage innovation. You will fail unless you have inner resilience (an inner attitude to get back on your toes and keep marching ahead and not let failure shake you). He was open to the idea of putting time and energy into developing a curriculum that unleashed creativity in Shell staff using meditation practices. That was like a 'godfather'—a pivotal role.	Tech Venture Group (venture capital) and GameChanger (an early angel investor) had been interfacing during 2001. I was in the Tech Venture Group from 1998 to 2002, then went to GameChanger. Belief in the entrepreneurial hero quickly became even more deeply embedded. At early stages, crazy ideas—the challenge was, you have to be good technologically but the key barriers to revolutionary innovation are social: how people get connected to each other—they're all social dynamics. The mechanics we know how to do but inter-human dimensions are key.

All these things are formative and laid the groundwork that allowed me to respond to Mandar. |

Innovation is like pulling together an orchestra, a jazz ensemble—everyone has to play their role. That's how I relate to my own idea. The idea of providing meditation techniques to my colleagues at Shell to help reduce workplace stress and improve interpersonal relationships had crossed my mind in 2005 when I became a meditation teacher of the Art of Living Foundation. Since 2005, I had taught thousands of people from all walks of life so I knew the power and benefit of meditation practice for developing personal development but needed a cook, some spices, somebody to taste and someone like Russ to have trust in my capabilities. Often I was challenged by my GameChanger team mates on the value of facilitating innovation learning workshops. I was surprised how a 'novel' idea like EMPOWER did not meet with their curiosity and support but perhaps it was because it was not a traditional technology innovation idea. Russ played a strong supportive role by participating in the programme and helping to bring EMPOWER to life and unleash my own creativity!

We need chemists and physicists and engineers but also people with different cultural perspectives ... Mandar is technical but has been a social intrapreneur from the beginning. His passion. I get geeked out over somebody with a new cool catalyst.

I like to apply what I know about social systems to make things happen. Better World, AWARE programme—Mandar's personal passion for energy is social and human. Used his background in petroleum engineering to talk geeky but it's personal/social, his passion. GameChanger has been supported a long time ... that gave me room and freedom to operate. Mandar wanted to explore some new dimensions.

After spending the first two years learning about innovation management and the GameChanger programme, I realised that a vibrant innovation culture would require many roles that staff can choose to play and not just generating new innovative ideas. That's why I designed the EMPOWER programme to empower participants to identify personal blockers to innovation and understand the different roles required in the innovation process that they could choose to play.

If you had asked me in 2010 what the number one problem for innovation was for Shell, it was cultural. Earlier in my career, there was permission to do crazy things. I felt over time that the space to be different had shrunk in the company. Mandar had this passion through EMPOWER programme to apply mindfulness/breathing to create space for innovation. That empowered Mandar but also pushed back a constraining force on innovation in Shell in general.

After 15 EMPOWER workshops and with over 400 graduates from the programme, we have many testimonials of how participants have incorporated the meditation techniques in their personal and professional life. Participants have also shared how the programme has helped them think innovatively, come up with novel ideas and improve personal and interpersonal relationships.

I think overall, things aren't signed sealed and delivered yet. In the process of supporting him for opportunities ... getting recognised [e.g. League of Intrapreneurs Award], he'll be more successful—'social intrapreneurs' term bought him more mileage.

I think we're about there (although I've retired). I am very proud that we've now secured a special role for Mandar in Shell where his successes are both validated and institutionalised. We've also got new champions for Mandar ... 'succession planning' for mentors—people with power who can do something ... I've learned in GameChanger—the heart of the process works really well and we're generally well regarded for doing that. I've learned how hard it is depends less on where we are in the organisation than who you plug into—personality traits, belief systems, ways of working.

Here is what other social intrapreneurs had to say about 'godparents':

> 'Boss creates space to pursue new projects, acts as board advocate for CR, pushes innovation.'

> 'His former boss, who is today director at a different company, helped him a lot to frame his sustainability initiatives in a more business[-like] manner ... Access to senior management is really important. You need a godfather inside the organisation who helps you to get things done.'

> '[Management sponsor] supported this [social intrapreneur's] idea, put [social intrapreneur] in touch with right people and connected various projects locally.'

> 'I talk two hours every three weeks to CEO and tell him what I think should happen. He believes in what I am doing—he is my sponsor.'

> 'He [manager] gave her plenty of discretion and autonomy.'

A resourceful manager can also function in a hybrid role as social intrapreneur and godparent:

Cassiano Mecchi: An agent for change

Cassiano Mecchi, then with Danone Brazil, sees himself as a social intrapreneur and change-agent to help other change-agents to pull together the wherewithal of time and resources and connections to make a difference, giving permission and encouragement to other employees to be social intrapreneurs.

The loss of a manager who is a key project sponsor or 'godparent' can have a major impact and may require significant adaptations to ensure a social intrapreneurial project survives:

> 'Microfinance unit [was] just getting into stride at time of 2008 banking crisis. [Social intrapreneur's] senior sponsor made redundant; and massive retrenchment. To survive, microfinance moved into Emerging Markets Division.'

Managers can also have a *disabling* impact on social intrapreneurism in an environment that is highly politicised, subject to severe economic pressures or where sustainability is not perceived as an issue requiring urgent attention:

> '[The social intrapreneur's] immediate boss was transferred to this department because she did not succeed as a commercial manager. She had little knowledge of CSR and gave [the social intrapreneur] few possibilities for development. Once [she] managed some projects which created more visibility her boss felt uncomfortable.'

> 'CEO ... had the job to get [company] out of the red. He was zero sympathetic to sustainability ... he was neutral to it. Apathetic management.'

> 'Difficult to change mentality of Board/SMT...[parent company] doesn't have sustainability policy ... Board at risk mitigation stage ... store managers/HQ don't have any KPI for sustainability.'

> 'I think the biggest barrier is the mentality of management. Management supposes a system of planning and control. This is the logic of business schools for the last 150 years. It believes that if I plan something, I can later control and I will have good results.'

Resources

Our literature review found that a key enabler for intrapreneurship is resource availability, including capital, time, knowledge, skills and slack resources in general (Anderson *et al.* 2004; Hostager *et al.* 1998; Kuratko *et al.* 1990, 2005; Mantere 2005). Of particular importance is time, as the innovation process is often non-linear and iterative, building on learning from past experience (Anderson *et al.* 2004; Christensen 2005; Hornsby *et al.* 1993; Kuratko *et al.* 1990). The organisation needs to match the resource requirements of the intrapreneurial project with the resources that are available, not only within the organisation, but also within its network (Christensen 2005; Kuratko *et al.* 2005; Narayanan *et al.* 2009).

Disabling factors in this category are lack of resources (Kuratko and Goldsby 2004), as well as high employee turnover (Anderson *et al.* 2004).

From our interviews, it appears that companies can support social innovation with a wide variety of resources and these are often blended together:

Innovation infrastructure

Several companies invested funds in internal networks that provided a focus for assessing, initiating, supporting and celebrating social innovation projects through different stages of development.

For example, Philips created an innovation board with funds and a work-time release scheme for which groups of employees with social intrapreneurial ideas could bid.

> '[Company] invested £2.5 million in innovative charitable bonds to fund the Future Business Centre—a business incubator for social enterprises ... employees will act as mentors and board members for the social enterprises incubated through Future Business. Have created an internal Yammer—the enterprise social network.'

> '[Company] has now invested in a Social Intelligence/Insight Unit alongside its more traditional Customer Intelligence/Market Insight function ... Four years ago, [company] committed €200 million for microfinance and now has one million customers across South America.'

> '€2 million programme (Blue Camp) for innovation. If good, can join and constantly search to find good candidates—pitch your ideas—jury selects—is part of management fast-track programme ... mentors for management development cohort.'

> 'Recently we introduced the filter of ideas. First you have the stage of the idea. This can come from any person in the company. If this idea is approved it gains resources to go from idea to concept. If the concept is approved, it turns into an initial project.'

> '[Head of Knowledge & Innovation] can call ad hoc innovation Task Force Board to assess crazy ideas ... Name and fame innovators—public recognition.'

> 'In addition to the innovation labs they have two organisations. One is iConnect—ideas that come from partners and internal business groups; and the other is CoI (CoInnovation network) ... now they adopted the 'consortium' business model, connecting companies in the field (seeds, fertilisers, irrigation, insurance etc.) that normally don't interact ... social interaction in the platform is a way to encourage people to share their ideas.'

'More to do on how this [sustainability] is translated through the organisation … pockets of action where the bottom up is working fantastically.'

Project teams for innovation projects can cross department boundaries and need
to be flexible over time:

'Someone above who played chess and took care to put the right
pieces together was very wise to set up this structure for [social intrap-
reneur] to grow. The structure was very Frankenstein—we put the VP
for R&D, a manager in supply chain and a team of one trainee and one
intern.'

'In meetings with the innovation team they usually ask all participants if
they have any idea for new products. They then bring that to marketing
and if the idea is interesting the initiator is challenged to develop a more
detailed proposal.'

In some companies CR departments and initiatives can provide the focus for
developing social innovation projects and integrating them with core business
operations:

'Positioning the CR department as a Programme Management Office …
mainstream the insights from these new units into mainstream business
decision-making … developed a model of "relate/incubate/translate" to
help [company] do this.'

'CR Academy is an internal resource.'

'Improvisational' accounting

Lucas Urbano, Danone, Sustainability Manager

At time of our research Lucas was in charge of sustainability projects
at Danone in Brazil such as the Kiteiras project experimenting new
forms of inclusive business by implementing a direct sales model.

One striking aspect of social intrapreneurism was the degree of
improvisation, a kind of financial 'jazz', required by social intrapreneurs and their
colleagues to fund projects within corporate accounting systems.

Some companies, such as Danone, create special financing mechanisms for social
innovation projects. Danone incorporates sustainability into accounting with a
'Green CAPEX', which gives a sustainability project an extra year to pay off. The
company also created an Ecosystem Fund in the belief that 'a strong Ecosystem
makes a strong business'. This fund invests in projects that aim to strengthen the
value chain through social inclusion. These projects have to benefit low-income

families and the invested funds have to be managed by an NGO involved in the project.

In Brazil, Danone embarked on the Kiteiras Project, aiming to increase sales by applying a direct sales model. The company aims to create 420 jobs for women entrepreneurs selling 700 tons of yoghurt a year. By 2013 the project had already created 220 jobs and 345 tons of yoghurt had been sold. The monthly income of the women increased on average by R$225, roughly US$100 extra a month.

Other social intrapreneurs highlighted financial resources as a major challenge:

'Budget always an issue.'

'Officially there were no resources provided.'

Amortising innovation costs across the organisation can help support innovation projects that might otherwise remain unresourced.

'At [Company] there is one entity with one bank account...to develop innovative ideas.'

'Working in cross-functional teams is really easy at [Company] ... [the social intrapreneur] suggested a project and the directors liked the idea of doing a study on how to connect [the company's] products and biodiversity. They asked how much does it cost? He answered about €40.000. He then asked if they would cover 50% of the costs and they agreed. He knew, however, that the study would cost half as much and thus had it financed by corporate headquarters ... Resources do not seem to be a problem if the business proposition is clear and if it creates value in terms of sales, reputation or branding.'

'Budgets are not formalised but lots of examples of resource investment in innovation—e.g. Project Eden [waste water treatment].'

'We are paid by the Brazilian [Company] Foundation. Important aspects of our shared value creation strategy are (1) Nutrition, (2) Water and (3) Local Development ...We have a few projects such as our [company] ship in the Amazon, collaborations with farmers etc. but I still find it hard to create the business case for it.'

'There is little budget for disruptive innovation, so they are not thinking about the farmers, for example, but on how to make money out of a challenge.'

While rules governing initial funding of projects could vary, some interviewees suggested that to secure and sustain investment in social intrapreneurism, a viable business case for investment should be developed and criteria for assessing business benefit agreed:

'The most interesting outcome of research would be, where is the business impact? The business context needs to be very clear.'

'Selection of projects for development depends on articulating the business case.'

Companies can offer modest Research and Development funds to employees to enable them to 'buy out' some of their own time to work up a social intrapreneurship proposal or to fund other costs associated with testing the idea. This could incorporate staged payments, so that only the most commercially promising projects and those with the greatest positive societal impact come through to secure larger financing for launch and subsequent expansion. Vodafone, for example, now encourage employees to bid competitively for internal innovation funds. Marks and Spencer has a similar fund for employees to bid competitively to help with implementation of their ambitious extension of Plan A to make Marks and Spencer the most sustainable major global retailer by 2015.

Organisational processes and structures

The main components of organisational structures and processes as discussed in the literature are: organisational design, teamwork, management systems and organisational capabilities.

An organic, lean, flat organisational design as seen in project-based or matrix organisations is considered an enabler for intrapreneurship (Anderson *et al.* 2004; Christensen 2005; Narayanan *et al.* 2009). Such a design allows cross-functional teams to work autonomously on innovation projects (Anderson *et al.* 2004; Antoncic and Hisrich 2003; Brunaker and Kurvinen 2006; Christensen 2005; Mantere 2005; Narayanan *et al.* 2009; Stopford and Baden-Fuller 1994).

In order to maintain control and at the same time steer the development of innovation projects, authors argue that management systems play a central role in providing policies and procedures, formal evaluation and, in the case of success, the distribution of rewards (Antoncic 2007; Christensen 2005; Kuratko and Goldsby 2004; Mantere 2005). Open and high-quality communication plays a major role in translating the vision into strategic plans and targets as well as creating consensus on individual and team performance targets (Antoncic 2007; Brunaker and Kurvinen 2006; Honig 2001; Kuratko and Goldsby 2004; Mantere 2005). Intrapreneurship also profits from organisational capabilities such as previous experience in innovation and business venturing (Narayanan *et al.* 2009).

Several of these organisational attributes from the literature review were also mentioned by our interviewees.

Egalitarian structures support social intrapreneurism

Returning to the idea of creativity, flow and ideational fluency (raised in the section earlier in this chapter on Dialogue), the concept of ideational fluency is associated with flatter associative hierarchies in individuals (Mednick 1962) and it appears from our literature review and interviews that flatter organisational structures may also be more conducive to developing ideational fluency supporting social intrapreneurism in companies than hierarchical organisations.

The decentralisation of both the organisation as a whole and responsibility for innovation can have a positive effect on social intrapreneurism:

> 'There is an openness for innovation as the organisation is decentral[ised]—lies in the responsibility of the regional CEOs. This decentralisation in the regions depends on culture. [Company] attracts more entrepreneurial people.'

> 'Innovation "always part of culture because [organisation is] very decentralised." People see their mainstream/day jobs in broadest way—so they take initiative.'

> 'Technical teams and innovation teams work closely with marketing and with product development ... very decentralised company ... much of the innovation is developed in partnership with operating companies.'

> '[Company] has a special characteristic: we attract a lot of good people. We attract people with a restlessness to make some difference in the world. And many times people get frustrated because they confront this situation. Processes, bureaucracy ... The biggest challenge is the find a way to finish with that. [Company] is an open environment. The people want to work here and want to create different relations and want to make a contribution. So our environment triggers this.'

> '[In the energy sector (vs. pharma)] innovation is a broader responsibility at [Company with no department. of innovation] ... more coming from people working on the issues on a daily basis.'

Employee share ownership—another manifestation of egalitarianism—was cited as a 'major' driver of intrapreneurism and also helped to promote a 'sharing culture'.

Our literature review found that organisational structures and processes can disable intrapreneurship if the organisational design is highly centralised, bureaucratic and hierarchical (Anderson *et al.* 2004; Hisrich 1990; Kuratko and Goldsby 2004; Singh 2006), and also if there is a narrow view of innovation as the task of the R&D department, and the tendency of creating silos (Christensen 2005). Teamwork obstacles revolve mainly around an excessive focus on job descriptions, resulting in difficulty in forming teams (Kuratko *et al.* 1990). Obstacles presented by management systems are excessive controls (Antoncic 2007) and strategic inconsistency in vision, targets, evaluation and rewards (Mantere 2005). Finally, hierarchical communication (Kuratko and Goldsby 2004) and mechanistic management (Narayanan *et al.* 2009) are also perceived as potential disablers of intrapreneurship.

Power imbalances and bureaucracy impede 'flow'

Again, the literature review findings resonated with many of the comments of our interviewees. The immersion of our social intrapreneurs in both the operational practices of their respective disciplines (e.g. marketing, supply-chain management), combined with their awareness of social and environmental issues, enhances their capacity to develop commercially applicable social innovations. Colleagues who work in formal R&D and innovation teams do not necessarily enjoy such advantages.

> 'At [Company] the power is concentrated in the hands of the directors. The environment is hierarchical, centralised and autocratic. Everything needs the approval of the directors. Other companies offer more space for autonomous decision-making ... If you are flying below the radar you will stay a long time in the company.'

> 'Organisational hierarchy/structure can be a disabler if lower ranks block the way for good ideas to flow through to top management; good communication/'storytelling' is needed to create impact with Boards.'

> 'There are hierarchical gaps as they were implementing a flatter organisation—however, the experience distance between the levels is too great. At the same time he [VP, Supply Chain] is not sure if the people would like more power.'

> 'We are far away [from sources of innovation] but have a strong motivation to create an innovation environment. [Company] is still a hierarchical organised company, we still have bureaucracy, stiffness, authorisations, so we are experiencing the clash of the two perspectives.'

> 'The business model is very procedural, with a lot of ambiguity and hierarchy, which slows things considerably. As we are in a small unit we can speed up things quite a lot, which is not true for other areas.'

> 'Big challenge in current environment where need more approvals than previously ... like EU ops of other US companies—focus on survival.'

> 'The teams do not need to take a lot of decisions—the director does. It would be good to free directors from operational duties and to distribute the power more equally.'

Organisational changes can also impact on the innovation process:

> 'Lot of M&A [Mergers & Acquisitions] in the last few years ... could give foundations for more structured conversations with employees than was possible in the past ... Level in organisation where people might come up with ideas, may not know I exist cf their management teams.'

This social intrapreneur highlighted the need for self-confidence and alliance-building skills to counteract the disabling effects of a hierarchical environment:

> 'We are organised in a matrix form. Therefore, I have many bosses and people to consult with. So the ability to form alliances and to align different people is very important. The difficulty is in permeating the organisation with its current culture. There is a strong hierarchy here

and power is centralised. You need to have the guts to walk into a director's office.'

Innovation processes

Some companies have started to actively challenge their employees to contribute to their innovation pipeline by suggesting projects that not only generate business but also value for society. Some of the examples in Table 4.6 are already well known, but we feel this is a trend in companies that aim to explore the power of social intrapreneurism or open innovation in general.

Table 4.6 Companies that challenge employees to develop shared value

Company	Process
General Electric	**Ecomagination** According to the company, 'Ecomagination is GE's commitment to build innovative solutions for today's environmental challenges while driving economic growth'. In 2010 GE set the goal of growing the revenue of certified ecomagination products at twice the rate of total company revenue. This goal was met in 2012 when ecomagination revenue reached US$25 billion and reduced greenhouse gas emissions by 4.88 million metric tons. In order to meet the goal GE invested US$1.4 billion in R&D[8] GE also launched a programme called Eco-Treasure Hunts, which involves employees in a competition about energy savings. After 200 such Eco-Treasure Hunts the company was able to save US$150 million in energy bills (Russell 2012)
Odebrecht	**Prêmio Destaque (Highlight Prize)** The Odebrecht Group of Companies has run the Prêmio Destaque since 1992 in order to highlight projects that add value to the business. In the Social Responsibility category the company looks for projects that create positive impacts in communities or the environment. The prize encourages employees to share best practices, which then are fed into the company's knowledge management system. Ricardo Lyra affirms 'As we work in a very decentralised way, it is important that the good work we do, e.g. in Alagoas, is available to be replicated in Rio Grande do Sul.'[9]

8 See GE's Ecomagination Report at http://www.ge.com/globalimpact/ecomagination.html#! report=top, accessed 7 January 2014.
9 Translated from http://www.odebrechtonline.com.br/materias/01401-01500/1435/, accessed 8 January 2014.
10 See http://www.shell.com/global/future-energy/innovation/game-changer/what-is-gamechanger.html, accessed 8 January 2014

Shell	**GameChanger**
	Shell believes that 'some people can't stop dreaming up ideas to make things better' and in order to engage with them launched the GameChanger initiative. They invite people to submit their ideas on increasing energy production, carbon management, energy conversion, storage and distribution, as well as fuelling transportation. The company invests in the good ideas that are presented. See our profiles of social intrapreneur Mandar Apte and his 'godparent' Russ Conser, who managed the programme (see Ch. 4, Table 4.5).[10]
Natura	**Cocriando Natura**
	Natura believes in the power of collective creation and launched in 2013 the programme Cocriando Natura. Natura gives a challenge such as 'relationship between mother and baby' or 'transparency' and involves people with an interest working on this topic either in meetings or online. Afterwards the company shares its learning in the process.
IBM	**IBM Innovation Jam**
	IBM has transformed the jazz 'jam' into an art, engaging more than 300,000 employees in innovation and problem-solving. In 2006 IBM opened the process to everyone and assembled more than 150,000 people from over 100 countries. As a result, the company launched ten new businesses with seed financing of US$100 million.[11] The innovation jams are held online and are a way of crowdsourcing new ideas.

Strategy

Our literature review found that characteristics of an enabling strategic approach to intrapreneurship are: proactivity, a clear customer orientation, materiality, long-term perspectives and enhancing organisational capabilities.

Proactivity is primarily expressed by prospective environmental scanning, integrating diverse socioeconomic, political and commercial trends into the company's strategy (Anderson *et al.* 2004; Antoncic 2007; Kanter 1983; Lombriser and Ansoff 1995; Stopford and Baden-Fuller 1994; Zahra 1991, 1993).

Along the same lines, proximity to customers (Antoncic 2007; Roberts and Hirsch 2005) is considered an intrapreneurial enabler, with some authors reporting that firms occasionally 'camp' at customer sites for extended periods of time to better understand their needs (Christensen 2005: 314).

11 See https://www.collaborationjam.com, accessed 8 January 2014.

Clearly, organisations can demonstrate material impacts of intrapreneurial activities, whether these are new products or services, new clients, processes or new business ventures (Antoncic 2007; Antoncic and Hisrich 2003), which normally go along with a diversification strategy (Antoncic and Hisrich 2003; Narayanan *et al.* 2009).

A favourable strategic approach to intrapreneurship is also based on a long-term perspective (Christensen 2005; Kuratko and Goldsby 2004), which allows the organisation to learn and build organisational capabilities.

Companies are discovering both the risks and opportunities emerging in an operating context characterised by greater transparency, connectedness, global markets where manufacturing is more visible to consumers and demands for accountability from a wider range of stakeholders (Marcus 2012). Because social intrapreneurism is usually a strategic activity, features of corporate strategy could act as enablers and disablers of social intrapreneurism.

With the backing of senior management, social intrapreneurs were empowered to pilot projects that were developed into completely new business models:

> 'We could provide access to [company's] expertise and specific services on disaster risk reduction, poverty alleviation ... Rather than doing it as a normal part of our business, [the social intrapreneur] and I developed this new model for the way the business should be operated.'

> 'My fundamental philosophy is that if you really want to achieve system-level change, you need to embed that deep within the business, not just in headquarters ... this was about being much more strategic and business aligned and integrated—connecting CR with broader value drivers. Be innovation-driven in that approach. Big focus on business innovation ... if you want to achieve a social impact, find an economically viable way of delivering that. You'll find a quantum difference in that thinking.'

> 'The differentiation is critical because my product is typically 20% more expensive than the marketplace—that's all down to the ethics, the adult labour, living wages, health and safety ... We need a mark which differentiates. And it is commercially successful. It's starting to differentiate us from people who don't support this standard.'

Among the necessary strategic capabilities are employee competences (Amo and Kolvereid 2005; Christensen 2005; Jennings, Cox and Cooper 1994; Mantere 2005), access to networks (Christensen 2005; Mantere 2005; Narayanan *et al.* 2009) and experience with innovation (Antoncic 2007; Narayanan *et al.* 2009).

Conversely, strategic disablers are short-termism (Christensen 2005) and an orientation to task-design (Mantere 2005). We saw evidence of this among our social intrapreneurs:

> 'Our Brazilian CEO [name] has strong leadership, which gives emphasis to short-term and "show me the money" culture. We do not have a leader such as Fabio Barbosa who would inspire more sustainability.'

'The mentality here at [company] is business and short-term. My dream would be that in future we will receive more demand for collaboration from internal departments. My colleagues don't see sustainability in their P&L [Profit & Loss]'

External environment

One of the key points of divergence from our literature review on innovation and our interviews with social intrapreneurs was that the latter cited their connections with external organisations, whether these were NGOs, suppliers or other commercial partners or government agencies, as being instrumental in the instigation or development of their social intrapreneurial activities. The connections with these external contacts fulfilled a variety of important functions:

- They raised awareness of a range of sustainability issues that were material to the business

- They facilitated the creation of a business case for the development of social intrapreneurial activities that could be presented to senior managers

- They helped to legitimise the activities of social intrapreneurs with both internal and external stakeholder audiences

- They helped in development of cost- and time-effective operational plans for piloting social intrapreneurial projects, sometimes by providing technical advice

- They helped in assessing the outcomes, costs and benefits (social/commercial) of projects

Here are some of the examples cited:

'In 2000, [Corporate Affairs specialist had] conversations with UNDP in New York on the topic of "Small Island Insurances". Realised that due to a lack of insurance, there is less investment and growth and ultimately human development. Brought that topic internally. Did a study with GTZ [now GIZ] in Laos, India and Indonesia. India and Indonesia were suitable candidates for a [microinsurance] pilot. Indonesia started as in 2004 there was the tsunami.'

'[Interview subject] co-created a Cambridge CR Forum with other companies and academics etc., in Cambridge [to] expose sustainability problems to forum for open-source solution.'

'So we see a combination of areas to create new products and services. For example, we tracked malnutrition of patients and developed an iPad application which helps people to do a diagnostic, track developments and have access to nutritionists and potential solutions. So innovation now comes from a combination of factors ... There are two sources for innovation, (1) Globally, and (2) Locally. We run open innovation programmes with local universities. We launched ten products in 2011, most of it was renovation.'

In one company, the Programme Manager CSR and Mobility who is also Chair of the Innovation Board reports key external connections are with WWF (endorsement of mobility plan); other NGOs ('my trend watchers, for example, interpret future EU laws'); Imperial College (for European Union Seventh Framework Programme for Research bid); a doctor (on mobility scan); and University of Aachen (partner to build electric vehicle for €5,000).

Cross-departmental connections within the company can also be a useful part of a social intrapreneur's network for tracking different CSR issues and instigating social innovation projects:

> 'At [company] here I am operating always in partnership with more technical colleagues and keep a low profile with communication ... we have a sustainability department which is concerned with environmental issues. The area is therefore more technical and focuses on water and energy ... CSR department does take care of social programmes and our shared value creation initiatives.'

Social intrapreneurism networks can be shaped by market and political forces, the sustainability issues that are material to the business and the presence/absence of stakeholders generally.

Changes in packaging for one company were instigated in conjunction with a client (Wal-Mart) and government ('new law of solid waste'). Partners included CEMPRE (solid waste), the internal procurement department and suppliers researching packaging material.

> 'We work with local governments, universities...with UN, WTO, whoever is there as a stakeholder. Groups of independent advisers.'

> '[Retail company] got into sustainability because [we were] pushed ... NGO pressure re buying from AP&P. Now partnered with Rainforest Alliance. USA Environmental Affairs team have partnership around packaging and energy. Few [partnerships] with academics locally— mainly student projects ... Trade Consortium—environmental certification for office products; 24 global suppliers partnered with—looking at packaging.'

> 'Partners in these [innovation] projects are not typically IT-related. In mKRISHI, for example, they work with a consortium model—among partners there are agro-food companies, NGOs, agricultural universities, village entrepreneurs.'

> 'Working with Utrecht City Council on cement-free concrete; strong regulatory/government, private investor pressure; collaboration with professor from Technical University Delft, Eindhoven University, Sustainable Concrete Initiative.'

The shape of partnerships can vary across countries within a single corporate group:

> '[Beer manufacturer] was involved in industry initiatives (responsible drinking; Partnerships for Water; supply chain). In India there was a partnership with Confederation of Indian Industries and Indian NGOs (water recycling/training farmers). In South Africa [the company worked] with WWF and local authorities—replaced trees to reduce water consumption. In 2011 there was knowledge-sharing among all people in water partnerships.'

Social innovation can also be pursued through peer networks. One social intrapreneur helped to set up banking sector networks in Netherlands to promote dialogue among CEOs of retail banks.

In some instances, social innovation activity can be supported by channelling corporate resources externally to social entrepreneurs. Together with ESADE and now also with the PwC Foundation, BBVA (the Spanish financial sector company) has launched Momentum to help ten Spanish social entrepreneurs with the aspiration and potential to grow, to do so successfully. The Shell GameChanger programme invests in novel early stage inventions that could impact the energy system, helping their inventors progress these to 'proof of concept' stage. Similarly, an energy company supports the innovation work of universities and research institutions.

Sustainability initiatives need to be well executed; otherwise, they might backfire. One company collaborated in a project with one NGO 'without listening to other NGOs'. According to the social intrapreneur the company learned, in retrospect, that technical expertise is very important.

Suppliers can be critical partners in social innovation:

> 'In our supply chain we help farmers to do better, e.g. in Kakao we want to grow 3% globally—so we need to grow production in order to fulfil this goal …We have 31 production facilities in Brazil—P&G, for example, has three. So we have a lot of impact in our local value chain. We need to do this in order to continue to operate … Also our sales need to continue and the clients are expecting sustainability.'

> 'We have a big impact in local communities and therefore try to create fidelity with our farmers and local suppliers helping them to improve productivity and quality … There is a lot of market pressure for sustainability.'

> '[We] talk to recycling companies; materials suppliers; local government/ national government. Less with NGOs.'

Culture and partnerships

Cultural attitudes can shape (positively and negatively) the formation of potentially useful external partnerships.

A Dutch retailer where one social intrapreneur worked had expected to handle technical sustainability issues in house. The social intrapreneur 'would like to work more with NGOs but the company is rather old school', so the company works with students in house instead.

> '[I] went to a sustainability dinner and each course you moved table and introduced yourself to new people. When I said that I work for [airline company] I got a negative reaction.'

> 'We still have the mentality of inside–outside. Who works for [company] is inside, partners are outside.'

Accenture: creating an enabling environment for social intrapreneurism

One organisation that has created an enabling environment for innovation, including social intrapreneurism such as Accenture Development Partnerships (see more at pages 83–88) is the multinational management consulting, technology services and outsourcing company Accenture.

Variously described by senior executives as a 'talent factory', a 'talent shop' a 'talent machine' or a 'talent multiplier', the organisational culture is very much about recruiting, nurturing and retaining talented staff.

'We have no other wealth than our people,' says Armelle Carminati-Rabasse, then HR director now Chief Resources Officer at Unibail-Rodamco.

> We have no factories, we have no sales staff, we have no distribution networks, we have no physical products. We have a single brand. Our products are the vibrant talents that serve us. That is why we pay very specific attention to the way we build our human capital.

Mark Spellman, global head of strategy for Accenture and head of the High Performance Institute (an internal think-tank developing thought-leadership pieces for Accenture) adds:

> We have two hundred and fifty thousand people. We are growing at 10% each year and we have 10% attrition. What that means is that you are recruiting fifty thousand people a year so you can actually move the show forward.

Jill Huntley, head of Corporate Citizenship describes the Accenture culture as one 'where employees look for ways to do things better: it's hard-wired to find better ways to develop capabilities.'

Human resource practices are designed to make these 50,000 new recruits effective quickly, as well as ensuring that all 250,000 people have a range of opportunities for continuous professional development. While the objective is to ensure consultants are kept occupied with client-facing work, there will be downtime as client projects evolve and workloads vary. Any downtime must be used productively for continuous professional development (CPD) or business and project development. Individual employees can, therefore, propose projects to research potential opportunities. They must find an internal sponsor, able and willing to sign off a certain amount of their time to investigate the idea.

Accenture's flagship global corporate citizenship programme Skills to Succeed is now also structured to create opportunities for employees to volunteer their personal and work time and do so in ways that will also enhance CPD and potentially also bring insights from social innovation developed through Skills to Succeed back into the rest of the business.

Skills to Succeed work on microinsurance projects in Cambodia, for example, has subsequently helped the firm with work for a major insurance company client.

Mentoring and coaching is a major part of Accenture's *modus operandi:* several of the company's innovation programmes have mentoring included, and, in practice, the requirement to get a formal sponsor for your personal 'downtime' project makes these sponsors mentors too.

It is increasingly being recognised inside the company that working in ADP, or Skills to Succeed or negotiating external placements can help your career progression. Spellman argues:

> By spending some of your time engaged around one of those platforms, actually that would accelerate your career because I think you get a richer, more varied set of experiences. For example, you can spend three years working at a big oil company in London or you can spend two years working in the oil company and then go off and spend a year working in Guatemala trying to help out an NGO. You will probably end up being a more rounded and more interesting consultant by having done the two plus one than you would by just doing the three years in the oil company. I would argue that you actually get better, more rounded people. We are in a world where I think increasingly you need a combination of analytical and emotional intelligence skills, and the differentiator is increasingly the emotional intelligence and the collaborative skills and the ability to work cross-culturally both geographically and sectorally: the analytics are necessary but not sufficient.

Would those 50,000 new Accenture hires this year hear top leadership, or the middle managers they would be more likely to come into more direct contact with, say this? Spellman is honest in terms of **management and leadership**:

> The straight answer is: it's a mixed bag as one would expect. You would get some pretty consistent messages from the top about the value of those platforms and why it's important. I think the operational realities of what happens when you hit the ground is different: some will give you the message and some perhaps won't and I think it varies quite a lot geography by geography—so I would say an opportunity to improve! One thing that I would say though is, particularly in an organisation like ours, the more that you have had people who have had that experience of two years in London and one in Guatemala and who have then been successful in their own right and are working their way through the system then obviously they become your ambassadors as well so it's an evolving process.'

Overall, however, senior executives emphasise the importance of innovation and talent development, the importance of individuals being proactive in their own career and skills development, and the organisation's openness to innovation.

This is reinforced by **resources** being available to support innovation including social intrapreneurism. There is an annual global innovation competition that has run since 2006, where employees can compete with new business ideas and winners share cash awards to develop their proposals. The 2012 competition generated 325 entries from 18 countries. According to Huntley, there has been a conscious effort in recent years to focus on innovation with potential for social good. There is also an annual innovation awards scheme where people compete with their existing project work. Various country units also run innovation competitions. France, for example, has run *chaîne d'innovation* (innovation chain) where joint teams composed of employee volunteers, volunteers from client companies, MBA students and students from art, design and architecture schools, work together over a six-month period in order to try to shape a new idea. In Accenture Spain, there is a year-round employees' innovation competition. Individual business units also have budgets for R&D and market and talent development, which employees can pitch for.

Organisational structures and processes are designed to foster teamwork, knowledge-sharing and innovation. The fast-changing nature of client consultancy means that individuals will find themselves in teams that are constantly forming and re-forming, amoeba-like. Of course, even in an organisation specialising in ICT to back up knowledge management, there are challenges in keeping 250,000 employees in the loop. The Strategy practice team are experimenting with a virtual Thought Leadership Café that aims to replicate what happens in a real café: people come together, sit down, have a cup of coffee and start discussing ideas. The Thought Leadership Café enables individual employees anywhere in the world to tap in their ideas and find other people interested in collaborating to develop them. Mark Spellman believes this could stimulate more social intrapreneurism, especially if it creates more possibilities to tap the social consciousness of Accenture's generally youthful employee base. Huntley says:

> It used to be down to individuals with resilience, persistence, sheer bloody-mindedness. Nowadays, social intrapreneurism is easier to do as part of a formalised programme because there are more places around the world where joint ventures between Accenture and non-profit organisations are occurring like Numerique in Cambodia.

Thus innovation linked to talent development is at the core of Accenture's own strategy. Bruno Berthon, who heads Accenture's global Sustainability practice, which emerged out of Berthon's own social intrapreneurism, argues that having a menu of different ways that Accenture employees might be able to spend some time working with non-traditional clients, such as *pro bono* assignments, corporate citizenship programmes like Skills to Succeed, tours of duty with ADP, innovation competition and approved client-downtime projects, helps to stimulate social innovation:

> We've realised that social innovation can be a very attractive innovation model in the sense of innovation for new business models which are quite difficult to innovate normally; but by working in new environments which cannot afford a classic business model or which don't have the required infrastructure you're forced to invent a different kind of business model; and you learn through that interesting sort of experience that you can transform into a sustainable business model.

They also create more opportunities for employees to work with NGOs, development agencies, clients etc. and thus tap external environment and understand better the elements of societal as well as business change. Mark Spellman argues that 'in a converging world where complex problems need more than just policy makers, more than just business and more than just civil society that becomes a very interesting backdrop for entrepreneurs and intrapreneurs to flourish.'

The 'enabling environment' within Accenture provided Julika Erfurt, a manager at Accenture's Strategy Practice, with an opportunity to develop a new client services stream focused on ageing and demographic change.

Julika Erfurt: adding ageing and demographic change to Accenture's client services

Salvador Pozo

Like many of her generation growing up in Eastern Europe, Julika Erfurt was politicised at a very early age. She was born in what was then East Germany in 1979 and spent her childhood in Leipzig, where the demonstrations against the East German Communist Party that are often seen as the beginning of the end of the Cold War began. Julika was at school with the children of a number of the opposition leaders; her classes were often cancelled in favour of intense political debates; and she and her parents joined the weekly demonstrations demanding freedom of speech, free elections and freedom to travel.

TENOR SAXOPHONIST SIMON ALLEN IS SHOWN SOLOING WITH THE STAN TRACEY OCTET WHILE OTHER FRONT LINE MEMBERS (LEFT TO RIGHT) MARK NIGHTINGALE (TROMBONE), MARK ARMSTRONG (TRUMPET), SAM MAYNE (ALTO SAX) AND NADIM TEIMOORI (FOREGROUND) LISTEN INTENTLY. SOCIAL INTRAPRENEURS, LIKE SKILLED MUSICIANS, PAY CLOSE ATTENTION TO EACH OTHER'S PLAYING SO THAT THEIR OWN SOLOS CONTRIBUTE TO A LARGER, COHERENT MUSICAL 'CONVERSATION'.

The Berlin Wall came down just before Julika's eleventh birthday. After reunification, she saw some of the negative consequences as unemployment soared locally, and family breakdowns and even suicides increased in her community. At McGill University she took degrees in Political Science and Anthropology. Her passion for justice and equality were further developed by two spells in Sri Lanka, working under the guidance of an anthropologist connected to the NGO Centre for Poverty Analysis (CEPA), with the support of the German international development agency GTZ (now GIZ). As Julika describes that time:

> I spent time in factories in the free trade zone near Colombo and then in the south of the country. I was mainly working with young female workers and it was a real eye-opener. I had gone there imagining these places were sweatshops and, instead, I found the women workers often saw them as giving them freedom and independence.

Julika joined Accenture in 2005 where she continued to study and reflect on the challenges and opportunities of sustainable development.

> About six years ago, it dawned on me that everyone in my team was talking about the environment, but I didn't hear so many people talking about the challenges of ageing and demographic change. I had a spell ill and was off work, and this gave me the time to read and reflect further.

Recovered and back at work, she started conversations with her Strategy Consulting colleagues and with other colleagues in the Accenture Sustainability Practice. She was able to pitch for time to develop her knowledge and expertise about ageing and demographic change. The Institute for High Performance, Accenture's internal think tank, and the Sustainability practice became internal 'sponsors' and introduced her to the Doughty Centre for Corporate Responsibility at Cranfield as well as John Elkington and his Volans colleagues. Together they were able to organise a series of roundtable conversations, hosted at Accenture as the 'Second Half Network' where individuals and organisations interested in the interface between demographic change and sustainability and entrepreneurship could develop thinking and action.

Through these roundtables, client work in multiple countries and the publication of thought-leadership papers for Accenture, Julika built up a profile as the 'go to' person for demographics questions. While she is unclear whether this might one day morph into a separate consulting practice, for now she knows her social intrapreneurism has found concrete expression in the consulting work she does to help clients see the opportunities of the 'silver economy'.

In Chapter 3 we introduced the story of Priscila Matta, a social intrapreneur at Natura in Brazil (pages 89–93) and posed the question of how best she could secure company buy-in for her ideas. Having examined the range of ways that companies can respond to social intrapreneurs in their midst and what makes an enabling environment, we pick up Priscila's story again.

Natura: how Priscila got the music started

Like a great jazz musician, Priscila has done her 'woodshedding' as an anthropologist. She has spent years learning to 'listen' to, and develop a deep understanding of, the perspectives of others.

Her anthropological skills allowed her to understand different communities, one of which was the community of people working for Natura. She understood that succeeding in this executive meeting meant getting sign-off for the next steps in designing the real strategy to resolve the distressed relationship with the community of Palmeira do Piauí. She also understood that the lack of knowledge was the main reason for Natura's resistance to move forward on the case: 'At the beginning Natura did not know what to do. They had the right values, but no know-how to address this type of issue.'

Priscila was also an 'insider' at Natura and had developed a deep sense of the company's values and principles. The challenge was to hear the 'voices' of both the company and the community and 'improvise' a solo that reflected, and would make sense to both of them.

Her presentation therefore needed to show Natura the first practical steps that could be taken in order to resolve the issue without further putting Natura's business and reputation at stake. With this in mind she designed her presentation, knowing at the same time that a visit to the community would significantly change the strategy she was presenting.

Her assessment of Natura's executives was correct and her strategy to convince them worked. During Priscila's presentation the executives could clearly see the quality of her approach. They also recognised the need for her to visit the community. The work she had done in the past months combined with the quality presentation gave the executives the confidence to approve her approach. Priscila had successfully completed the first milestone—she gained the executives trust and was allowed to start her work with the community.

When Priscila arrived at Palmeira do Piauí in October 2008, her first step was to make a diagnosis, so that she could understand how the situation had evolved from 2006. Joined by another independent anthropologist (as required by the Brazilian Management Council of Genetic Heritage in cases of access to genetic heritage and associated traditional knowledge), she spoke to many members in the community, whose story then started to be unveiled. Originally, the people of Palmeira do Piauí did not sell anything to people outside. Their community was based on a subsistence economy. Little by little, this situation started to change, as minor amounts of buriti oil and sweet roots were sold to small-scale traders at low prices. At that time, the income generated by these sales did not yet affect the social fabric of the community.

Priscila then realised that the upcoming distribution of benefits could potentially damage the community and create greed as well as resentment. It was almost impossible to identify who were the 'holders' of the knowledge related to the buriti oil production process, and in different ways, the buriti plant represented a means of living to most of the people in Palmeira do Piauí, who rarely know how to read and write. Consequently, it was very complex to explain what the new Brazilian 'Biodiversity Law' meant for them. Differences between the business and the community languages and the novelty of the subject made it hard to approach the issue. However, they did understand that Natura wanted to share some benefits concerning the commercial research using the buriti oil sample purchased from Palmeira do Piauí in the past. As a result, everybody wanted to have a part of that. Different lists had been set up in order to distribute the benefits and it was difficult to sort out who rightfully had a claim to receive a share. People were literally fighting for money. Although Natura wanted to respect the social and political organisation form of that group, the company wanted to follow its principles and conduct a process without fights and local discussions.

Priscila's first action to halt the fight for money was to announce that the money would be distributed to the benefit of the community and not individual members, strengthening the sustainable use of biodiversity and environmental conservation, according to Natura's principles and the Convention on Biological Diversity (CBD).

This ingenious solution was a brilliant 'solo' on Priscila's part and provided a theme that would resonate with both the company's executives and community leaders.

> My first strategy was to say: there will be no money, but instead benefits in terms of environmental conservation, community building etc. This eliminated from the process all the people who were only interested in getting some money, so that we could start working with the people who really worked with the buriti oil and had an interest in fostering the community.

A focus on biodiversity conservation actions, and on the strengthening and appreciation of the buriti oil producers, would also help to maintain the social fabric in the community, and potentially provide every member with the conditions to increase their quality of life.

In order to decide what type of project could be developed to share the benefits with the community, Priscila then set up a broad-scale community engagement process. Such dialogue is a form of intrapreneurial 'jamming', giving community members an opportunity for their 'voices', and their ideas, to be heard.

The community and Natura approved the benefit-sharing plan in November 2009. Initiatives included training courses for the handling and conservation of buriti areas, social strengthening and organisation, appreciation of buriti oil producers' knowledge and improvements in production. This approval was the result of a broad-scale public participation process clearly focusing on the community's needs.

Natura partnered with the NGO Instituto Ecológica (IE). IE was made responsible for managing the resources related to the benefit sharing, and for guaranteeing that investments would focus effectively on the appreciation of the local way of life, the sustainable use of biodiversity and environmental conservation actions within the Palmeira do Piauí community.

By recruiting IE to the 'ensemble', Priscila demonstrated her skills as a 'bandleader', bringing an entirely new voice into the music-making and enriching the partnership.

'JAM SESSIONS' IN SMALL CLUBS—SUCH AS THIS 2012 'JAM' AT THE AJANI GRILL & JAZZ PLACE IN LONDON,
WHERE ALTO PLAYER CAMILLA GEORGE IS SHOWN SOLOING WITH BASSIST TOM MOORE AND GUITARIST
GRAHAM GARSIDE COMPING BEHIND HER—ENABLE TALENTED MUSICIANS TO CONNECT AND TRY OUT NEW
IDEAS IN FRONT OF AN AUDIENCE OF INTERESTED LISTENERS.

SIMILARLY, COMPANIES CAN STAGE THEIR OWN IN-HOUSE 'JAM SESSIONS', PROVIDING PROTECTED
ENVIRONMENTS WHERE LIKE-MINDED EMPLOYEES CAN TRY OUT, AND PLAY WITH, NEW INTRAPRENEURIAL
PROJECT IDEAS.

At the end of the process Priscila was happy to see that she had gained the
respect of the people of Palmeira do Piauí and helped Natura build a trust relationship with the community. From the very beginning she engaged with her colleagues inside on the different approaches to resolve the issues with the Palmeira
do Piauí community. She knew that part of the success was due to the excellent
collaboration with people inside Natura. The legal team helped her design robust
contracts with the community, which did not have an official representation such
as a cooperative. The community engagement team helped talk through different scenarios, so every time Priscila went to the community she was prepared for
whatever outcome the situation presented. Due to Natura's in-sourcing of the
management of community relationships her team had grown to a total of ten
people. All of them contributed to Priscila's success and all shared the experiences from the Palmeira do Piauí case. In a way Priscila replicated the public-
participation process internally in order to share learning and to equip Natura to
avoid similar issues in its relationships with communities in the future.

Additionally, Natura approved a new Policy of Sustainable Use of Biodiversity
and Traditional Knowledge in 2008, which was fully implemented in 2009. This
document established the use of biodiversity as an important component of sustainable development within Natura, and includes[12]:

12 Natura's Annual Report 2008.

- The appreciation of ethical and transparent relationships with stakeholders
- The application of the well-founded principle of prior consent
- The harmonious use of traditional knowledge and scientific rigour in the development of products
- Establishment of networks
- The appreciation of cultural heritage and traditional knowledge
- Minimisation of impacts
- Sustainable handling
- Certification
- Sharing of benefits
- The appreciation of work
- Fair price based on a sound value-chain analysis

Therefore, Priscila concludes, Natura learned a lot from the relationship with Palmeira do Piauí people:

> The company has learned a lot, the level of understanding for local communities is very high, and the learning resulted from previous errors and the continuous formation of its workers. Today, more and more people inside Natura understand this line of work. Natura is always on the look to improve and do more to fully follow its principles.

Marcelo Cardoso agrees that the values of Natura are a strong source of innovation:

> 'At Natura innovation came from the genesis of the company. As Natura has its essence and corporate values which reflect aspiration to contribute to humans millennium goals, that is an impulse because these values are always contemporary. Even in the case of Natura, which listens little to the consumer and many of the things Natura did was when not listening to the consumer. EKOS for example, consumers thought the product was very ugly, strange packaging, it wasn't in the same line of design. Our innovation culture is in this sense of bringing to life our vision and the experience of well-being (*bem-estar*) to the consumer and to society. Innovation comes more from the reason of being and less from market dynamics.'

However, Marcelo recognises that Natura attracts talent but also recognises some obstacles in the innovation process:

> We attract a lot of good people. We attract people with a restlessness to make a difference in the world. But many times people get frustrated because of processes and bureaucracy. I think the biggest barrier is the mentality of management. Management supposes a system of planning and control. This is the logic of business schools for the last 150 years. It believes that if I plan something, I can later control and I will have good results. In a world in which we live in great uncertainty, where things can change in terms of weeks, now something can happen in the Middle East, something can happen. This changes how you view business. Fukushima, Italian debt, climate change, environmental crisis, terrorism... this destroys management and the belief that you can plan something and control. The biggest challenge is the find a way to finish with that. And in the heads of leaders, you need to change that, they need to control, they think they

cannot share information, competition ... The biggest obstacle is the mental model of the persons.

Priscila's case demonstrates that she felt frustrated because she was not allowed to visit the community in the beginning. However, the management's hesitation expresses another point Marcelo Cardoso considers relevant: 'It can't be too easy; there needs to be some resistance. Here we lead as well with the maturity of persons. There are many immature persons and they desist at the first sign of resistance.'

Print the Model of Social Intrapreneurship on an A0 poster. Take some green, yellow and red sticky notes. The green notes are for leverage factors, the red represent barriers and the yellow other relevant issues you consider important. Think about the enabling environment, passing from organisational culture, strategy, top leadership support, Human Resource practices, resources and collaboration with external organisations noting leverages, barriers and other relevant factors and you'll have a pretty good picture of what the enabling environment of your company looks like. You might want to do this exercise with your team.

Summarising the enablers and disablers

Table 4.7 summarises all the enablers and disablers we identified within the literature and theory (T) as well as with the interviews with social intrapreneurs (I).

Table 4.7 Summary of enablers and disablers

Factor	Enablers	Disablers
Culture	Values: Values (T, I) Vision (T, I) Empowerment: Autonomy (T, I) Experimentation (T, I) Risk-taking (T, I) Problem-solving with co-workers (T, I) Tolerance for failure (T, I) Social awareness (I) Dialogue/'café culture' to promote ideational fluency/'flow' (I)	Values: Incongruent values (I) Either/or CSR mind-set (philanthropy vs. profitability) Empowerment: Scepticism (I)

Human resource practices	Personnel development: Valuing employees' skills and knowledge (T, I) Seeing employees' potential (T, I) Training (T, I) Volunteering support: Involving employees in CR (I) Personal innovation time (I) Group innovation/brainstorming sessions Knowledge management Rewards: Financial (T, I) Non-financial (recognition) (T, I) Blended HR management methods (I)	Personnel development: Change-resistant employees (T) Lack of collaboration (T) Difficulties in getting to know co-workers (T) Obstacles to SI action (I)
Management and leadership	Guide: Vision and values (T, I) Giving importance to innovation (T, I) Commitment to sustainability (I) Sponsor: Encourage risk-taking (T, I) Tolerance for failure (T, I) Providing resources (T, I) Delegating authority (T, I) Creating protected space for experimentation (I) Facilitator/'godparent' (I) Skills Long-term thinking (T) Quality communication (T, I) Experience with innovation (T) Framing business context for social innovation (I)	Guide: Not providing direction (T) Values (I) Scepticism (I) Succession (I) Personal/political ambition (I) Excessive management control (I) Sponsor Loss of sponsor Skills Short-term thinking (T, I)
Resources	Resource availability (T, I) Time (T, I) Innovation infrastructure (I) CR support (I) 'Improvisational' accounting (I)	Lack of resources (T, I) Employee turnover (T)

Organisational structures and processes	Organisational design: Flat (T, I) Decentralisation (I) Communication-enabling (T, I) CR unit (I) Size (I) Teamwork: Cross-functional teams (T, I) Management systems: Strategic consistency (T) Formal evaluation (T, I) Organisational capabilities Experience in innovation (T, I)	Organisational design: Bureaucracy (T, I) Silos (T, I) Centralisation (I) CR unit (I) Size (I) Teamwork: Difficulty in forming teams (T) Innovation as the exclusive responsibility of R&D (T) Management systems: Strategic inconsistency (T, I) Lack of formal evaluation (T, I) Excessive control (T)
Strategy	Proactivity Environmental scanning (T, I) Social diagnosis (I) Customer orientation Proximity to customers (T, I) Material impact (T, I) Triple bottom line strategy (I) Long-term perspective (T, I) Capabilities Employee competencies (T) Access to external networks (T&I) Experience in innovation (T&I) Piloting projects (I) Alternative business model development (I)	Task-design orientation (T) CR as 'philanthropy and volunteering' (I) Financial bottom line strategy (I) Short-term perspective (T&I) Aversion to risk (I) Exclusive eco-efficiency focus (I)
External environment (I)	Networks NGOs Development agencies Leading authorities Universities Expert forums Other social intrapreneurs Cross-sector coalitions Business peer networks Supply chain networks Societal pressures: From stakeholders From governments From customers Recession Recognition Awards	Competitors' greenwashing NGOs/local communities' philanthropic expectations Cultural barriers to external partnerships (inside/outside mind-set) Societal pressures Recession

Note: T = factors identified from intrapreneurship theory; I = factors identified from interviews with social intrapreneurs and their colleagues.

Putting it into practice

Mark Thain joined Barclays in 2007, initially as a Finance Business Partner and became Associate Director, Global Community Investment in 2009. He was integral to a strategic review of Barclays' corporate citizenship activity, which had been evolving since the millennium from corporate philanthropy to more business-focused corporate citizenship. Mark proposed, and now leads, the Barclays Social Innovation Facility (SIF) as Vice President of Social Innovation at Barclays.[13]

At a Shared Value Summit, he explained how the company's 'shared value' approach enhances its competitive edge (Thain 2013):

> I think 'shared value' gives us a competitive edge in three main ways in Barclays:
>
> First of all, it opens up a whole new opportunity set for us. It forces us to think in new ways about our products and services, which drives innovation and growth.
>
> Second way is … the really interesting relationships it helps to build with our stakeholders. That's with clients or other corporate partners or other NGOs and governments; it's a whole new way of having conversations with them and starts to drive deep new relationships.
>
> And the final area is employee engagement … getting the employees to get excited and involved in some of our programmes, or recruiting the next generation of top talent who are increasingly focused on this type of area. They're trying to find areas they can work that line up with their own values.
>
> The shared value approach has differences in one main way for me and that's a focus on longer-term sustainability. It's not about maximising profits in this quarter or looking back at the previous quarter's results. It's really looking forward to the next 15 to 20 years—looking at where the business is going to be in the long-term.

The following example illustrates how development of the Barclays SIF Innovation Facility has enabled the bank to start promoting social intrapreneurism within the company.

13   Source: interview with co-author, 21 October 2013.

Social Innovation Facility: how Barclays is promoting social intrapreneurism

As a financial institution we have expertise, knowledge, networks, products and services that are critical for economic and social development. But we need to focus on what can be achieved if we combine those assets, with the expertise and resources of like-minded corporates across different sectors (Group Chief Executive, Antony Jenkins).[14]

The £25 million Barclays Social Innovation Facility (SIF) grew out of a strategic review of Barclays' long-established and substantial philanthropic and community-investment programmes in 2011. While these programmes had evolved substantially since the millennium and become much more strategic, with fewer and bigger programmes more closely aligned to the business such as financial literacy and help for small businesses, it was felt that Barclays—like any business—could have much more societal impact through core business.

Hence, the SIF was created to provide 'proof of concept' support to business teams across Barclays to prove innovative commercial solutions to social challenges through research and development, investment in new technologies and assistance with testing and piloting of new concepts; if successful, businesses will scale. It is seen as an internal version of the DFID Challenge Fund referred to on page 73.

Experimenting with social intrapreneurism projects, which the SIF is designed to promote, will generate pilots that provide 'proof of concept', which can then be rolled out on a larger scale to create greater impact.

Strategising to achieve sustainable business and societal goals, as Barclays have done here, is vital to ensuring that social intrapreneurism projects have a life beyond the pilot phase.

Structure of the SIF

All propositions are embedded and delivered within business teams, with a heavy focus on collaboration and partnership, both within Barclays and externally across different sectors, regions and industries. The SIF is open to all businesses within Barclays, with relevant propositions that meet the SIF criteria.

Each project is evaluated against four funding criteria:

1. **Business impact.** Does it create long-term economic value to Barclays? Grow revenues? Reduce costs? Drive client connectivity? Open up new markets?

2. **Social impact.** Does it contribute in a measurable way to society? Address a specific social or environmental issue? Benefit an identifiable community or group?

Accounting for social and environmental, as well as economic, value created by a social intrapreneurism project helps to change or sustain a corporate mindset that recognises a broader spectrum of value creation beyond generating purely

---

14 Barclays news, 27 September 2013, http://group.barclays.com/news/news-article/1329930723898, accessed 9 January 2014.

financial returns. This is vital to ensuring a social intrapreneurism activity continues to be supported, even in the midst of an adverse economic climate.

3. **Scalability.** Does it have long term growth prospects? Leverage for products across multiple regions/sectors/businesses? Potential to apply new technologies? Broad consumer insights?

4. **Strategic alignment.** Does it complement Barclays' strategy? In line with current or future business strategy in the region? Contribute to becoming the 'Go-To' bank? Demonstrate purpose and values in action?

All proposals must be owned and embedded within a business team who will take on full responsibility for delivering projects and deploying resources.

Proposals for SIF support are considered by a Governing Council made up of senior members from the different Barclays businesses as well as the corporate board. Current members include vice chairmen from the investment banking and corporate businesses alongside the retail director from Barclays business in Africa, the Head of the Group Design office and the Managing Director responsible for Marketing, Brand and Citizenship.

The Governing Council members are potential 'godparents' for social intrapreneurs and are people who can play roles as power brokers, networkers, translators (of raw ideas into corporate purpose and strategy), coaches/listeners, sustainability advocates, fielders of challenges, prudent risk-takers and diplomats. See the section above on 'The Magic of Dynamic Duos' (pages 122–24) for a more detailed description of godparents and their relationships to social intrapreneurs.

In addition to directly funding projects, the SIF can also provide internal risk guarantees, and support in accessing cross-sector external partners, subject matter experts and relevant knowledge-sharing forums. The SIF plays an important role in gaining sponsorship and advocacy within business units through SIF governing council members and senior leaders and through sharing of internal best practice across Barclays business units and regions.

Knowledge-sharing, especially across teams, is what can drive generation of the new ideas that can then be developed into viable projects. Companies need to cultivate café culture (see Ch. 7)—create an environment where it is safe to 'think crazy stuff in any position and in any meeting', as Cassiano Mecchi (when at Danone) said—to ensure that, as in jazz improvisation, great ideas can emerge and flow freely.

While the availability of funding was initially seen as the key, in practice, non-financial support, including the backing of the 'heavy hitters' on the Governing Council, has proved particularly important. Regular progress reports on individual SIF-supported projects are provided to the Council who can also be asked to help tackle organisational blockages.

Barclays has committed to investing a total of £25 million through the SIF and by the end of 2013 had supported a portfolio of 12 projects. In addition to receiving proposals from across the bank, SIF is also working to proactively accelerate a pipeline of proposals within a number of high priority areas that lock together sizeable commercial value and significant social impact. These include developing the new products, technologies and business models that will support increased access to financial services in emerging markets, investigating the role that mainstream banks can play in growing the impact-investing sector and supporting Barclays clients in driving economic inclusion by transforming their supply chains.

Networking with clients and others outside the organisation—with a view to developing external partnerships for projects—is a crucial step in building an external enabling environment for social intrapreneurism.

How the SIF helps build an enabling environment within Barclays for social intrapreneurism

While the SIF began before the new Barclays leadership launched the bank's new purpose and values, these have helped to reinforce the case for the SIF. Further initiatives planned to help stimulate a more enabling environment within Barclays for social intrapreneurism include developing an internal version of the League of Intrapreneurs Innovation Lab (several Barclays would-be social intrapreneurs and the head of the SIF attended the inaugural Lab); creating formal secondment programmes to temporarily place Barclays employees within SIF supported projects; and encouraging senior leaders who participate in experiential learning programmes to think about social innovation/shared value ideas during their immersion. The SIF also has an existing fellowship programme within the investment banking business that offers high-performing analysts or associates a six-month secondment to the central SIF team.

Growing people through personal development programmes such as the Social Intrapreneur Lab, experiential learning and SIF Fellowship secondment initiatives helps prepare aspiring social intrapreneurs for leadership roles in sustainable innovation projects.

However, to ensure a return on such programmes, companies need to cultivate café culture and humanise the organisation—promoting an atmosphere of egalitarianism and generosity (a 'vibe' found in great jazz clubs)—so that people feel that they can share ideas freely (e.g. in any corporate 'jam session') and contribute to the development of others' projects (i.e. acting as good 'sidemen'), knowing that their contributions will be recognised and appreciated.

5

External enabling environment

External organisations and networks

Over the past two decades, an international architecture to raise awareness of, and support for, social entrepreneurs and social enterprise has emerged, thanks to the pioneering work of a number of individuals and organisations. Prominent among these have been Bill Drayton and the Ashoka Foundation he created; the AVINA Foundation; Klaus Schwab, founder of the Davos World Economic Forum, through whose Schwab Foundation social enterprise has featured at the WEF; Jeff Skoll and the Skoll Foundation, which in turn has created the Skoll Centre for Social Enterprise at Oxford's Said Business School, and the annual Skoll World Forum on Social Enterprise; and John Elkington and Pamela Hartigan, with their book *The Power of Unreasonable People* (2008).

We are now starting to see an analogous burgeoning of an international architecture to raise awareness of, and support for, the growth of social intrapreneurism. Among the early pioneers are John Elkington, Maggie De Pree and Alexa Clay who co-authored the 2008 SustainAbility Field Guide to Social Intrapreneurs; Gib Bulloch, the social intrapreneurial founder of Accenture Development Partnerships (ADP) and his ADP colleagues; again Ashoka and the League of Intrapreneurs, which began as an international competition to find social intrapreneurs and is now evolving into a loose coalition of interested individuals and organisations, grouped around Alexa Clay, Maggie De Pree, ADP and Ashoka.

Social intrapreneurs often feel alone inside their companies swimming against the current. External networks and groups help in finding people with similar ideas and values. External groups such as business schools, social innovation networks, NGOs, CR coalitions, venture philanthropists and awards all play roles in helping social intrapreneurs to succeed with their ideas and achieve shared sustainability goals. These external partners create stages for experimenting and discussing projects as well as potentially finding allies. Table 5.1 shows some of the partner organisations that were identified in our research interviews as having aided the progress of social intrapreneurism projects.

JAZZ MUSICIANS OFTEN EXPERIMENT WITH DIFFERENT INSTRUMENTAL MIXES IN THEIR ENSEMBLES TO GET A PARTICULAR COLLECTIVE SOUND THAT COULD NOT BE ACHIEVED OTHERWISE. HERE, THE BYRON WALLEN QUINTET (PERFORMING AT HERTS JAZZ CLUB) HAVE INCLUDED A TUBA AND OMITTED A PIANO TO CREATE AN UNUSUAL BRASS SOUND: (LEFT TO RIGHT) OREN MARSHALL (TUBA), JULIAN SIEGEL (TENOR SAX), BYRON WALLEN (TRUMPET), NEIL CHARLES (BASS), TOM SKINNER (DRUMS).

SIMILARLY, SUCCESSFUL SOCIAL INTRAPRENEURISM PROJECT TEAMS INCLUDE PARTNERS OUTSIDE THE INTRAPRENEUR'S COMPANY AND EVEN BEYOND THE CORPORATE SECTOR. WORKING ALLIANCES WITH NGOS, FOR EXAMPLE, CAN PRODUCE NOVEL, POWERFUL SOCIAL IMPACTS.

Table 5.1 External partners working with social intrapreneurs

NGO	Government agencies	Educational	Commercial
Second Nature (environmental NGO)	GTZ (German government developmental agency) (now GIZ)	University of Birmingham	The *Guardian*; the *Daily Telegraph* (media partners)
Forum for the Future (not-for-profit consultancy)	Inter-American Development Bank	C.K. Prahalad (University of Michigan professor and business guru)	Asociación Peruana de Turismo
Hadoti Hast Shilp Sansthan (Indian NGO providing welfare services)	UK DFID Challenge Grant	Aspen Institute	
WWF Australia			
MicroEnergy International			
Instituto Ecológica			
Conservation International			

Social innovation networks

Social innovation networks such as Impact Hub[1] attract social entrepreneurs as well as social innovators inside business organisations. By offering a co-working space and short courses on social innovation these networks give members access to necessary training and people to 'bounce' ideas off.

A number of the social innovation incubators including Impact Hubs in Amsterdam, London, Mexico City, Sao Paolo and Zurich have run events for aspiring and emerging social intrapreneurs and their supporters.

Lara Toensman created a one-year social intrapreneurship programme at the Impact Hub in Amsterdam comprising the participation in a learning group of 12 social intrapreneurs, ten 4-hour workshops, key note events, monthly meetings and access to the global Impact Hub community.

1   http://www.impacthub.net/.

In Brazil the Impact Hub in São Paulo has partnered with the leading business school in Latin America, Fundação Dom Cabral, to assist social intrapreneurs in designing their projects, overcoming internal resistance and honing their entrepreneurial skills. The feedback from participants describes the value they ascribe to the course:

> 'I was inspired by the other persons who are merging sustainability and business within their organisations.'

> 'It helped me to mature my ideas.'

> 'Nurturing my soul.'

> 'Gaining a new identity as social intrapreneur understanding that it is possible to do social innovation within companies.'

This feedback reinforces the need of social intrapreneurs to get together with others who share the same vision and values, and try to use business for the common good.

NGOs

Peter Schwartz and Blair Gibb (Schwartz and Gibb, 1999) classify NGOs according to their interactions with corporations, which range from adversarial campaigning to partnerships. A logical extension of a partnership approach is collaboration with social intrapreneurs. Some of our interviewees already collaborate with NGOs in the realisation of their projects; for example, in the aim to reduce emissions and comply with new recycling regulation, Lucas Urbano at Danone Brazil partnered with the Ipê Institute and CEMPRE, which brought their technical expertise to the table.

Where companies have already embraced social intrapreneurship, NGOs can help with market research, awareness-raising sessions with employees, hosting field visits and providing technical support under contract with the company. Where a company has yet to move beyond the compliance or risk-minimisation stages of CR, the NGO may be more productive by encouraging any members of the NGO working inside large companies to consider enacting their commitment to the goals of the NGO at their place of employment.

For NGOs, social intrapreneurs can be a route to increasing their own impact substantially and extending their reach. Conversely, engagement with NGOs, for example, through volunteering programmes, can create benefits for the volunteers and the companies for whom they work.

Corporate responsibility coalitions

Business-led CR coalitions are defined as:

> Independent, non-profit membership organisations that are composed mainly or exclusively of for-profit businesses; that have a board of directors composed predominantly or only of business people; that are core-funded primarily or totally from business; and whose dedicated purpose is to promote responsible business practice (Grayson and Nelson 2013).

There are such coalitions in at least 70 countries, including more than two-thirds of the world's 10 largest economies. Additionally, there are multi-stakeholder CR coalitions such as the national chapters of the UN Global Compact in around 90 countries.

Many of these coalitions have traditionally focused on CEOs, main board directors and specialist CR directors. Many, however, also have employee volunteer programmes focused on harnessing employee time and expertise for charitable and community projects; and separate workplace campaigns. A powerful extension of these current programmes and campaigns would be to include social intrapreneurship as another example of how to engage employees and how employees can contribute to sustainable development. Indeed, the corporate responsibility coalition CSR Europe has teamed up with Ashoka and the BMW Foundation to raise awareness of, and capacity for supporting, social intrapreneurism among their corporate members and national CR coalition partners.[2]

Awareness-raising and capacity-building

A number of specific social intrapreneurism initiatives have emerged in recent years such as:

- **Action-learning programmes to capacity-build social intrapreneurs,** such as the Aspen Institute First Movers Fellowship Program (see Fig. 5.1)

- **Social intrapreneurship awards for individuals,** such as the League of Intrapreneurs Award described below

---

2 http://www.csreurope.org/european-social-intrapreneurship-programme.

Figure 5.1 Aspen Institute First Movers Program

Source: First Movers

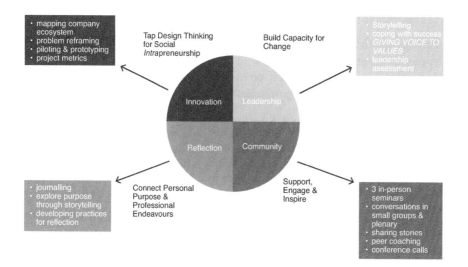

Fellowship Themes
with Sample Skills & Activities

- mapping company ecosystem
- problem reframing
- piloting & prototyping
- project metrics

Tap Design Thinking for Social *Intrapreneurship*

Build Capacity for Change

- Storytelling
- coping with success
- *GIVING VOICE TO VALUES*
- leadership assessment

Innovation Leadership

Reflection Community

- journalling
- explore purpose through storytelling
- developing practices for reflection

Connect Personal Purpose & Professional Endeavours

Support, Engage & Inspire

- 3 in-person seminars
- conversations in small groups & plenary
- sharing stories
- peer coaching
- conference calls

Aspen Institute First Movers Program

First Movers is a fellowship programme launched by the Aspen Institute's Business and Society Program in 2009, which 'serves as an innovation lab for exceptional individuals in business today who are implementing breakthrough strategies to create profitable business growth and positive social change'. It is a yearly programme consisting of three intense residential seminars, between which First Movers work on their social intrapreneurial ideas within their companies. The programme is built around four pillars: Innovation, Leadership, Reflection and Community (see Fig. 5.1). Participants have to be nominated and then have to seek the endorsement and financial support of their employers to take part in the programme. Since the first cohort was recruited in 2009, nearly 90 individuals have participated in First Movers, from companies such as Citibank, Coca-Cola, Dow Chemical, IBM, Microsoft and Wal-Mart. They include James Inglesby from Unilever (page 51) and Paul Ellingstad from HP (page 37).

The success factors for the programme (Aspen 2012) include:

- The quality of the group that Aspen recruits each year. Fellows are informed and inspired by others

- The programme design, which brings together leadership, innovation, and advancing a company's capacity to integrate social and environmental value into its core strategy

- The focus on deep personal exploration and emphasis on personal reflection

- The requirement that Fellows must have at least two thought partners within their companies who help them conceptualise their projects and strategise about navigating organisational dynamics

- The rigorous focus on a project that is both innovative and strategically significant for the company grounds the learning

Perhaps significantly, First Movers have found that many participants' projects change significantly during the course of the programme.

Joanna Hafenmayer Stefanska, an Aspen First Mover Fellow in the second cohort (2010), reflects on her participation in the programme:

> The careful selection of Fellows, an exceptional faculty and approach created a space for deep insight and break-through ideas. Next to everyday instruments of an intrapreneur—such as storytelling, prototyping, strategising internal support etc.—the programme allows enough time for personal reflection and exchange with Fellows. And that's where most of the magic happens.
>
> In my experience being a social intrapreneur is a hard and extremely rewarding job. There are tools that help—learning about some of them in the process of education, would be highly valuable. One of the main roadblocks I perceive in many cases is that people don't really believe that change is possible and desirable. Who should tell them?[3]

The League of Intrapreneurs

In 2012 Ashoka's Change Maker programme launched the League of Intrapreneurs. Between September 2012 and January 2013 the League received more than 200 submissions and presented four winners from 11 finalists. The winners are pioneering game-changing models for business and society and are profiled on Fast Company's blog Co.EXIST; they received consulting support from Accenture Development Partnerships to further their work. The League of Intrapreneurs created visibility for the winners and for the movement of social intrapreneurs in general.

More recently, the League of Intrapreneurs Awards competition has spawned a League of Intrapreneurs Lab[4]—an intense three-day programme followed by three months of mentoring provided by ADP and other Lab directors. The pilot Lab was hosted at the Said Business School, Oxford, UK, in October 2013 with participants from Barclays, GSK, SAB Miller and Novartis and speakers from League supporters and partners including Business Fights Poverty and Leadership Laboratories.

---

3 Based on author's exchange in October 2013 with Joanna Hafenmayer Stefanska, former intrapreneur at Microsoft and now Founder and Managing Director of MyImpact focusing on realising meaningful careers (www.myimpact.net).
4 League of Intrapreneurs Lab: promoted on Business Fights Poverty website at http://intrapreneur.businessfightspoverty.org/take action/the-intrapreneur-lab/

One aspect of networking, whether it is externally such as through First Movers and the League of Intrapreneurs or internally within the company—is the opportunity to develop self-knowledge. ('It is important for people to understand their own thresholds, tolerance of sticking around through everything.') Social intrapreneurs have to discover whether it is better for them to stay in the company, move to another company, strike out as a social entrepreneur or go to an NGO.

Athlon's Kenan Aksular used participation in an executive programme run by Nyenrode Business School, CSR in Action, to help find like-minded managers in large companies; he describes himself as a natural networker: 'It is always give and take. I keep in touch with NGOs, my trend watchers (for example, to interpret future EU laws), universities (students, innovators), the EU, local government, customers and suppliers.'

In practice, social intrapreneurship is going to need action from many different players. Otherwise, according to one experienced corporate sustainability manager:

> Will intrapreneurship be the next CSR? I.e. will every company tolerate having an ambitious intrapreneurship programme but just like CSR will ultimately keep it behind a glass wall for people to peer in and be proud of but not let it truly change how the business makes its day-to-day profits. The very best businesses won't do this, they'll let the intrapreneurship programme inspire, influence and re-skill its whole organisation. But a sustainable society/economy needs more than just a few companies to become sustainable. It needs everyone to! So intrapreneurship might need positioning as a 'phase' in the journey to build a truly sustainable organisation rather than an end in itself.[5]

Social entrepreneurship networks

Organisations engaged in the field of social entrepreneurship such as the Social Enterprise Coalition in the UK, Ashoka and the Skoll World Forum are often used by social intrapreneurs for inspiration, to start thinking outside the box and get some hints on the implementation of new business models. The work of social entrepreneurs might inspire social intrapreneurs to leverage the potential of their employers. Our social intrapreneurs already include many examples, such as applying the microfinance model created by the Grameen Bank to insurance companies such as Allianz. Social entrepreneurs could also become part of the value chain of existing businesses, as in the case of the Grameen–Danone partnership.

5 Personal communication with co-author David Grayson.

The Grameen–Danone Foods Joint Venture

Franck Riboud, Chairman and CEO of Groupe Danone, was inspired by the example of Grameen Bank and approached Muhammad Yunus with an offer of collaboration. With this top-management champion, things started to move quickly. In 2005, talks between Riboud and Yunus led to the idea of manufacturing highly nutritious affordable products that would improve the diet of rural Bangladeshis, primarily children, as 56% of these children under the age of five suffer from moderate to severe malnutrition. In addition to the social contribution, it was understood that the Grameen–Danone joint venture would create income opportunities for people in rural Bangladesh.

In 2007, only two years after the initial talks, the new Bogra factory processed around 6,000 litres of milk a day, employed 50 local people and produced 3,000 kg of Shokti Doi (Bengali for 'energy') yoghurt, which is sold by 300 'Grameen Danone ladies' within a radius of 5 km. The yoghurt provides 30% of a child's daily requirements of vitamin A, iron, zinc and iodine. The Danone team involved in setting up the plant was clearly given room to experiment. They had to skip the usual standards of plant set-up and experiment in order to make the venture cost efficient as well as beneficial to the local communities. However, this 'Yunus Inside' corporate social innovation strategy was clearly not an act of charity or philanthropy. Emmanuel Marchant, Managing Director of Danone Communities, said: 'This is not about charity for us. This is about business and building our brand' (Black 2009). Grameen-Danone Foods is considering rolling out this concept into Africa and Latin America. The experiment has taught Danone a lot about how to produce with simpler and thus lower cost structures, and TV advertising featuring Muhammad Yunus has proved to be a very successful strategy to market Danone products in Bangladesh.[6]

Business schools

Business schools can also provide an environment that caters for the social intrapreneur's learning needs. Our interviews clearly demonstrate that there is a demand for programmes on social innovation and social intrapreneurism, as well as change management:

> 'I've always carried on with continuing professional development—I did an IOD diploma in Company Direction, became a chartered director—the triple bottom line really struck a chord. This was something I came to at university—probably only 20 years ago that people started to talk about it in the mainstream.'

6 For the business benefits of the Grameen–Danone Partnership see: B. Kiviat (2010). We also recommend the video of Muhammad Yunus explaining the partnership as well as the concept of a social business at: http://www.youtube.com/watch?v=AV4WQV32ijs.

Some of our interviewees participated in the University of Bath's Masters' Programme in Responsibility and Business Practice (now relocated to the Ashridge Management School, also in the UK), where they learned how to think about business and responsibility together. Others currently participate in the Aspen Institute's First Movers Fellowship Program, described above.

Such programmes provide social intrapreneurs-in-development with mutual support and reassurance, contacts and access to technical expertise, capacity-building and problem-solving opportunities, mentoring and career support, awareness of sustainability issues and possible solutions, and technical and soft-skills training.

An increasing number of business schools now offer courses to MBA and other Master's degree students in social entrepreneurship, social innovation and how to be a change-maker. Stanford's Center for Social Innovation within the Graduate School of Business, for example, offers MBAs the chance to focus on social and environmental leadership during their MBA by providing 'courses and activities designed to build knowledge in areas such as non-profit management, public policy, sustainable business practices, social entrepreneurship, cross-sector collaborations, and the role of each sector in creating social and environmental value.'

INSEAD runs a change-makers' 'boot-camp' weekend off-campus and early in the MBA programme. These types of course offer a ready-made vehicle to present the idea of social intrapreneurship and to explain that being a social intrapreneur is one of range of ways to be a change-maker for sustainable development.

Emma Stewart PhD is Head of Sustainability Solutions at Autodesk, a world leader in 3D design software for entertainment, natural resources, manufacturing, engineering, construction and civil infrastructure. In 2009, Emma founded Autodesk's Sustainable Design Living Lab programme, which uses Autodesk facilities as a testing ground for new software to rapidly green existing buildings, and the next year she was invited to become an Aspen First Movers Fellow. She was subsequently invited to join the Professional Faculty at UC Berkeley's Haas School of Business and create and teach a new course, launched in September 2013, on 'Intrapreneurship for Sustainability: Driving Change from within Corporations'.

All these initiatives are also a way for business schools to demonstrate that their education can contribute to a more sustainable future and is not narrowly focusing on short-term profits.

Several international business schools have faculty researching social intrapreneurism or associated ideas of corporate social innovation and corporate social entrepreneurship. In addition to the institutions of the authors (Cranfield School of Management [UK] and Fundação Dom Cabral [Brazil]), these include IESE (Spain), INSEAD (France), Nyenrode (Netherlands) and Ross School of Business, University of Michigan (USA).

Social innovation consultants

The work of SustainAbility (2008) in publishing *The Social Intrapreneur: A Field Guide for Corporate Changemakers* has been pivotal in creating a new movement. The original team of the guide has now spread: while Alexa Clay initiated the League of Intrapreneurs working at Ashoka, Maggie De Pree founded her own consulting firm, The Human Agency, supporting companies to unleash the potential of social intrapreneurs. Similarly, organisations such as Forum for the Future and Volans in the UK, Aoka and Artemisia in Brazil, endeva and the Wuppertal Institute in Germany, and many others aim to help companies to design more inclusive and sustainable business models.

6
Impacts of social intrapreneurism

As illustrated by our social intrapreneurship model (see Fig. 2 in the Introduction), the work of social intrapreneurs generates impacts for the individual, for the company and for society.

Impacts for the social intrapreneur

Many people ask us what happened to the social intrapreneurs after their projects had been implemented. From the experiences of our interviewees we categorised the following scenarios:

- **Head of the new business.** As a consequence of their intrapreneurial activity these social intrapreneurs become head of the new business unit

- **The serial intrapreneur.** These social intrapreneurs get their motivation from new projects and challenges. They are not made for running an established business unit and get bored by activities, which have become standard operating procedures. So they start all over again with new projects

- **Turning social entrepreneur.** Some of the social intrapreneurs we interviewed set up their own social enterprise. Some did this as co-founders, for example, Michael Anthony, others do this on their own

- **Turn academic.** These social intrapreneurs usually want to dedicate more time to the topic of social innovation, social entrepreneurship or sustainable business

- **Change companies.** Some of our social intrapreneurs have changed companies for diverse reasons

Table 6.1 gives some examples of what happened to the social intrapreneurs in our network in recent years.

Table 6.1 Social intrapreneurs: where are they now?

Social intrapreneur	Company	Individual impact
Michael Anthony	Allianz	**Promotion** When embarking on the Microinsurance project Michael was officially Senior Climate Change Advisor. In 2008 he was promoted to Head of Microinsurance and since 2011 he has been Head of Emerging Markets Development with a focus on Agricultural Insurances **Turning social entrepreneur** In 2011, parallel to working at Allianz, he co-founded Boond Inc., a social enterprise that aims to provide affordable clean energy and other development goods (such as water purifiers) to rural areas in India
Priscila Matta	Natura	**Promotion** Priscila now leads a team at Natura that is responsible for managing relationships with traditional communities. As she is pursuing her PhD in Anthropology, she is likely to become an academic in the future
Stefan Koch	E-ON	**Change companies** Now Management Financial Sustainability Relations at Bayer
Cassiano Mecchi	Danone	**Change companies** Cassiano now works at Google Ireland
Liliane Pellegrini	BASF	**Turning academic** Liliane now works at a university with ties to social innovation
Lucas Urbano	Danone	**Promotion** Lucas was trainee in the sustainability department and now heads Danone's Project Management office
Mark Siebert	Siemens	**Change companies** Now works at publishing company Elsevier in the Netherlands **Serial intrapreneur** In his new role, Mark still works on social innovation projects such as Open Online Courses and Open Access for Academics in Developing Countries

Gib Bulloch	Accenture	**Head of new business** Is now heading Accenture's Development Partnership Programme.
Carrina Gaffney	The Guardian	**Change companies** Is now Business Development Director at B-corp Volans
Christel Scholten	ABN Amro	**Turning social entrepreneur** Christel founded BB Naturals in Brazil–a company focussed on sustainable baby care. She also consults companies on their sustainability strategies
Nick Hughes	Vodafone	**Turning social entrepreneur** Runs M-KOPA which provides affordable solar power to Kenyan households, using the M-PESA mobile payments system developed at Vodafone
Susie Lonie	Vodafone	**Changed companies** Susie now works as a Mobile Payments Consultant at SJL Consulting Services Ltd.[1]
Jo da Silva	Arup	**Heads new business** Jo is now Founder and Director of Arup International Development
Chris Harrop	Marshalls Plc	**Still a director** Chris has been Group Marketing Director and Sustainability Director at Marshalls for more than ten years now. Since 2011 he has been a non-executive director for the Ethical Trading Initiative and since 2012 heads the UN Global Compact UK network
Dorje Mundle	Novartis	**Promotion** Dorje joined Novartis in 2004 as Corporate Responsibility Manager and is now Group Head Corporate Responsibility
Hugh Saddington	Telstra	**Turning academic** Hugh left Telstra in 2012 to do a one year full time Master's programme in sustainability **Changed companies** In 2013 he served as Head, Corporate Strategy at Sydney Water **Turning social entrepreneur** Setting up a new company aiming to 'change the way that Australians pay and fund their dental treatment'

1 Taken from Susie Lonie's Linked In profile at http://www.linkedin.com/pub/susie-lonie/45/824/796.

As many examples show, they still play the jazz of sustainable business, either still in the same band or in different ensembles and big bands. This demonstrates that this emerging group of change agents cares deeply about their personal legacy or, as one of them was quoted in the SustainAbility guide (2008: 58): 'The minute I'm no longer solving the problem, I'll leave the company.' Just as playing music itself is one of the biggest impacts for jazz musicians, creating social impact is the most important thing social intrapreneurs expect to see. If this comes additionally with new roles and benefits, all the better.

Impacts for the company

It is basically impossible to launch a social intrapreneurship project within a company if you are not able to outline the business case. Table 6.2 sets out some arguments we found in the initiatives that were driven by the social intrapreneurs within our network.

Table 6.2 Social intrapreneurism: company impact

Impact	Useful indicators	Example
Increase sales	Sales Market penetration No. of customers No. of products and services sold	Allianz was able to attract millions of new customers for their microinsurance business around the world
New products and income streams	No. of new products launched Income from recent products	At Natura it takes roughly six months to develop a new product from idea to being sold to the consumer; 65% of Natura's sales comes from products developed in the last 2 years
Reducing costs	Variable costs Fixed costs	By simply replacing bottled water from the canteen Jason McBriarty was able to reduce sourcing costs at Levi Strauss & Co by US$40,000 per year
Attract and retain talent	Voluntary turnover rate	Due to Natura's vision, values and corporate environment the company's staff turnover is at 4% while the average of cosmetics companies in Brazil is 8%. ADP helps to retain top talent within Accenture
International roll-out	Market penetration	Vodafone's M-PESA has been rolled out to countries such as India, South Africa and Tanzania. Odebrecht's Acreditar Program has been applied in several other countries

However, some companies are also aware of the intangible value that social intrapreneurism creates, such as reputation, creating a socially responsible image, spontaneous media reporting, increased employee satisfaction, better working climate and reducing the liability of 'foreignness' when operating or entering in new international markets.

In talking about all these market-relevant benefits one should not forget that social intrapreneurism helps to shape the identity as well as legacy of the organisation. It comes back and provides a potential answer to the existential question of 'Why does your company exist?' Or in terms of the social intrapreneur: 'Why do you get out of bed in the morning? And why should anyone care?'

Accenture Development Partnerships founder Gib Bulloch noted that in terms of direct benefits, the first generation business case for ADP was very much around recruitment, retention and skills development. It became clear that many people were staying with the firm largely for the opportunity to do an ADP project. Or had done an ADP project and came back more engaged and more inspired. Attrition levels for those returning from ADP assignments were 2% less than the company average.

As mentioned earlier in the 'Enabling environment inside companies' section in Chapter 3, some companies, such as Danone, employ 'improvisational' accounting mechanisms (Danone's Green CAPEX) to ensure that social intrapreneurism projects have the opportunity to achieve proof of concept and that the full spectrum of social, environmental and economic value created can be accrued.

Most of the projects illustrated in this book deliver a sound business case. The big question is, however: Does social intrapreneurism affects the mainstream business in significant ways? To date our answer is still negative: we have found no business in which significant spill-overs change the way business is done in general.

Even one of the most advanced companies, GE, defining growing sales targets for Ecomagination products, has not yet achieved 100% of sales coming from more sustainable products, services and business models. Some companies are on the way—defining innovation structures in which sustainability is integrated—and thus it can be expected that an ever-greater proportion of product offerings come from more sustainable forms of production. At some companies the projects of social intrapreneurs are still a niche offering and it remains unclear if this part of the business might inspire other areas to integrate shared value strategies in general. This is definitely on our agenda for future research and we are watching carefully how the projects of our social intrapreneurs develop over time.

Impacts for society

Finally, social intrapreneurism does not only impact on company results but also on society and is thus a practical way to create what Porter and Kramer (2011) termed 'shared value'. As they state, 'The concept of shared value—which focuses on the connection between societal and economic progress—has the power to unleash the next wave of global growth' (ibid.: 65).

In similar vein the SustainAbility guide argues that sustainability issues such as financial exclusion can be seen as opportunities to create solutions to 'help the have-nots become bankable, insurable and entrepreneurial' (SustainAbility 2008: 22). Table 6.3 gives examples of some of the societal impacts created by social intrapreneurism.

Table 6.3 Social intrapreneurism: societal impacts

Impact	Example
Financial Inclusion	By launching M-PESA, Nick Hughes gave access to financial services making it much easier and safer for Kenya's population to do financial transactions. Today approximately 17 million Kenyans are using the service. This is quite significant, considering that Kenya has a population of 19 million
	Allianz microinsurances, created by Michael Anthony, cover basic risks such as life and health issues for people at the bottom of the pyramid. The Allianz products now cover these risks for millions of people in Indonesia, India and other developing countries
Income for communities	Priscila Matta helped Natura to create a process that shares the revenues of successfully developed products based on the traditional knowledge of communities and local biodiversity with those communities
Health issues	Dorje Mundle at Novartis started to develop health treatment for the bottom-of-the-pyramid markets that in India now reach 44 million people. An additional 2.5 million people have attended local health orientations
Professionalisation of the social sector	Gib Bulloch convinced Accenture that their impact on society is in their core business: consulting. By consulting NGOs and other civil society organisations they professionalise their approach and thus leverage the good work these organisations are delivering
Environmental Issues	Leonardo Vitoriano da Silva at BASF in Brazil showcases with the CasaE—an eco-efficient building—how chemical products can reduce energy and water consumption in the construction sector
Housing and security	Jo da Silva provides disaster relief and a place to stay for people affected by natural disasters
Access to essential products and services	Stefan Koch worked at E.ON to create energy solutions for disadvantaged communities in developing countries

If you follow discussions about social entrepreneurship, you will know that the major topics are measuring social impact and reaching scale. Muhammad Yunus founded Grameen Bank in 1983 and received recognition in 2006 in the form of the Nobel Peace Prize. By 2006, and therefore after 23 years, Grameen had an estimated 7.3 million customers. Compare that to the impact of, for example, M-PESA, which after one year had more than a million customers and within eight years attracted 17 million subscribers. Novartis shared-value projects in India attended to more than 44 million patients within five years of existence. So the major difference between social entrepreneurship and social intrapreneurism is scale, or as Gib Bulloch states: 'Affecting even small change in large organizations can lead to significant positive social impact' (SustainAbility 2008: 15).

So social entrepreneurs might learn a lot about how to scale their initiatives by collaborating with social intrapreneurs. At the same time social intrapreneurs might learn a lot about measurement of social impacts from social entrepreneurs. That might be the reason why 'systempreneurs', such as John Elkington, seem so excited about bringing social entrepreneurs and social intrapreneurs together.

New technologies connect intrapreneurs to create large-scale impacts

Social media channels such as Facebook, Twitter and YouTube have been recognised as key catalysts in the rapid spread of ideas which can act as precursors to large-scale action. The most salient example of this confluence of social media reach, speed of spread and powerful ideas sparking a mass movement has been the 'Arab Spring' of 2011, in which social media helped shape political debate, spread democratic ideas across international borders and facilitated the online revolutionary conversations that sparked major action on the ground (Howard et al. 2011).

Mobile phone technologies have also played an important role in delivering key services in under-served markets, as has been demonstrated in the examples of TCS mKRISHI (Ch. 1, pages 44–45) and Vodafone/M-PESA (Ch. 2, pages 70–75).

What we are now seeing is a proliferation of innovative social intrapreneurial ideas that are spreading across sectors and 'catching fire' through working partnerships, facilitated by social media and other new technologies.

A powerful example of this is the adaptation of the M-PESA project to deliver low-cost medical insurance in Kenya. The PharmAccess Group—an alliance of not-for-profit organisations committed to 'making good health care accessible in Africa, contributing to healthier populations and social and economic development'[2] —recently partnered with Safaricom and the M-PESA Foundation to continue working towards its long-term goal of improving access to healthcare for low-income sub-Saharan Africans. Onno Schellekens, Managing Director of the PharmAccess Group, is very enthusiastic about M-PESA: 'These kind of solutions truly revolutionise access and equal opportunity for the poor.' Les Baillie,

---

2 PharmAccess, 'About Us', http://www.pharmaccess.org/RunScript.asp?page=261&p=ASP%5CPg261.asp.

Executive Director of the M-PESA Foundation, noted the power of cross-sector partnership when he was invited by PharmAccess and the Amsterdam Medical Center in April 2013 to tell the M-PESA success story to partners, students and representatives from charitable organisations in Amsterdam: 'Introducing low-cost medical insurance in Kenya is something that the M-PESA Foundation has been looking into for a couple of years but hasn't been able to get started,' he said. PharmAccess, the M-PESA Foundation and Safaricom are now going to work together to develop mobile health products such as health insurance for low-income Kenyans.[3]

As technological advances reduce the costs and improve accessibility to connective technologies such as smartphones and social networks, the opportunities for social intrapreneurs to take their innovative ideas to scale will be greatly enhanced. We expect to see many more ideas 'catch fire' in the future as intrapreneurs and their partners connect up in 'big bands' to address the global challenges we outlined in Chapter 1.

---

3   PharmAccess, 'Les Baillie tells "M-PESA Story" in Amsterdam', 7 May 2013, http://www.phar maccess.org/RunScript.asp?page=24&Article_ID=254&AR=AR&ap=NewsArticleDetail.asp&p= ASP\ Pg?4 asp

7

Recommendations and practical tips

All our research, the interviews with social intrapreneurs and their godparents, and our own learning journey since 2009 enable us to give some recommendations and practical tips for aspiring social intrapreneurs and managers who want to tap into their potential.

For social intrapreneurs aspiring to be 'bandleaders'

Know who you are and what really matters to you

This may seem obvious but it's harder than it looks. All of us cultivate romanticised images of who we are—or could be—with desirable attributes such as attractiveness, power, popularity, wealth, compassion and generosity ... the list goes on and on.

The journey of the social intrapreneur can be exciting and fulfilling but, like other challenging life adventures, it can be long and arduous as well. So it is worthwhile taking time at the beginning (and the middle and the end) to do a reality check on *you*. Understand your passions, your 'big ideas', your strengths, as well as your weaknesses, in knowledge and temperament.

PROVIDED THEY HAVE DONE THEIR SHARE OF WOODSHEDDING, JAMMING AND PAYING THEIR DUES, JAZZ MUSICIANS CAN BECOME BANDLEADERS AT ANY AGE. TRUMPETER LAURA JURD, SHOWN LEADING HER OWN OCTET AT A 2013 HERTS JAZZ CLUB CONCERT WHILE STILL IN HER EARLY TWENTIES, HAD ALREADY WON THE 2011 DANKWORTH PRIZE FOR JAZZ COMPOSITION, WITH THE WINNING PIECE PREMIERED AT RONNIE SCOTT'S JAZZ CLUB IN LONDON, AND GARNERED THE 2012 WORSHIPFUL COMPANY OF MUSICIANS YOUNG JAZZ MUSICIAN AWARD.

SIMILARLY, SOCIAL INTRAPRENEURS CAN LEAD THEIR OWN PROJECT TEAMS EVEN AT A COMPARATIVELY YOUNG AGE IF THEY HAVE EARNED THE TRUST OF THEIR MANAGERS AND OTHER COLLEAGUES. WRITING IN *THE GUARDIAN* (20 SEPTEMBER 2013), EMMA STEWART OF AUTODESK NOTED THAT 'WITH LOTS OF TECHNOLOGY SAVVY YOUNG EMPLOYEES, THE NEW CROP OF SOCIAL INTRAPRENEURS IS LIKELY TO GROW IN NUMBERS AND INFLUENCE.'

First, do you *really* want to be a social intrapreneur? This will involve a lot of extra 'woodshedding' work that may not be (and most likely isn't) part of your job description and for which you may not be rewarded.

To realise his vision of creating Accenture Development Partnerships, Gib Bulloch was required to forgo the normal perquisites of salary and status enjoyed by his peers in a major management consultancy. Other social intrapreneurs we interviewed echoed the theme of self-sacrifice in pursuit of their dream.

If your goal is the fastest possible progression up the corporate ladder and you want to maximise your earnings, the experiences of others suggest that becoming a social intrapreneur may not be a smart career goal. This is not just a job; it is a vocation.

So ask yourself these questions:

- How important is the idea to me?

- How much personal time and energy am I prepared to invest?

- What types of role do my skills and temperament suit me to play?

- In terms of my discretionary time to push things that matter to me, where am I likely to have most effect?

- Am I prepared to lose my job if this doesn't work out?

Even if you decide that being a social intrapreneur is not for you, there can still be ways inside or outside the business where you could make a positive social and/or environmental contribution without the intense commitment that being an intrapreneur entails.

> Not everyone is born to be a risk taker or an entrepreneur but that does not mean they are not capable of coming up with a product or an idea that is powerful enough to change the shape of a business sector or an industry. The key for decision-makers is to be receptive and willing to listen to the ideas of junior employees—they might just have a concept which will catapult their company way out in front of the competition.

> Company leaders should always be aware of the talent and innovation that may be lurking undiscovered within their own organisation. Intrapreneurs are a very special breed capable of working within the hierarchy of an organisation but also have the ability to act and think outside the box (Caan 2013).

Identify your passion, your big social intrapreneurial idea

And if you don't already have something, can you get an idea from the following examples?

- Existing company–NGO partnerships (e.g. Marks and Spencer's Oxfam voucher to spend on new clothes if old ones taken to an Oxfam store, which in turn led to idea of Shwopping, came from an M&S Finance team staffer)

- If you reflect on your **volunteering or extramural interests** outside work, does that suggest something? Or else volunteer; seek a short secondment with a company partner NGO operating in the field you are interested in?

- Remembering Peter Drucker's maxim that 'every social problem, every global issue, is a best opportunity in disguise' and thinking about your company's core competences, where are there business opportunities 'in disguise' for your company? You might want to look at the emerging post-2015 United Nations Sustainable Development Goals for inspiration[1]

- Has your employer identified challenges the company is facing in embedding sustainability, for example, as Unilever has summarised its current difficulties in fully implementing its Unilever Sustainable Living Plan?[2]

- Is there research commissioned or sponsored by the company that has not been pursued? One social intrapreneur has used an MSc thesis co-sponsored

---

1 http://sustainabledevelopment.un.org/index.php?menu=1300.
2 http://www.unilever.co.uk/sustainable-living/uslp/

by her employer as the basis for her project for low-cost, prefab homes for base-of-pyramid markets

- Look inside and outside your company for opportunities for experiential learning programmes that you might apply for, to help you to locate your passion such as Leaders Quest. For example, Graham Simpson went on GSK's Pulse programme and saw the need for simple diagnostic tests

- It might also be revealing to compare the sustainability challenges your company or sector is facing and how the current innovation pipeline responds to those challenges. While working for a big consumer brand company in Brazil, we realised that management defined lower- and middle-class segments as growth opportunities but virtually none of their innovation projects catered for these customers

Once you have identified your passion, follow it. But also be prepared to adjust your idea in the light of experience. First Movers say that many of their participants have changed their ideas during the programme, sometimes fundamentally. Indeed, one of the most successful social intrapreneurism projects, Vodafone's M-PESA, started out proposing a very different model.

Be prepared for a lot of 'woodshedding'

You will need to do lots of work—both within and beyond your 'day job'—to ensure you have acquired a deep knowledge of:

- **Your business and industry,** its core purpose and mission; how it creates value, both for investors and other stakeholders, drawing on the power and resources of its unique extended community, and how it serves society at large

- **Your profession or function,** for example, marketing, engineering, procurement, and how it serves, or impacts adversely on, others in your sphere(s) of influence

- **Sustainability issues.** Whether you're interested in climate change, human rights, poverty or other societal issues, you need to understand how you and your business can contribute to addressing these issues. The best way is to go to the roots of the problem, which might be down the supply chain at manufacturers in Asia, for example

It may be helpful to engage one or more partners from a charity or not-for-profit organisation to help you think this through. This can enable you to develop a 'helicopter view' of the 'system'—how businesses (and entire industries), NGOs and governments working together can improve the quality of human life in specific ways, whilst minimising adverse environmental impacts.

Watch and learn how senior executives make decisions and how they argue. It might be interesting to interview some successful corporate change agents and see how they did it. You might also pitch your ideas to a friend working in finance to see how to express yourself better in financial language.

Sharpen your own business understanding, your business acumen. Really understand the drivers, pressures, priorities and challenges of your key commercial constituencies. This is fundamentally important. In order to do that, you really need to be getting out there and forming relationships with key people in the organisation at different hierarchical levels. Commercial folk, country heads, management heads of different operations, global corporate functions, whatever is relevant to what you want to drive. Form good-quality relationships—understand their world. Then identify how your agenda maps onto theirs and how to contribute to their success (Dorje Mundle of Novartis).

Not everyone wants to start out by doing their deep thinking with others, however. Like 'woodshedding' musicians, many prefer working through their ideas in private, as Chris Harrop, Group Marketing and Sustainability Director at Marshalls, did when he was developing Fairstone (Harrop n.d.), the company's range of sustainably sourced Indian sandstone products:

I don't network with people and talk about these things ... I like reading and things that challenge my brain. I also like taking models and working through them, have the business become more successful by using those models.

Once he began to research his ideas, Chris did what others had not done: he travelled to the developing world to understand in depth how supply chains worked.

Gifford Pinchot, who first coined the term 'intrapreneur' and 'intrapreneurism', recommends 'working underground as long as you can. Publicity triggers the corporate immune system.'

Pay your dues

Trust is paramount in all business dealings, no more so than when you are pitching a truly new idea that will require others to support you. Only by 'paying your dues' in an organisation—performing well enough, long enough—will you earn the confidence of your peers and managers to risk investing corporate time and resources in any pilot project you propose.

Jo da Silva, the founder of Arup International Development, noted that, along with presenting 'a diagram that explained the spectrum running from philanthropy to major business opportunity', which she presented at Arup's Annual Group Meeting, what helped persuade directors to back her project was that 'I was an insider coming in with a big idea. There was a long-term relationship. I could present that in a business framework. This isn't about making money but it's not about philanthropy, either.'

Paying your dues includes being a good 'sideman' and 'comping' for (accompanying) others as well as 'soloing'. Supporting the ideas and projects of your colleagues, as well as advancing your own ideas, immerses you in the political ebb and flow of daily corporate life. Think beyond scoring points for your own ideas in the short term to building up the organisational knowledge and social capital you will need to launch your project later on. As Maggie De Pree points out, 'negotiating the system' is an essential component of the 'Cubicle Warrior' toolkit.[3] Become, as Maggie advises, not a martyr but a 'graceful warrior'.

Be prepared to share any kudos received and share credit widely. Heed the wisdom of Deng Xiaoping: 'It doesn't matter what colour the cat is as long as it catches mice.'

Join in with your corporate 'jam' sessions

Every team or organisation will have created the equivalent of 'jam sessions', such as brainstorming meetings (face to face or online), often in environments where people can relax informally, such as a corporate café or perhaps an off-site location. These are the places and times where you will have opportunities to try out new ideas, bounce them off others, play with them and refine them.

Nicolai Tewes, Senior Vice President Corporate Affairs at Allianz, describes how corporate culture can support the flow of ideas:

> You need a culture of dialogue, people able and willing to listen and discuss ideas. Interest to know how things are seen from the outside ... There is a genuine interest to talk, debate listen, consult with externals.

By immersing yourself in the ongoing stream of dialogue in your organisation— speaking the language of others, which reflects your understanding of them—you are more likely to be heard and less likely to activate the 'corporate immune system', which Gib Bulloch has identified as

> the aspects of HR, culture, strategy and process discipline that are unleashed like anti-bodies against any initiative that dares to be different. They act as the corporate's defence mechanism and when combined, can often provide sufficient inertia to maintain the status quo.

Start building your 'band'

> If you want to travel fast, travel alone; but if you want to travel far, travel with others (American Indian proverb).

While you are paying your dues, comping or soloing and being a 'sideman', you need to start thinking about building a community that could support the

---

3   League of Intrapreneurs, Cubicle Warrior Toolkit, 'Negotiating the System', http://www.leagueofin trapreneurs.com/toolkits/negotiating-the-system, accessed 7 January 2014.

development of a project idea. A collaborative community is another essential component of the 'Cubicle Warrior' toolkit.[4]

You will be instinctively drawn to like-minded people who (1) share your interests in sustainability issues and innovation; (2) possess useful skills, experience, temperament and networks that complement your own; and (3) might be prepared to work with you on developing a pilot project. These are the people with whom you might start a small project 'band' to develop a pilot project. Begin to map out your stakeholders, based on these criteria.

While some suggest 'networking' is only one letter different from 'not working,' networking is a crucial aspect of being a successful social intrapreneur. Two good books on networking are *Networking: The Art of Making Friends* (Stone 2001) and *The Ultimate Guide to Successful Networking* (Stone 2004).

Mike Barry, who is now Director of Plan A as 'how we do business', at UK retailer Marks and Spencer and Chairman of the international CR coalition World Environment Centre, describes how he spent his first few years at Marks and Spencer before the launch of the Plan A for embedding sustainability by building up his internal networks and talent-spotting managers destined for fast-track promotion.

Arun Pande, who oversaw TCS mKRISHI project to help small-scale Indian farmers, advises: 'It is important to build a team by convincing them to own your idea. Always be with them/defend them if they violate processes or rules in letter [but] not in spirit.'

Among the first people you recruit should be one or more 'godparents'. As stated earlier, this is a person, usually a senior manager (perhaps your own line manager), who can act as a power broker, networker, translator, listener, coach and mentor, who is open to your challenging ideas and prepared to take intelligent risks to test your ideas and establish 'proof of concept' and provide air-cover. As Gib Bulloch notes, 'Intrapreneurship can be lonely and isolated. The presence of a senior supporter, confidante or coach has proven to be crucial to success.' As it is so essential, be sure that you have backup godparents in case your support changes roles or companies.

Godparents can also cover for you when you apply the entrepreneur's motto that 'it is easier to ask forgiveness than it is to get permission'. Remember, ask for advice before asking for resources. And be smart about taking the advice when you have asked for it. If you do not have one or more godparents already, does the company have any mentoring or high-flyer, fast-track development programme that you could tap into to find a godparent?

---

4 League of Intrapreneurs, Cubicle Warrior Toolkit, 'Building Community', http://www.leagueofintrapreneurs.com/toolkits/building-community, accessed 7 January 2014.

Pick the A-Team, but don't recruit in your own likeness

One of my biggest learnings is the fact that to be successful you need to be surrounded by a great team of people. I'm lucky that I really have the 'A Team' in Accenture. The context we work in seems to act as a lightning rod for talent and I couldn't handpick a better and more capable team of people than the ones I have to work with now. It's important to take people who are good at the things you are not good at, or interested in the things that you're less interested in. Diversity in my mind is what makes great team (Gib Bulloch, Accenture Development Partnerships).

Recruit 'band members' from beyond your company

Remember that your 'band' does not have to be restricted to people working inside your company. We discovered from our research that one of the defining characteristics of successful social intrapreneurs is that they can connect and collaborate with key contacts *outside* their organisation, often working in other industries or sectors, in helping them build momentum for a project.

One instance is Hugh Saddington of Telstra working with WWF Australia described in Chapter 1 (pages 39–41). In another example, Chris Harrop worked with journalists from UK broadsheet papers to help make the case for using responsibly sourced materials that did not entail the use of child labour in producing the Indian sandstone used in Marshalls' products:

> I arranged for *Guardian* and *Daily Telegraph* journalists to go to India independently to see it [the child labour situation]. In both those cases they had full-page articles in those newspapers on the issue and, gratifyingly, what I was doing about tackling the problem. This is using basic marketing to communicate and drive an issue through. You can use marketing in a positive way—but greenwash will be found out.

Working with partners in different organisations and sectors can be extremely challenging. Organisations such as The Partnering Initiative offer short courses to help build the skills and knowledge needed for collaborating with multiple stakeholders.[5]

---

5 The Partnering Initiative 'Essential Skills for Effective Partnering', http://thepartneringinitiative .org/w/professional development/certificate in partnering-practice/, accessed 8 January 2014.

Compose new pieces for your 'band' to perform

When you have done your preparatory woodshedding, earned the trust of your peers and managers by 'paying your dues' in the organisation and supporting others' projects and tested your initial ideas in corporate 'jam sessions', you will be ready to present a 'composition' of your own—a pilot project proposal—which you can invite your fellow 'band members' to support and perform.

SKILLED JAZZ COMPOSERS ARE GREAT STORYTELLERS, ABLE TO ENGAGE AUDIENCES WITH A WIDE RANGE OF EXPERIENCES IN HIGHLY NUANCED FORMS. BILLY STRAYHORN'S FAMOUS FINAL COMPOSITION, 'BLOOD COUNT' - PERFORMED HERE BY CHRISTIAN BREWER (ALTO), ANDREA POZZA (PIANO), LUKE STEELE (BASS), STEVE BROWN (DRUMS) - COMMUNICATED THE SUFFERING, ANGUISH AND HOPELESSNESS OF HIS BATTLE WITH ESOPHAGEAL CANCER BY WRITING THIS MOURNFUL BALLAD. STRAYHORN'S MUSICAL COLLEAGUE, DUKE ELLINGTON, WAS SO MOVED BY THE COMPOSITION THAT HE NEVER PERFORMED IT AGAIN AFTER RECORDING IT IN A STUDIO SESSION (SOURCE: www.allmusic.com/song/blood-count-mt0010956393).

WE FOUND THAT SUCCESSFUL SOCIAL INTRAPRENEURS ARE ALSO GREAT STORYTELLERS, INSPIRING THEIR COLLEAGUES TO TAKE ACTION WITH NARRATIVES THAT APPEAL TO THE HEART, ALONGSIDE A SOLIDLY CONSTRUCTED BUSINESS CASE THAT APPEALS TO THE HEAD.

However, it will help if your 'composition' (a form of storytelling) is as appealing as possible to your 'audience'—initially a limited number of close peers and managers in a small, trusted ensemble—and, just as important, to you. 'Storytelling: 70% of my job!' (Gib Bulloch, Accenture Development Partnerships).

Drawing on the principles of great corporate storytelling presented in a Doughty Centre 'How To' Guide on knowledge management (McLaren and Spender 2011), which in turn builds on the work of Van Riel (2000), ask yourself if your composition/story shows the C.A.R.D.S: is it:

Coherent?

Does it evoke the company's purpose and character, taking key stakeholders and (business and sustainability) challenges into account?

Is it compelling enough to get you up and eager to work on it every day?

Authentic?

Would the proposed project fit the company's true values and purpose? Does pursuing social intrapreneurism fit with what you truly value, your long-term career goals and your own skills and abilities?

You will no doubt be preparing a 'business case' for your idea, which is the rational analysis of how your project could make, or save, money, or create value for the business in ways that are more difficult to quantify (e.g. building reputation, creating goodwill with customers and other stakeholders). This is the appeal to the *head*.

This is one of the differences between what a social entrepreneur and a social intrapreneur needs to do. The late Malcolm Lane, who, as head of Tata Consultancy Services, saw many would-be social intrapreneurs, used to complain how frequently they simply had not done their homework or thought about how their idea was good for the business. So develop a business case.

Hugh Saddington, General Manager, Market Strategy and Analytics, Telstra Enterprise and Government, overcame initial scepticism about the relevance of climate change to the company, by co-producing a White Paper on using information communication technology and sustainability with WWF Australia (Saddington and Toni 2009). By engaging WWF, Saddington was able to take the 'heat' out of an internal political debate through presentation of facts by a reputable not-for-profit organisation.

However, presenting an idea that also appeals to the *heart*—resonating with others (and you) on an intuitive, emotional level can be just as, perhaps even more, powerful than a numbers-based business case on its own. This is especially true if it is a genuinely new idea whose potential financial value to the company is unknown but which nevertheless ties directly to the company's core purpose in a direct way.

When appealing to the top directors of global engineering consultancy Arup to create a start-up within the business to 'focus exclusively on working in developing countries on projects that contribute to social well-being and are sustainable in the environmental sense', engineer Jo da Silva cited the 'key speech' by founder Ove Arup in 1970[6] that had inspired her to join the firm in the first place. This speech highlights the importance of a humanitarian approach to business, uncommon in 1970, which proposed:

---

6 'Ove Arup's Key Speech, 9 July 1970', http://www.arup.com/Publications/The_Key_Speech.aspx., accessed 6 December 2013.

[there are] two ways of looking at the pursuit of happiness: One is to go straight for the things you fancy without restraints, that is, without considering anybody else besides yourself. The other is: to recognise that no man is an island, that our lives are inextricably mixed up with those of our fellow human beings, and that there can be no real happiness in isolation. Which leads to an attitude which would accord to others the rights claimed for oneself, which would accept certain moral or humanitarian restraints. We, again, opt for the second way.

Translated into the jazz metaphor, Jo had done her full share of woodshedding, jamming and paying her dues as a 'sideman' before proposing her new composition to the corporate 'big band'.

Relevant?

Is it relevant to the company's current business or sustainability activities?

Does it build on any existing company–NGO partnerships or existing corporate programmes that would make adoption easier? For, example: the Marks and Spencer Oxfam voucher scheme led to the idea of Shwopping, proposed by an M&S Finance team staffer.

Does it address challenges identified by your company in embedding sustainability? The Unilever Sustainable Living Plan[7] integrates sustainability into the company's strategy, brands and innovation. A significant proportion of the research and development budget is committed, via the Unilever Ventures initiative, to finding sustainability-led technologies.

Does it resonate with the individual(s) in your audience? Depending on your audience, you may have to appeal to head or heart—or both. This requires being a great listener, which by now you should have become through participating in corporate 'jam' sessions. Be ready to tailor your style of 'music' for different audiences. Specific tips from social intrapreneurs include the following:

Xerox's Dab Godamune advises that it is easier if you are proposing something entirely new, rather than a better way of doing something that the company already does, because with the latter there may be vested interests against you—in which case, avoid being too critical of the status quo.

Chris Harrop, Marshalls, says:

You've got to really understand the issues. It's really easy to say bonded labour is a problem. You've got to visit, understand, deeply analyse what's going on...come back and convert those issues into messages and language that resonate with people in the UK, your board, your organisation. This must never be seen as a personal moral crusade.

Is it relevant to what you do within the organisation? Is it part of your 'day job' or social/environmental projects you already support, perhaps through volunteering?

---

7   http://www.unilever.com/sustainable-living/.

Dynamic?

Will it be possible to adapt your idea in response to ongoing dialogue with your colleagues and other project stakeholders or other changing conditions?

Sustainable?

Will your project create value that balances both business needs, stakeholder demands and sustainability objectives over time?

Creating social or economic value is not enough. To be truly sustainable, you need to demonstrate how your project would save the company money or make it money, or otherwise help the business.

> Key lesson? Almost disguise social aspects and present as helping business to grow revenue—can still talk about sustainability but emphasise business—then people happier to talk (Hugh Saddington, Telstra).

> Charity doesn't work; but enabling people in developing countries to work their way out of poverty, that's what really works—has to be balancing the social, economic and the environment (Chris Harrop, Marshalls).

Be a great bandleader

Running a social intrapreneurism project, according to those we know who have done it, requires persistence and resilience in the face of adversity as well as generosity and a range of other emotional and social intelligence capabilities.

Here are three quotes from social intrapreneurs who have all survived their share of organisational challenges during their corporate careers:

> It's quite lonely, you live on self-belief and determination (Jo da Silva, Arup International Development).

> Don't give up—this is where dogged determination comes in. In the early days, I was accused of all sorts by competitors, trade associations, the media. It would have been easy to sweep it under the carpet (Chris Harrop, Marshalls).

> Know which policies you can bend or break—how close to wind you can sail without getting sacked! (Gib Bulloch, Accenture).

All three of the individuals quoted above are still working in their organisations, suggesting that perhaps what matters most is not whether the sustainability mindset of the social intrapreneur is aligned with organisational culture, but whether the social intrapreneur is able to recognise fully the cultural challenges they face in developing their new projects and have the skills and emotional intelligence required to overcome these.

Don't change companies; change the company you're in

Gib Bulloch offers this additional piece of advice to aspiring social intrapreneurs who may be experiencing frustration or loneliness:

If you're seeking a new challenge or if you want to have more social impact and meaning from your job, don't change companies, change the company you're in. Many people reach a stage in their careers or jobs where they're looking for a bit more meaning from their work. They want to do something different or are frustrated with the role they're in. I would argue that rather than going down the normal route of sharpening the résumé and simply changing jobs, the potentially more impactful option would be to change the company—or sector—in which you are working.

That may sound a bit glib and I'm not overinflating the amount of change we've had in Accenture, but small positive change in large organisations equals impact. People are often most effective at doing that when they've been in a company for a few years. Who else knows the key people as well as you do? You've developed an internal network and know how to cut corners on policy and often who the right people are to get things done. Often these people are not the most senior. Social Intrapreneurs will be most effective when they've got these qualities—and they can't be developed overnight in a new company. Experienced employees should think carefully before needlessly squandering that potential for change.

Be true to your goals, but be flexible and realistic about the ways to achieve them. Never give up! There will always be people who will say no. If you approach a brick wall, step back—you may find it's not made of brick or not so big. James Inglesby of Unilever faced great initial scepticism from country management in Ghana but now they are huge supporters.

In the case of Eagle Lager, NGOs had expected that SABMiller would adopt a philanthropic approach. Ian Mackintosh resisted; 'not wanting to create dependency', he 'wanted to produce the relationship of a "willing seller" and a "willing buyer".'

Be determined to make it happen where you think it's right for the organisation. Hugh Saddington of Telstra advises 'perseverance—there were times when it felt like I was fighting a guerrilla war inside the organisation'. Ask yourself: Am I prepared for reverses and rejections? Am I prepared to carry on when others say 'no'? Could I modify my proposal so as to neutralise objections when I meet them?

Building personal resilience: a view from a social intrapreneur-turned-coach

A former social intrapreneur at Virgin's corporate foundation, Virgin Unite, Heidi Kikoler[8] dedicates her time now to championing social intrapreneurs as a Leadership Coach.

For intrapreneurs navigating the system of brick walls without a roadmap, Heidi reinforces the importance of actively cultivating one's personal resilience:

> We must remember that we aren't born resilient, but rather we have the amazing ability to become resilient and bounce back from enormous adversity. The most effective way to do this is through self-accepting and non-judgemental self-observation. A deeper understanding of how we uniquely think, feel, and behave will enable us to create personally relevant strategies to stay resilient and effective.

Heidi suggests that the benefits of deepening your self-awareness go well beyond resilience as it can bring much needed clarity around what an individual wants to achieve in his or her career and life. For intrapreneurs, this can help reinforce their self-belief and ground their sense of purpose.

To begin building your resilience, Heidi suggests you answer the following questions either in the moment of adversity, or better yet in advance of it:

- What am I thinking?
- What am I feeling?
- How am I behaving?

Once you've observed these three things, she recommends you ask yourself this next question in order to enable you to apply your observations in a constructive, forward-moving way in the future:

- How do I want to respond differently next time?

Heidi also recommends that intrapreneurs sharpen their knowledge around positive psychology because even what may appear to be the simplest of tricks can have a profound impact on cultivating resilience, and generating positive emotions that have a range of benefits for intrapreneurs including enhanced creativity, personal magnetism and ultimately happiness.

Let go

The hardest moment can come when and if you need to hand over the leader's baton to a new bandleader who can take your band in an entirely new direction to ensure it grows to scale.

8 See www.heidikikoler.com.

Roberto Bocca, who spent four years developing the BP Renewables business and grew it to 400,000 customers—at that time the biggest such business in the world but still tiny by BP standards—was forced to relinquish his fledgling operation to a member of his Indian staff team to continue developing it. But he was philosophical about the outcome, observing that if he had not been in BP, he would never have had the opportunity to start the business in the first place. The experience enabled him to make the transition to the World Economic Forum, where he became Senior Director, Head of Energy Industries.

Athlon's Kenan Aksular recognised that while it might be better for his career to be running the Mobility Scan consulting business he set up, his forte is start-up and early-stage intrapreneurship: 'I'm stuck at start-ups/earlier stages of new business development.'

Be prepared for adversity and recognise that despite your seeming success, you may still find 'events, events' undermines you and means that, like Roberto Bocca or Tom Nieuwenhuijzen of Van Nieuwpoort Group, you have to resign or are made redundant; or simply that as the project grows, it needs different types of people with a different skill set. Nick Hughes at Vodafone came to this conclusion in 2009 when he decided to leave the company and start a social enterprise, M-KOPA.

Gifford Pinchot has suggested in his Intrapreneur's Ten Commandments[9] (which he says apply also to 'ecopreneuring and social intrapreneuring') has as his first commandment: 'come to work each day willing to be fired' (although he later modified this with the advice: 'don't ask to be fired; even as you bend the rules and act without permission, use all the political skill you and your sponsors can muster to move the project forward without making waves').

Ask yourself: Once the project is developed, am I prepared to hand it over to others to keep it running? How will I ensure that my project will survive and prosper, even after I've moved on to another project or company?

We end this section with quotes from some great jazz bandleaders embodying a range of practical tips for leadership in almost any walk of life:[10]

> Running a band is a 24-hour-a-day job. A bandleader needs the heart of a hobo and more stamina than a gold rush pioneer ... I consider good health a major requisite for anyone that wants to be a bandleader (Vaughn Monroe).

> The trick ... lies in keeping your balance. Only one person can make you lose it. That's yourself (Benny Goodman).

---

9   The Pinchot Perspective, 'The Intrapreneur's Ten Commandments', 20 November 2011, http://www.pinchot.com/2011/11/the-intrapreneurs-ten-commandments.html, accessed 8 JANUARY 2014.
10 'How to be a Bandleader: Quotes Selected by Christopher Popa', http://www.bigbandlibrary.com/howtobeabandleader.html, accessed 6 December 2013.

Don't play from habit. Read the notes and try to think that they are fresh and new ... Don't see whether you can do it better this time than you did last time. That's not the point. Instead, try to see how well you can play it, period. Use it as a challenge to your ability in itself (Artie Shaw).

There's one thing besides musical excellence that requires stressing ... And that's a well-rounded education. I don't mean merely the study of music theory and harmony... Anything that you can do to enrich that mind will help in the formulation of mature and interesting musical thoughts, adding depth to whatever you create (Paul Whiteman).

Kids take to music so naturally ... teach young kids the rudiments that they need to add to that natural rhythm and joy in music (Lionel Hampton).

A bandleader must improvise many things besides hot choruses ... Luck is everything, but it means nothing unless you're ready musically and morally to exploit it ... My own conception of luck can be defined as follows: being in the right place at the right time doing the right things before the right people (Duke Ellington).

The years of serious study I've had with legitimate teachers finally is paying off enabling me to write arrangements employing unusual, rich harmonies, many never before used in dance bands ... We were playing in the Meadowbrook early last spring [1939] and up front, all of a sudden, the band hit me. It was clicking. For the first time I knew it was playing like I wanted it to. It sounded wonderful. I didn't say anything—just drove home and told the wife. But I prayed it would last (Glenn Miller).

Work hard at bandleading, for it is gratifying work, indeed. Take what is in your heart, apply to the knowledge in your mind, add the skill in your hands, and there you have the best formula for how to become a bandleader (Xavier Cugat).

For managers learning to 'play the C.H.A.N.G.E.S.': seven habits to build successful social intrapreneurism

Based on our findings, we suggest the following habits that companies can practise to develop social intrapreneurism in their organisations.

1. Cultivate 'café culture'

Create time and space for people at all levels of your organisation to learn, think and talk about what is happening in the wider world and how your business can be a force for good in it. This needs to be embedded into your culture, not siloed into formal training programmes or restricted to top management tiers. Like the social intrapreneurs we interviewed, people should feel free to 'think crazy stuff in any position and in any meeting'.

2. Humanise your organisation to promote egalitarianism and generosity

Our literature and interview evidence tells us that social intrapreneurism flourishes in egalitarian environments with flat hierarchies. People unencumbered by bureaucracy and politically induced fear will be free to think about 'their mainstream day jobs in the broadest way' and are more likely to take responsibility for innovation, sharing their ideas and learning with others with improved results.

3. Account for the social and environmental, as well as economic, value you create

Conventional accounting rules and time-frames make it difficult to develop socially innovative projects. Managers of aspiring social intrapreneurs should look for ways to assess the social and environmental, as well as economic, value that their proposed projects can create. This will help free them from the organisational 'treacle' that can prevent a good project from getting off the ground and open the door to truly new ways of doing business.

4. Network inside and outside your organisation to create consortia for action

As our interviews showed, successful social intrapreneurs built alliances with partners outside, as well as inside, the organisation. Cross-border and cross-sector partnerships can form the basis for powerful consortia for change. Senior managers need to be open to working not only with people in other departments, suppliers and other business partners, but also with other organisations in other sectors in order for these partnerships to work.

5. Grow people into leadership roles for sustainable business

People given opportunities to develop self-confidence and skills for collaboration, to gain a deep understanding of the business and to 'do good' through volunteering and mentoring—and who are then recognised and rewarded for such behaviour—are more likely to develop into successful agents for social change, whether they become social intrapreneurs, 'tempered radicals' who effect change in more moderate ways, 'godparents' who facilitate the work of other change agents, or undertake other change agent roles.

6. Experiment with social intrapreneurism pilots that can be scaled up for impact

Our social intrapreneurs started with time-limited, small-scale projects, often in their spare time, at the margins of their organisations, which could provide proof of concept with minimal financial or reputational risk to the company before being scaled up further. While it is desirable to be able to predict or calculate return on investment for such projects, most pilots cannot be assessed against quantitative criteria and therefore alternative qualitative criteria will need to be used to define success.

7. Strategise to achieve sustainable business and societal goals

The ultimate goal is for leaders of the business to understand its wider societal purpose—encompassing the social and environmental, as well as economic, value it creates—and to develop business strategy, vision and values that encompass this more sustainable, as well as inspirational, purpose for the benefit of the business as well as society at large.

Jazz musicians learn to 'play the changes' of tunes: improvise musical lines in their solos that are appropriate to the sequence of chords of a particular jazz tune.

Managers who want to promote social innovation in their companies need to learn how to 'play the C.H.A.N.G.E.S.' described above (and Table 7.1 gives some questions for managers to ask when they are 'playing'). In other words, they need to cultivate the seven habits of managers that help create an 'enabling environment' for social intrapreneurism.

Table 7.1 Playing the C.H.A.N.G.E.S.: questions for managers

C.H.A.N.G.E.S. model	CEO, executive director, strategic business unit head or country manager	Human resource managers	Innovation and new business development directors	Corporate responsibility/ sustainability directors
Cultivate 'café culture' that D.A.R.E.S. (Dialogue/ Autonomy/ Risk-taking/ Experimentation/ Sustainability) to foster social innovation	Are current business activities, market conditions, company history (including any collective memory about how any previous social intrapreneurs were treated) and corporate culture enablers or disablers of social intrapreneurism? If you do a quick audit of your division by comparison with the description of the enabling environment (pages 103–61), are there any glaring gaps, where some provision needs to be improvised, and if so, how?	Do you have regular 'café culture' events for sharing ideas across teams? Do you have any cross-department idea/sharing events on a regular basis? Have you tried IBM jam sessions? Or co-creation sessions like Cocriando Natura?	Do you have a 'not invented here' mentality or are you open to ideas from any source?	Do you share your sustainability challenges with employees, suppliers and NGO partners, e.g. Unilever Sustainable Living Plan?
Humanise your organisation to promote egalitarianism and generosity	If you map your company/division on an 'employee engagement and corporate sustainability matrix' where are you located and what directions are you moving in: up and right (more engaged and more sustainable) or the opposite, or static? i.e. what is the environment for social intrapreneurism?	Could you build up an existing employee volunteering programme to give talented employees exposure to environmental and social issues, which might stimulate social intrapreneurism?	Do you facilitate social innovation in your innovation pipeline, e.g. Green CAPEX (capital expenditure) Danone?	Are you working with HR to grow employee volunteering programmes into capacity-building for social intrapreneurism?

C.H.A.N.G.E.S. model	CEO, executive director, strategic business unit head or country manager	Human resource managers	Innovation and new business development directors	Corporate responsibility/ sustainability directors
Account for the social and environmental, as well as economic, value you create	Do you account fully for the costs as well as the value that your company creates?	Have you incorporated achievement of sustainability goals into appraisals, compensation and promotion decisions? (see Danone)	Do you account for the social and environmental impacts that your new products and services create, e.g. 'green' design, lifecycle accounting?	Are you promoting true-cost accounting and integrating reporting to investors? Can you account for the full range of value (tangible and intangible) for your sustainability initiatives so your leadership team recognises their strategic importance?
Network inside and outside your organisation to create consortia for action	Are you a member of corporate responsibility coalitions or other stakeholder initiatives? Do you bring ideas from these groups into your company?	Do you send people to conferences where they can learn about social innovation? Are you integrating board membership of NGOs, coalitions, or initiatives such as LeadersQuest, ADP into development programmes?	Do you create 'open innovation platforms' that engage external stakeholders such as NGOs, e.g. Shell Energy Challenge?	Do you send people to conferences where they can learn about social innovation? Are you integrating board membership of NGOs, coalitions, or initiatives such as LeadersQuest, ADP into development programmes?

Grow people into leadership roles for sustainable business	Is there a particular team within your reports that might be enthusiastic about piloting a programme to encourage social intrapreneurism? Are there any existing activities such as a successful sustainability team that might be built upon? Which of your lieutenants will instinctively understand what social intrapreneurism is all about, and run with it? What forthcoming events and diary dates do you have where I might talk about social intrapreneurism e.g. a staff webinar, a management development programme for high-flyers?	Does the company have any existing people development strategy that might be expanded to include social intrapreneurism? Does the company already have, or is there potential to experiment with experiential learning programmes that aspirant social intrapreneurs could benefit from? Do you have a mechanism to match potential social intrapreneurs with potential 'godparents' to form 'dynamic duos' in your organisation?	Do you recognise achievements in social innovation in your corporate awards and recognition schemes, e.g. GE Ecomagination?	How can you best help potential social intrapreneurs to find mentors and resources to develop their ideas? How do you identify potential social intrapreneurs in your own team and elsewhere in your organisation who could be helped by working with you or by personal development programmes?
Experiment with social intrapreneurism pilots that can be scaled up for impact	Does your growth strategy include any ideas to create 'shared value' through social intrapreneurism pilots?	Are there existing talent development programmes (internal or commissioned from external providers such as a business school or other executive education provider) where ideas about social intrapreneurism might be introduced?	Could you promote an internal innovation fund to draw out and nurture potential social intrapreneurs?	How can you best inform employees about global sustainability challenges, where the company is most needing help and new ideas to achieve its sustainability goals, and where you see the most fruitful areas for shared value innovation?

C.H.A.N.G.E.S. model	CEO, executive director, strategic business unit head or country manager	Human resource managers	Innovation and new business development directors	Corporate responsibility/ sustainability directors
Strategise to achieve sustainable business and societal goals	Any existing corporate programme, public commitment, 'BHAG' (big, hairy, audacious goal), strategy, corporate value, KPI (for your division) that you could link a drive on social intrapreneurism to?	Any existing corporate programme, public commitment, 'BHAG' (big, hairy, audacious goal), strategy, corporate value, KPI (for your department) that you could link a drive on social intrapreneurism to?	Any existing corporate programme, public commitment, 'BHAG' (big, hairy, audacious goal), strategy, corporate value, KPI (for your division) that you could link a drive on social intrapreneurism to?	Any existing corporate programme, public commitment, 'BHAG' (big, hairy, audacious goal), strategy, corporate value, KPI (for your division) that you could link a drive on social intrapreneurism to? How might social intrapreneurism fit in to your strategy for embedding sustainability in the company?

8
The way ahead

It has taken more than two decades for social entrepreneurism to be widely recognised. Is it possible for the socialisation of the idea of, and development of good practice in, social intrapreneurism to be accelerated?

THE SIMULTANEOUS EVOLUTION OF POETRY AND JAZZ DURING THE 1920S EVENTUALLY LED TO THE ART FORMS BEING FUSED INTO A SINGLE GENRE, 'JAZZ POETRY', WHICH 'DEMONSTRATES JAZZ-LIKE RHYTHM OR THE FEEL OF IMPROVISATION'. THIS 'OUTSIDER' ART FORM CONTINUED TO EVOLVE THROUGH THE 'BEAT GENERATION' AND HAS BEEN ADAPTED IN MODERN TIMES INTO HIP-HOP MUSIC AND LIVE POETRY EVENTS KNOWN AS POETRY SLAMS (SOURCE: EN.WIKIPEDIA.ORG/WIKI/JAZZ_POETRY). THIS 2011 PERFORMANCE AT LONDON'S PIZZA EXPRESS JAZZ CLUB FEATURES PIANIST TIM LAPTHORN (PIANO) AND POETS RICHARD DOUGLAS PENNANT AND HANNAH SILVA.

WHILE SOCIAL INTRAPRENEURISM IS A COMPARATIVELY NEW FORM OF BUSINESS ACTIVITY, THE AUTHORS ANTICIPATE THAT THIS, TOO, WILL EVOLVE OVER TIME IN RESPONSE TO THE CHANGING SOCIOPOLITICAL LANDSCAPE AND THE EMERGENCE OF NEW BUSINESS MODELS.

Awareness-raising

One of the factors driving increased awareness of social entrepreneurism was the interest of the Schwab Foundation and discussion of the topic in the World Economic Forum. Already, social intrapreneurism has been discussed in Davos in 2013 and in the WEF China 2013 meeting. Undoubtedly, regular further discussion in such fora where many of the global elite and global opinion-formers meet to share and develop ideas, would help to speed up awareness-raising as participants and journalists covering the event spread the messages they have heard.

Creating an enabling environment for social intrapreneurism and social innovation more broadly

A few individual consultancies and corporate responsibility coalitions are starting to help companies to explore how to create an enabling environment. This process could be accelerated if a group of leading multinational companies could be persuaded to commit publicly to social intrapreneurism, and to a joint action-learning programme where they would share their experiences and challenges and explore potential solutions for creating an enabling environment for social intrapreneurism in their own organisations. Such an action-learning research club would carry greater credibility and profile if it were coordinated by: a high-profile organisation such as the WEF; one of the leading corporate responsibility coalitions such as Business for Social Responsibility or the World Business Council for Sustainable Development; leading business school(s); or a global consultancy. Ideally, such collaboration would optimise the latest online information and communications technology to facilitate the capture, storage and retrieval of good practice; and the emerging learning would be made publicly available via the Internet and subsequently through capacity-building training programmes for corporate heads of learning, talent development, innovation, HR, strategy, new business development etc.

Awareness-raising with potential social intrapreneurs

Ideally, in parallel with this awareness-raising and capacity-building for companies, there would be increased promotion to potential social intrapreneurs themselves. This could be through further competitions and award schemes like the League of Intrapreneurs. There are now around 50 Impact Hubs with a further 50 expected to be operational by 2015 (Bachmann 2014). More Impact Hubs around the world could run courses and clubs for social intrapreneurs. Student organisations such as AIESEC, oikos International and Net Impact, and student-run conferences such as Emerge (hosted at Said Business School, Oxford) and the annual 'Doing Good and Doing Well Conference' on responsible business at IESE (Barcelona) could profile social intrapreneurs regularly.[1]

Net Impact and oikos International are global student networks aiming to bring sustainability into management education. AIESEC also has some interest groups on sustainability. Their alumni are a natural source of social intrapreneurs as their members are convinced that business can be used as a positive force for good. At their universities they have already learned change-making skills in trying to convince university administration to integrate sustainability in their course offerings. Some Net Impact alumni who qualify as social intrapreneurs are featured in a Net Impact (2009) publication called *Making Your Impact at Work*.

Net Impact has several 'professionals' chapters for alumni now working. It is possible that some of these individuals may be aspiring or emergent social intrapreneurs. Apart from encouraging them, Net Impact could profile such members to inspire others.

By making social intrapreneurism a regular theme of their conferences, publications and activities, student organisations such as oikos International and Net Impact could raise awareness of the idea of social intrapreneurism, build networks and potentially create learning collateral that local chapters could use. Members could also suggest social intrapreneurism as a topic for classes, to their faculty.

The world's business schools could include courses on social intrapreneurism in their MBA and specialist Masters programmes, as well in specialist executive leadership programmes.

Supporting individual social intrapreneurs

Being a social intrapreneur, especially in the early stages, can be very lonely. Capturing and disseminating more practical advice and tips like the League of Intrapreneurs *Cubicle Warrior Toolkit* and creating more peer-to-peer learning and support networks like the League of Intrapreneurs Lab and First Movers, in different parts of the world—again, perhaps linked to the WEF or some of the corporate responsibility coalitions or the Impact Hubs or business schools—and sharing curriculum and case studies online, could also accelerate adoption of social intrapreneurism. Impact Hubs in particular could also facilitate match-making between social intrapreneurs and social entrepreneurs: see below.

---

1 http://blog.iese.edu/dgdw/.

External partners for social intrapreneurs

In describing various social intrapreneurs and their projects, we have identified a number of external partners (see pages 162–72) that have been crucial to the successful ones. For these external partners, social intrapreneurs can be a route to increasing their own impact substantially and extending their reach.

NGOs

As Gib Bulloch from Accenture Development Partnerships has written:

> Most large charities or NGOs will have tens if not hundreds of thousands of supporters each giving $10, $20, $50 or more each month as part of their commitment to a cause they are passionate about. Some will work in the public sector, some in the non-profit sector. But many will work in the corporate sector. And of them, a handful may even be latent social intrapreneurs—people who are well networked internally. Who knows the rules of the corporate and when to bend or even break them? They know that influence doesn't always mean you've memorized the hierarchy of an organisation chart. They know how to cut corners to get things done and are willing to take career risks for a cause they are passionate about. The smart NGO CEO will consider less about chasing philanthropic dollars—more about how to mine their donor database for the latent social intrapreneurs—the herds of latent 'Trojan Horses' residing deep undercover in the corporate world, awaiting a cause and a call to action (Bulloch 2013).

Imagine a group of innovative social enterprises and charities either individually or as a consortium offering some tailored, experiential management development placements with them for selected high-flyers from their corporate partners and other multinationals. Or those same social enterprises and charities with entrepreneurial ideas related to their core mission, using social media to help them talk directly to supporters working in relevant multinationals and encouraging them either to take up the ideas themselves or find co-workers who might relish such an intrapreneurial challenge.

Imagine too a 'dating service' for social intrapreneurs and external partners (NGOs, international development agencies etc.) working in the social intrapreneurs' areas of interest: a model suggested by Meg Jones who works for the International Trade Centre, a joint agency of the UN and the World Trade Organization, mandated to help SMEs in developing countries achieve export success.

NGOs might consider identifying and targeting their members/supporters working for multinational companies and encouraging them to explore social intrapreneurial ideas relevant to the work of the NGO.

NGOs might also work with existing corporate partners to run experiential learning programmes like the IBM Corporate Service Corps or GSK Pulse (Ch. 4, pages 117 and 118) that might stimulate social intrapreneurs within the corporate partners? Indeed, NGOs may already be working with key individuals in their corporate partners who might have, or might be encouraged to develop, social intrapreneurial ideas, with the help of an NGO.

International development agencies

International development agencies have long recognised that it is better to teach a community to fish than to give them fish, and that, therefore, business and broader economic development are fundamental to sustainable development. Providing early-stage funding to support proof of concept, as the DFID Challenge Fund did for M-PESA in Kenya (see page 73), could be an effective way of fast-tracking economic development.

Do agencies already have a funding mechanism that could potentially be used to support social intrapreneurs? Are there any existing, effective promotional mechanisms to bring such a fund to the attention of potential applicants?

We recognise this is a fast-developing field and one that would benefit from further research. As researchers ourselves it might be seen as special pleading to recommend further research. However, we do believe that the proposed efforts to raise awareness, promote, capacity-build and share emerging good practice, will be greatly enhanced if accompanied by action research. There are a number of researchers internationally who might be invited to help refine and develop the starting propositions in Box 8.1. We hope that such a research agenda might be sponsored by one or more foundations or consortia of companies, perhaps organised through a coalition such as ABIS to manage a coherent research programme.

Box 8.1 Future research

Based on our work, we would identify several topics for further inquiry. Specifically, future research might explore more rigorously:

Social intrapreneurs

- More on the backgrounds, mind-sets, behaviours and skills of individual social intrapreneurs, their journeys, and the things that helped them to succeed
- The specific chains of causality between elements of the social intrapreneur's life history (early influences, values, personality characteristics, career choices)
- Longitudinal studies on what happens to social intrapreneurs and to their ideas; and the differences among social intrapreneurs and their company circumstances, between those whose ideas succeed and those whose don't; and whether there are common determinants of success or failure
- How do social intrapreneurs overcome the dichotomy of either business or philanthropic benefits?

- How do social intrapreneurs recognise and exploit opportunities? Especially in the face of adversity?
- How do social intrapreneurs get attention and enact their projects? How do they orchestrate resources (from the self, the organisation and the external environment)?
- What is the right timing for introducing a social intrapreneurial idea to an organisation? What are the time-frames and trajectories of social intrapreneurship?
- What are the different narratives used by social intrapreneurs (from insight to scale)?
- How do successful social intrapreneurs network?
- How does an intrapreneurial project become collective?
- Do intrapreneurial projects transform whole companies to become more sustainable or will they always be niche offerings?
- How do individuals sustain themselves through the intrapreneurial journey? What is the role of emotions and self-regulation?
- How do social intrapreneurs succeed in specific sectors?

Why have we not yet found many social intrapreneurs working in Asia? That may be because our networks do not reach very well into Asia or it may be because Asian corporate cultures do not encourage brainstorming or intrapreneurship and are much more respectful of authority and hierarchy—the antithesis of intrapreneurship. There is, of course, a contrary thesis that social intrapreneurism sits well with the more communal philosophical traditions of Asia.

Nor have we yet found any serial social intrapreneurs (and unpicked whether they are more likely to be serial social intrapreneurs inside the same firm or by moving from firm to firm). We also do not know whether serial social intrapreneurs, if they exist, do things in the same topic area, for example, child labour or climate change, or pursue different themes.

How easily do social intrapreneurs become 'close relatives' or vice-versa? To what extent does this depend on the attributes of the corporate/external 'enabling environment' versus the attributes of the individual (skills, experience and motivation)? To what extent do people have preferences for undertaking sustainability work? Do these reflect personality traits that could be modelled and assessed via tools similar to Belbin or Myers Briggs personality assessment tests?

What do social intrapreneurs need—mind-sets, skills and resources (including allies and mentors)—and how can these be acquired? Are any routes proving particularly effective in developing these?

Enabling environment

- What creates an enabling environment for social intrapreneurism and employee engagement for sustainability more generally? What would an ideal enabling corporate environment look like? What are the kinds of practical things that companies can do, and are doing, to stimulate such an enabling environment?
- Nature versus nurture: to what extent can social intrapreneurs be developed through external intervention?
- What are the variety of roles and characteristics of the individuals who act as 'godparents' (sponsors/mentors) to social intrapreneurs?

- If you want to promote the concept of social intrapreneurism to potential social intrapreneurs, what are the best ways? Perhaps a supporting alliance is needed between CR practitioners, HR practitioners and senior managers? Do internal/external award schemes help to incentivise their projects?
- What can companies do to enable people in a wider variety of job functions (e.g. accountancy, legal, facilities management) to engage in social intrapreneurial behaviour?
- Do companies that have reached higher stages of CR maturity provide a more supportive environment for social intrapreneurs than others? It could be argued that an integral part of embedding CR within business purpose and strategy is an intensive form of employee engagement, and that encouraging social intrapreneurship is one sophisticated way for companies to do this
- How do companies ensure that social intrapreneurial changes endure rather than fade with the departure of their protagonists and their supporters?

Impacts

- Which type(s) of social and economic value can be created through intrapreneurial processes?
- What are the long-term impacts for business and society of social intrapreneurial activity? And are there critical success factors for which projects successfully go to scale and those which do not?
- Do social intrapreneur's projects stay isolated business units or do they change the way business is done as a whole (spill-over effects)?

In short, social intrapreneurism, and employee engagement for sustainability more generally, is fertile ground for theoretical and applied researchers; and especially for cross-disciplinary teams who can bring together knowledge of corporate sustainability, innovation, employee motivation and engagement, social entrepreneurism and leadership.

Expanding the international architecture for social intrapreneurism

How might this supporting architecture develop? Imagine a world in which:

- Corporate responsibility coalitions run awareness-raising and good practice sharing for member companies; and potentially include social intrapreneur category in any CR awards programmes they might run

- Business schools teach social intrapreneurism as part of any change-maker courses they might run for MBA students; and offer master-classes and executive education programmes in creating an enabling environment for social intrapreneurism

- Social enterprise Impact Hubs and equivalent centres around the world offer development programmes and peer support to aspiring and new social intrapreneurs

- League of Intrapreneurs or similar grouping develop as an open-source, online centre of excellence, offering case studies, how-to advice, signposting to further help, match-making to potential social intrapreneurial 'buddies,' and access to online and face-to-face training programmes

- International development agencies are willing to consider co-funding viable social intrapreneurial proposals and pump-prime capacity-building initiatives

Each of these things could happen organically. There are, however, opportunities to provide some light-touch coordination and strategic direction of efforts to go further and faster. Could an existing international foundation extend its remit to promote social intrapreneurism? Alternatively, is this a ready-made opportunity for a high-net-worth individual looking to achieve positive societal impact at scale to create a new venture to promote social intrapreneurism as, for example, the Skoll and the Schwab Foundations have promoted social enterprise?

In his best-seller, *The Tipping Point*, Malcolm Gladwell (2000) argues that ideas spread thanks to the existence of sales-people, connectors (brokers) and mavens (individuals able to see meaning and patterns and the big picture from seemingly random information). We need the resources to bring together sales-people, connectors and mavens for social intrapreneurism!

Conclusion
Towards a new way of doing business

Ultimately we envision that social intrapreneurism will become not merely a new approach to corporate responsibility and sustainability practice but a gateway to an entirely different way of doing business. An important perspective on this changing strategic landscape was offered by one of our expert colleagues, Penny Walker, in an interview:

> The question is not 'What is our CR strategy?' or 'What is our sustainability strategy?' but 'What does understanding sustainability mean for our organisational strategy?' Social intrapreneurs can help to answer this question through their experiments in triple-bottom line solutions.

With people such as social intrapreneurs, their 'godparents' and other partners leading the way, a growing number of large companies such as Unilever and other 'green game-changers' profiled by WWF (2012) in a recent report are transcending simple product and process innovation to completely transform their business models.

We believe that social intrapreneurs represent the leading wave of a business transformation movement that could go 'viral' if companies are prepared to invest time and resources in their own 'enabling environments' for social intrapreneurism, join up their efforts in corporate responsibility coalitions (see Grayson and Nelson 2012, 2013) and work with governments and NGOs to achieve shared value for the benefit of their businesses as well as the wider societies in which they operate.

BRITISH PIANIST STAN TRACEY (1926–2013) IS WIDELY CONSIDERED TO HAVE BEEN ONE OF THE WORLD'S
OUTSTANDING JAZZ MUSICIANS. ACCORDING TO *FINANCIAL TIMES* JAZZ CRITIC MIKE HOBART (7 DECEMBER
2013), TRACEY 'WAS A PIONEER OF EXTENDED JAZZ COMPOSITION AND HIS 1965 ALBUM JAZZ SUITE INSPIRED
BY DYLAN THOMAS' UNDER MILK WOOD' (SHOWN HERE BEING REPRISED WITH BOBBY WELLINS (TENOR),
ANDY CLEYNDERT (BASS), SON CLARK TRACEY (DRUMS) AND GRANDSON BEN TRACEY (NARRATOR) AT
HERTS JAZZ FESTIVAL 2012) 'ESTABLISHED UNDILUTED BRITISH MODERN JAZZ AS A VALUED ART FORM.
THE INTEGRITY AND OPEN-MINDEDNESS OF HIS 70-YEAR CAREER WON HIM THE RESPECT OF SUCCESSIVE
GENERATIONS OF MUSICIANS AS WELL AS CRITICAL ACCLAIM AND NATIONAL HONOURS; HE WAS AWARDED
THE CBE IN 2008'.

THOSE ASPIRING TO SOCIAL INTRAPRENEURISM AS A LONG-TERM VOCATION CAN TAKE INSPIRATION FROM
TRACEY'S EXAMPLE, A LIFE IN JAZZ 'AS INVENTIVELY CREATIVE AS IT WAS LONG'.

Social intrapreneurs generate social innovation and change by leveraging their organisation's capacity to address societal issues profitably. They are characterised by a mind-set to strive for societal value creation in a way that is attractive to business. They pursue societal value creation in a persistent, learning and outreaching manner and apply the skills of entrepreneurship and communication. Social intrapreneurs collaborate with NGOs in order to generate societal impact and obtain missing knowledge and skills at business schools.

Corporations interested in social intrapreneurship should be thinking of providing a supportive environment in which social intrapreneurs can develop and test their ideas. Crucial for their success are senior management sponsorship, an understanding of how business and society can be brought together and the creation of space for experimentation. NGOs are invited to explore their membership rosters for potential social intrapreneurs in order to leverage corporate activities to the benefit of society. Likewise, business schools have a role to play in inspiring and training social intrapreneurs, especially developing the entrepreneurial as well as communication skills they need to succeed.

In general, the phenomenon of social intrapreneurs might be a visible sign of people looking for ways to reconcile their social and working lives.

We suggested at the beginning of this book that social intrapreneurism might just be a gateway into a whole new way of doing business. Through the stories we have been sharing, we have also been trying to give some clues to what this new way might involve.

In concluding, we would like to draw together what might be some of the strands of this new way of doing business:

- Involving more varied and individualistic definitions of business purpose than defining purpose automatically as optimising returns to shareholders

- Having a sustainability culture that truly involves employees and other stakeholders; is more empowering and entrepreneurial; and embodies 'relationship thinking' and practice so that employees can 'bring their whole selves to work'

- Including effective networking and engaging with company alumni including retirees to continue to harness their wisdom and commitment, for example, as mentors to aspirant social intrapreneurs

- Doing more business activity through collaborations and also with a richer mix of business and other collaborators (public sector, NGOs, academic partners etc.)

- Embodying the Peter Drucker maxim that 'every social issue and global problem is a business opportunity in disguise' and creating profitable business from better management of social, environmental and economic impacts

- Measuring value in new and more holistic, long-term ways, accounting for social and environmental as well as economic costs and impacts

- Promoting a 'sharing economy' as well as an 'ownership economy' through servitisation of company products

Join our 'big band' and share your music

It has been a privilege and deeply energising to meet and interview social intrapreneurs, godparents and social intrapreneurism collaborators. We are all in the early stages of learning about social intrapreneurism: what encourages it? What makes social intrapreneurs tick? What impacts are they having?

We want to continue our own learning journey in further understanding and development of the emerging social intrapreneurism movement, and you can be part of our growing 'big band' to do this!

If you are a social intrapreneur, an aspiring social intrapreneur or a godparent, if you are part of a social intrapreneurism project or are trying to create an enabling environment for social intrapreneurism in your company, we would like to hear your story and your experiences—setbacks as well as successes—and, in turn, if you would like to join our mailing list, we will share with you periodic updates.

The Doughty Centre and Fundação Dom Cabral are seeking partners to help us to develop understanding of what works for more companies, leading to the production of master classes and how-to guides both for companies and for social intrapreneurs themselves. We also want to help develop a curriculum and resources materials for teaching social intrapreneurship in business schools.

Beyond the publication of this book, our aspiration as a team is to work with others to help build a very big band—a global 'community of practice' around social intrapreneurism, enabling corporate practitioners, academics, NGOs and other interested parties to continue to develop, share and apply our collective learning to enhance the quality and scale of social intrapreneurism. We hope to do this in a number of ways:

- By using our research to develop practical tools for prospective social intrapreneurs and managers wishing to cultivate social intrapreneurism in their own organisations

- By publishing case studies of individuals and companies that have been developing social intrapreneurism projects, highlighting successes, failures and lessons learned

- By supporting awareness-raising events—such as the Skoll World Forum on Social Entrepreneurship (http://skollworldforum.org/) and the League of Intrapreneurs

- By building online networks, such as the Portuguese-speaking Intraempreendedores Sociais[1] and Social Intrapreneurs Groups[2] on Facebook and the Social Intrapreneurs LinkedIn Group,[3] that enable the sharing of information among practitioners

- By teaching students in our own institutions: Cranfield School of Management, and Fundação Dom Cabral (Brazil) and further afield

- We look forward to connecting and 'jamming' with you on the world stage for social intrapreneurism. Please come and share your music!

---

1 https://www.facebook.com/groups/183408645051917/.
2 https://www.facebook.com/groups/599493373445519/.
3 lnkd.in/dnRMFow.

Appendix: Our research

We were originally inspired to investigate social intrapreneurism after reading SustainAbility's *The Social Intrapreneur: A Field Guide for Changemakers* (2008) and Net Impact's *Making Your Impact at Work: A Practical Guide to Changing the World from Inside any Company* (2009).

We began in 2009 by issuing a call for people who thought of themselves as social intrapreneurs or who knew someone who might be considered as a social intrapreneur to contact us. We issued the call through *Ethical Corporation* magazine, personal contacts and postings on websites and social networks focusing on social innovation and change. Initially we interviewed 25 putative social intrapreneurs working in a wide range of sectors to address a diverse range of issues from sectors such as:

Energy

Telecoms

Media

Financial services

Engineering consultancy

Management consultancies

Advertising and PR agencies

Logistics

Alcohol

Retailing

Construction

Developing business ideas to tackle, for example:

Banking services

Micro-enterprises

Agricultural development

Climate change

Waste

Water

Sustainable development

Child labour

In June 2010, David had the opportunity to present some initial findings at an International Research conference organised by the Centre for Social Impact in Australia, with a number of internal scholars in corporate responsibility including professors David Vogel and Sandra Waddock from the United States (CSI 2010). We also interviewed other researchers, consultants and practitioners studying and supporting the work of social intrapreneurs. The results were published in a Doughty Centre for Corporate Responsibility Occasional Paper, *Social Intrapreneurs: An Extra Force for Sustainability* (Grayson *et al.* 2011).

What was evident in our interviews with social intrapreneurs was that the environments in which they worked exerted a profound effect on their capacity for initiating, developing and sustaining projects that produced both commercial and social benefits. Some features of these environments mentioned by our interviewees—including culture, human resource management, access to resources, organisational processes and infrastructure, management and leadership behaviour, links with external organisations, and strategic focus on sustainability—appeared to be 'enabling' of social intrapreneurism in some forms. Other factors were 'disabling' and could disrupt the social innovation process in different ways, for example, by suppressing or pre-empting dialogue about sustainability, failing to provide senior support or sufficient time and resources to develop project ideas, or failing to recognise the value of social impacts created by the business.

In the second phase of our research, in addition to continuing to interview more social intrapreneurs, we, therefore, sought to identify key features of the 'enabling environment' for social intrapreneurism, including the presence of other colleagues who played influential roles in working with social intrapreneurs to bring projects to fruition. We contacted interviewees from our original group of social intrapreneurs to probe their original comments in greater depth as well as interview colleagues in their organisations—often 'godparents' who supported the development of social intrapreneurism in their organisations and could provide additional insights into the process.

Our research team also conducted a literature review to identify essential components of the organisational environment that enable or disable the process of intrapreneurship generally within firms as well as analysing data obtained from our interviews with social intrapreneurs.

With our key enablers and disablers provisionally identified, we then developed an interview protocol that we could use to probe these elements further. A further set of interviews was conducted with colleagues of our original social intrapreneurs—particularly individuals whom we thought would be in a position to comment on these enablers and disablers (e.g. HR directors, heads of innovation, other senior managers whom our social intrapreneurs identified as 'godparents' who facilitated the development of their projects)—as well as other experts (in NGOs, academia and business) working in the field of social intrapreneurism.

This involved in-depth interviews with people from more than 30 national and mainly multinational companies in the following sectors:

Management consultancy

Insurance

Information technology hardware and equipment

Engineering consultancy

Car rental and leasing

Chemicals

Banking

Food

Retailing

Energy

News media

Airlines

Building materials

Investment banking

Personal care

Pharmaceuticals

Health and wellness, audio, multimedia

Breweries

Diversified machinery

Electronics

Specialty retail

Consulting services—information technology

Telecommunications

Fast-moving consumer goods

Cleaning and facilities management

Additionally, experts in social intrapreneurship in the Netherlands, UK and the USA were consulted and team members benefited from speaking at or moderating conferences on social intrapreneurship at the Asian Institute of Management's Annual CSR Forum in Manila; for the British Council Japan and Volans with groups of visiting Japanese business and media representatives; for the Skoll Centre for Social Enterprise, Said Business School; and for events at The Hub in Amsterdam, London and Sao Paulo. This led to a second Doughty Centre Occasional Paper: *Creating Sustainable Businesses Through Social Intrapreneurism* (Grayson *et al.* 2013), launched at the awards ceremony for the League of Intrapreneurs.

Over the five years we have been investigating social intrapreneurism, one of our team, Melody, has repeatedly used analogies and metaphors from her interest in jazz to get points across in our team discussions. At the awards ceremony for the League of Intrapreneurs Melody spontaneously teamed up with another enthusiastic amateur jazz musician: Lionel Bodin from Accenture Development Partnerships. This led to further discussions about the insights from jazz for our understanding of social intrapreneurism both with Lionel and with jazz experts.

Throughout our work, we have benefited from the insights and experience of several individuals and organisations who have been studying and promoting social intrapreneurism, a number of whom have generously commented on earlier drafts of this book and are recognised in the acknowledgements. Finally, we have regularly shared our emerging ideas through blogs, articles and presentations, and we have benefited from feedback from these.

Still, *Social intrapreneurism and All That Jazz* can only be a snapshot of a fast-evolving movement, and by identifying some of the most obvious areas worthy of further research (Chapter 8), we hope we can stimulate further investigation and deeper knowledge.

References

Allianz (2013) *Microinsurance at Allianz Group 2013 Half Year Report*, Allianz SE, https://www.allianz.com/v_1381221496000/media/responsibility/documents/microinsurance_business_update_2013.pdf, accessed 6 December 2013.

Amo, B.W., and L. Kolvereid (2005) 'Organisational Strategy, Individual Personality and Innovation Behavior', *Journal of Entreprising Culture* 13.1: 7-19.

Anderson, N., C.K.W. de Drew and B.A. Nijstad (2004) 'The Routinisation of Innovation Research: A Constructively Critical Review of the State-of-the-science', *Journal of Organisational Behavior* 25.2: 147-73.

Andersson, L.M., and T.S. Bateman (2000) 'Individual Environmental Initiative: Championing Natural Environmental Issues in U.S. Business Organizations', Academy of Management Journal 43.4: 548-70.

Antoncic, B. (2007) 'Intrapreneurship: A Comparative Structural Equation Modeling Study', *Industrial Management & Data* 107.3: 309-25.

Antoncic, B., and R. Hisrich (2003) 'Clarifying the Intrapreneurship Concept', *Journal of Small Business and Enterprise Development* 10.1: 7-24.

Apte, M. (2013) 'EMPOWERing Innovation Culture at Shell Using Meditation', M-Prize, 3 January 2013, http://www.mixprize.org/story/empowering-innovation-culture, accessed 6 December 2013.

Aron, J-E., O. Kayser, L. Liautaud and A. Nowlan (2009) *Access to Energy for the Base of the Pyramid*, (Paris: Hystra; Washington, DC: Ashoka).

Aspen Institute (2012) 'The Aspen Institute First Mover Fellowship Program: Assessing the Impact December, 2012', public summary of independent evaluation by Dr. Shari Cohen, President of Intersections Resources, http://www.aspeninstitute.org/sites/default/files/content/upload/public_aspen_evaluation-final.pdf, accessed 6 December 2013.

Bachmann, M. (2014) 'How the Hub Found Its Center', *Stanford Social Innovation Review*, Winter 2014, http://www.ssireview.org/articles/entry/how_the_hub_found_its_center, accessed 7 January 2014.

Balch, O. (2013) 'The Car Hire Company that Wants Cars off the Road', Guardian Sustainable Business, 14 May 2013, http://www.theguardian.com/sustainable-business/car-hire-company-cars-off-road, accessed 30 October 2013.

Baptista, P., and S. Heitmann (2010) *Unleashing the Power of Convergence to Advance Mobile Money Ecosystems* (Washington, DC: IFC; Boston, MA: Harvard Kennedy School).

Berg, J.M., J.E. Dutton and A. Wrzesniewski (2008) 'What is Job Crafting and Why Does It Matter? Theory-to-Practice Briefing', University of Michigan Ross School of Business.

Bevan, S. (2012) *Good Work, High Performance and Productivity* (London: The Work Foundation).

Black, L. (2009) 'Pots of Gold', *The Guardian*, 18 February 2009, http://www.guardian .co.uk/society/2009/feb/18/liam-black-bangladesh, accessed 6 December 2013.

Bode, C.S., and F.M. Santos (2013) 'The Organisational Foundations of Corporate Social Entrepreneurship', *INSEAD Working Paper* 2013/07/EFE/ST/ICE, January 2013, http:// www.insead.edu/facultyresearch/research/doc.cfm?did=51663.

Brunaker, S., and J. Kurvinen (2006) 'Intrapreneurship, Local Initiatives in Organisational Change Processes', *Leadership and Organisational Development Journal* 27.2: 118-32.

Bulloch, G. (2012) 'Inside-Out Transformation: A Hybrid Business Model for a Converging World' (one of ten winning entries in the Long-Term Capitalism Challenge of the Harvard Business Review/ McKinsey M Prize for Management Innovation), http://www .managementexchange.com/story/isnide-out-transformation, accessed 6 December 2013.

Bulloch, G. (2013) 'Harnessing the Herd: Could Social Intrapreneurs Represent a "Trojan Horse" Strategy for Charities', Business Fights Poverty blog, 24 March 2013, http://community.businessfightspoverty.org/profiles/blogs/gib-bulloch-harnessing-the-herd, accessed 13 December 2013.

Business Green (2012) 'Unilever Boss: Climate Change Cost Company €200m Last Year', Business Green, 24 April 2012, http://www.businessgreen.com/bg/news/2169950/ unilever-boss-climate-change-cost-company-eur200m accessed 6 December 2013.

Business in the Community (2010) *Learning to Connect: Building the Café Culture Movement*, (London: Business in the Community).

Caan, J. (2013) 'Unleashing Passion: The Intrapreneur', Linkedin, 25 February 2013, www.linkedin.com/today/post/article/20130225132843-32175171-unleashing-talent-the-intrapreneur, accessed 7 January 2014.

Capell, K. (2009) 'SABMiller's Plan for Cheaper African Beer', *Business Week*, 8 April 2009. http://www.businessweek.com/globalbiz/content/apr2009/gb2009048_046722.htm, accessed 6 December 2013.

CSI (Center for Social Impact) (2010) Intersecting Transformations: Business and the Third Sector (Conference proceedings; Sydney: CSI, http://csi.edu.au/research/our-project/ intersecting-transformations-business-and-third-sector-december-2010/, accessed 7 January 2014).

Cheballah, A. (2013) 'M-Pesa Phenomenon Taken a Step Further', *Business Day*, 29 April 2013, http://www.bdlive.co.za/africa/africanbusiness/2013/04/29/m-pesa-phenomenon-taken-a-step-further, accessed 6 december 2013.

Christensen, K.S. (2005) 'Enabling Intrapreneurship: The Case of a Knowledge-intensive Industrial Company', *European Journal of Innovation Management* 8.3: 305-22.

Clay, J. (2013) 'The Rise of the Extrapreneur: Making Cross-sector Collaboration Happen', *Guardian*, 21 June 2013, http://www.theguardian.com/sustainable-business/rise-of-extrapreneur-cross-sector-collaboration, accessed 6 December 2013.

Climate Policy Initiative (2013) Climate Change Investment Totals USD $359 Billion Worldwide', press release, Climate Policy Initiative, 22 October 2013. http://climatepolicy initiative.org/press-release/climate-change-investment-totals-usd-359-billion-worldwide/, accessed 6 December 2013.

Corroto, M. (2011) 'Duos: When the Sum is Greater than its Parts', all about jazz, 10 March 2011, http://www.allaboutjazz.com/php/article.php?id=38941, accessed 6 December 2013.

CSI (Center for Social Impact) (2010) Intersecting Transformations: Business and the Third Sector (Conference proceedings; Sydney: CSI, http://csi.edu.au/research/our-project/intersecting-transformations-business-and-third-sector-december-2010/

Csiksczentmihalyi, M. (1990) *Flow: The Psychology of Optimal Experience* (New York: Harper and Row).

Deal T.E., and A.A. Kennedy (1982) *Corporate Cultures: The Rites and Rituals of Corporate Life* (Harmondsworth, UK: Penguin Books).

De Geus, A. (1997) *The Living Company* (London: Nicholas Brealey).

Dess, G.G., and G.T. Lumpkin (2005) 'The Role of Entrepreneurial Orientation on Stimulating Effective Corporate Entrepreneurship', *Academy of Management Executive* 19.1: 147-56.

DfID (Department for International Development) (2013) 'Making Sure Children in Developing Countries Get a Good Education', Gov.UK, 11 October 2013, https://www.gov.uk/government/policies/making-sure-children-in-developing-countries-get-a-good-education, accessed 5 November 2013.

Dunphy, D.C., A. Griffiths and S. Benn (2007) *Organisational Change for Corporate Sustainability: A Guide for Leaders and Change Agents of the Future* (London/New York: Routledge, 2nd edn).

Economist, 'Agents of change,' in *The Economist*, 31 January 2008, http://www.economist.com/node/10601356, accessed 6 January 2014.

Elkington J., and C. Love (2012) 'Social Intrapreneurs are Just as Important as Entrepreneurs,' Fast Company CoExist blog, 23 October 2012, http://www.fastcoexist.com/1680715/social-intrapreneurs-are-just-as-important-as-entrepreneurs, accessed 13 December 2013.

Elkington, J., and P. Hartigan (2008) *The Power of Unreasonable People: How Social Entrepreneurs Create Markets That Change the World* (Cambridge, MA: Harvard Business School Press).

O Estado de São Paulo (2009) 'Natura lucra com a Amazônia', *O Estado de São Paulo*, 3 December 2009.

Fordham, J. (2011) 'A Teenage Charlie Parker has a Cymbal Thrown at Him: Number 11 in our series of the 50 key events in the history of jazz music', *The Guardian*, 17 June 2011, http://www.theguardian.com/music/2011/jun/17/charlie-parker-cymbal-thrown, accessed 6 December 2013.

Gallup Inc. (2013) 'State of the American Workplace: Employee Engagement Insights for U.S. Business Leaders', Gallup, http://www.gallup.com/strategicconsulting/163007/state-american-workplace.aspx, accessed 13 December 2013.

Gates, B. (2008) 'World Economic Forum 2008', transcript of remarks by Bill Gates at WEF 2008, 24 January 2008, http://www.microsoft.com/Presspass/exec/billg/speeches/2008/01-24WEFDavos.mspx, accessed 13 December 2013.

Gazeta Mercantil (2000) 'Natura, de cara nova, amplia conceito de beleza', *Gazeta Mercantil* 7 April 2000.

Gladwell, M. (2000) *The Tipping Point: How Little Things Can Make a Big Difference* (New York: Little, Brown).

Gladwell, M. (2005) *Blink: The Power of Thinking Without Thinking* (New York: Little, Brown).

Gladwell, M. (2008) *Outliers: The Story of Success* (New York: Little, Brown).

Gleiser, P.M., and L. Danon (2003) 'Community Structure in Jazz', *Advances in Complex Systems* 6.4: 565-73.

Goleman, D. (1998) *Working with Emotional Intelligence* (New York: Bantam Books).

Grayson, D. (2013) 'Corporate Responsibility with Chinese Characteristics', *Ethical Corporation*, 11 July 2013.

Grayson, D., and A. Hodges (2001) *Everybody's Business: Managing Risks and Opportunities in Today's Global Society* (London: Dorling Kindersley).

Grayson, D., and A. Hodges (2004) *Corporate Social Opportunity: 7 Steps to Make Corporate Social Responsibility Work for your Business* (Sheffield, UK: Greenleaf).

Grayson D., and A. Hodges (2008) 'Corporate Social Opportunity: Taking Ethical Risks to Market', *Ethical Corporation*, 9 September 2008.

Grayson, D., and J. Nelson (2012) 'Sustainable Capitalism and the potential of corporate responsibility coalitions,' *Ethical Corporation*, 7 November 2012.

Grayson, D., and J. Nelson (2013) *Corporate Responsibility Coalitions: The Past, Present, and Future of Alliances for Sustainable Capitalism* (Sheffield, UK: Greenleaf).

Grayson, D., M. McLaren and H. Spitzeck (2011) *Social Intrapreneurs: An Extra Force for Sustainability Innovation* (Doughty Centre Occasional Paper; Bedford, UK: Cranfield University, School of Management, Doughty Centre for Corporate Responsibility, http://www.som.cranfield.ac.uk/som/dinamic-content/media/knowledgeinterchange/criticalguides/20110223b/Guide.pdf), accessed 6 December 2013.

Grayson, D., H. Spitzeck, E. Alt and M. McLaren (2013) *Creating Sustainable Businesses Through Social Intrapreneurism* (Doughty Centre Occasional Paper; Bedford, UK: Cranfield University, School of Management, Doughty Centre for Corporate Responsibility http://www.som.cranfield.ac.uk/som/dinamic-content/media/OP_Creating%20Sustainable%20Business%20Through%20Social%20Intrapreneurism_March%2013.pdf), accessed 6 December 2013.

Guilford, J.P. (1959) 'Traits of Creativity', in H.H. Anderson (ed.), *Creativity and its Cultivation* (New York: Harper and Row): 142-61.

Harop, C. (n.d.) 'Marshalls plc–Fairstone® Journey', http://www.marshalls.co.uk/sustainability/publications/pdfs/Marshalls_Fairstone_Rio+20_approved.pdf.

Hayton, J.C., and D.J. Kelly (2006) 'A Competency-Based Framework for Promoting Corporate Entrepreneurship', *Human Resource Management* 45.3: 407-27.

Hill, C.W.L, and G.R. Jones (2001) *Strategic Management: An Integrated Approach* (Boston, MA: Houghton Mifflin).

Hisrich, R.D. (1990) 'Entrepreneurship/Intrapreneurship', *American Psychologist* 45.2: 209-22.

Honig, B. (2001) 'Learning Strategies and Resources for Entrepreneurs and Intrapreneurs', *Entrepreneurship Theory and Practice* 26.1: 21-35.

Hornsby, J.S., D.W. Naffziger, D.F. Kuratko and R.V. Montagno (1993) 'An Interactive Model of the Corporate Entrepreneurship Process', *Entrepreneurship Theory and Practice* 17: 29-37.

Hostager, T.J., T.C. Neil, R.L. Decker and R.D. Lorentz (1998) 'Seeing Environmental Opportunities: Effects of Efficacy, Motivation and Desirability', *Journal of Organizational Change Management* 11.1: 11-25.

Howard, P.N., Duffy, A., Freelon, D., Hussain, M., Mari, W. & Mazaid, M. (2011). Opening Closed Regimes: What Was the Role of Social Media During the Arab Spring? Seattle: PIPTI. Retrieved May 22, 2012 from http://pitpi.org/index.php/2011/09/11/opening-closed-regimes-what-was-the-role-of-social-media-during-the-arab-spring/

HSRP (Human Security Report Project) (2012), *Human Security Report 2012* (Vancouver: HSRP, http://www.hsrgroup.org/human-security-reports/2012/overview.aspx).

Internet World Stats (n.d.)'The Digital Divide, ICT and the 50×15 Initiative', http://www.internetworldstats.com/links10.htm, accessed 6 December 2013.

Jennings, R., C. Cox and C.L. Cooper (1994) *Business Elites : The Psychology of Entrepreneurs and Intrapreneurs* (London/New York: Routledge).

Jones, R.A., N.L. Jimmieson and A. Griffiths (2005) 'The Impact of Organisational Culture and Reshaping Capabilities on Change Implementation Success: The Mediating Role of Readiness for Change', *Journal of Management Studies* 42.2: 361-86.

Joseph, M. (2013) 'Story of M-PESA: Michael Joseph Reveals how M-PESA Came to be in Kenya', thinkM-PESA.com, 3 April 2013, animation, http://www.thinkm-pesa.com/2013/04/story-of-m-pesa-michael-joseph-reveals.html.

Kanter, R.M. (1983) *The Change Masters: Innovations for Productivity in the American Corporation* (New York: Simon and Schuster).

Kesting, H., and M. Anthony (2007) *Hedging Climate Change: How Insurers Can Manage the Risk of Increasing Natural Catastrophes* (Allianz Dresdner Economic Research Risk Report; Munich: Allianz SE).

Kiser, C., and D. Leipziger (2014) *Creating Social Value: A Guide for Leaders and Change Makers*, with J.J. Shubert (Sheffield, UK: Greenleaf Publishing).

Kiviat, B. (2010) Danone's Cheap Trick', *Time Magazine*, 23 August 2010, http://content.time.com/time/magazine/article/0,9171,2010077,00.html (accessed 23 October 2013).

Knowledge@Australian School of Business (2011) 'Social Intrapreneurs: How Corporate Provocateurs Can Change the World', Social Impact, Knowledge@Australian School of Business, 27 April 2011, http://knowledge.asb.unsw.edu.au/article.cfm?articleid=1381, accessed 6 December 2013.

Knowledge@Wharton (2012), 'At Shell, a Grassroots Effort Aims to Nourish Innovation Via Meditation', Knowledge@Wharton, 1 August 2012, http://knowledge.wharton.upenn.edu/article/at-shell-a-grassroots-effort-aims-to-nourish-innovation-via-meditation/, accessed 6 December 2013.

Kuratko, D.F., and M.G. Goldsby (2004) 'Corporate Entrepreneurs or Rogue Middle Managers? A Framework for Ethical Corporate Entrepreneurship', *Journal of Business Ethics* 55.1: 13-30.

Kuratko, D.F., R.D. Ireland, J.G. Covin and J.S. Hornsby (2005) 'A Model of Middle-Level Managers' Entrepreneurial Behavior', *Entrepreneurship Theory & Practice* 29.6: 699-716.

Kuratko, D.F., R.B. Montagno and J.S. Hornsby (1990) 'Developing an Intrapreneurial Assessment Instrument for an Effective Corporate Entrepreneurial Environment', *Strategic Management Journal* 11.5: 28-49.

Lave, J., and E. Wenger (1991) *Situated Learning: Legitimate Peripheral Participation* (Cambridge, UK: Cambridge University Press).

League of Intrapreneurs (n.d.) 'Cubicle Warrior Toolkit: Negotiating the System', http://www.leagueofintrapreneurs.com/toolkits/negotiating-the-system.

Lombriser, R., and I. Ansoff (1995) 'How Successful Intrapreneurs Pilot Firms Through the Turbulent 1990s', *Journal of Strategic Change* 4.2: 95-108.

McGaw, N. (2013) 'Have a Real Impact; Keep Your Day Job,' HBR Blog Network, 8 February 2013, http://socialinnovation.ca/community/buzz/have-real-impact-keep-your-day-job, accessed 13 December 2013.

McKinsey (2013) *Towards the Circular Economy* (McKinsey & Co.).

McLaren, M. & Spender J (2011) *Supporting Corporate Responsibility Performance Through Effective Knowledge Management* (Doughty Centre How-to Guide; Bedford, UK: Cranfield University, School of Management, Doughty Centre for Corporate Responsibility).

Macrae, N. (1982) 'Intrapreneurial Now', *The Economist*, 17 April 1982.

Mantere, S. (2005) 'Strategic Practices as Enablers and Disablers of Championing Activity', *Strategic Organization* 3.2: 157-84.

Marcus, L. (2012) 'Aesop's Year in the boardroom,' LinkedIn.com, 18 December 2012, http://www.linkedin.com/today/post/article/20121218215334-60894986-aesop-s-year-in-the-boardroom, accessed 6 December 2013.

Mednick, S.A. (1962) 'The Associative Basis of the Creative Process', *Psychological Review* 69: 220–32.

Meyerson, D. (2001) *Tempered Radicals: How People Use Difference to Inspire Change at Work* (Boston, MA: Harvard Business School Press).

Meyerson, D. (2004) 'The Tempered Radicals', *Stanford Social Innovation Review*, Fall 2004: 14-23.

Meyerson, D., and M. Scully (1995) 'Tempered Radicalism and the Politics of Ambivalence and Change', *Organization Science* 6.5: 585-600.

Mirvis, P.H., and B. Googins (2006) 'Stages of Corporate Citizenship: A Developmental Framework', *California Management Review* 48.2.

Mitchell, N. (2013) '5 Ways Social Intrapreneurs and Entrepreneurs Can Learn From Each Other', Fast Company CoExist blog, 13 February 2013, http://www.fastcoexist.com/1681387/5-ways-social-intrapreneurs-and-entrepreneurs-can-learn-from-each-other, accessed 13 December 2013.

Morris, M.H., and D.F. Kuratko (2002) *Corporate Entrepreneurship* (Orlando, FL: Harcourt College Publishers).

Morris E., J. Winiecki, S. Chowdhary and K. Cortiglia (2007) *Using Microfinance to Expand Access to Energy Services: Summary of Findings* (Washington, DC: The SEEP Network, http://www.arcfinance.org/pdfs/pubs/Energy_Summary_FINAL.pdf, accessed 8 January 2014).

Mwangi, P.G. (2013) 'Latest M-PESA statistics', think-M-Pesa.com, Blog, 14 May 2013, http://www.thinkm-pesa.com/2013/05/latest-m-pesa-statistics.html#links, accessed 6 December 2013.

Narayanan, V.K., Y. Yang and S.A. Zahra (2009) 'Corporate Venturing and Value Creation: A Review and Proposed Framework', *Research Policy* 38.1: 58-76.

Navajas S. and Tejerina L. (2006) *Microfinance in Latin America and the Caribbean: How Large is the Market?* (Sustainable Development Department Best Practice Series; Washington, DC: Inter-American Development Bank, http://idbdocs.iadb.org/wsdocs/getdocument.aspx?docnum=866107, accessed 8 January 2014).

Net Impact (2009) *Making Your Impact at Work: A Practical Guide to Changing the World from Inside Any Company'* (San Francisco: Net Impact).

Odebrecht, N. (1983) *Survival, Growth and Perpetuity* (Salvador, Brazil).

Parker, S.C. (2011) 'Intrapreneurship or Entrepreneurship?' *Journal of Business Venturing* 26.1: 19-34.

Pinchot, G., and E. Pinchot (1978) 'Intra-corporate Entreprenuership', Tarrytown School for Entrepreneurs, available at http://www.intrapreneur.com/MainPages/History/IntraCorp.html, accessed 13 December 2013.

Porritt, J., and C. Tuppen (2003) *Just Values: Beyond the Business Case for Sustainable Development* (BT Occasional Paper; London: BT in association with Forum for the Future).

Porter, M.E., and M.R. Kramer (2006) 'Strategy and Society: The Link between Competitive Advantage and Corporate Social Responsibility', *Harvard Business Review* 84.12: 78-92.

Porter, M.E., and M.R. Kramer (2011) 'Creating Shared Value: How to Reinvent Capitalism and Unleash a Wave of Innovation and Growth', *Harvard Business Review* 89.1-2: 62-77.

Prahalad, C.K. (2004) The Fortune at the Bottom of the Pyramid: Eradicating Poverty Through Profits (Upper Saddle River, NJ: Prentice Hall).

Provost, C. (2013), 'Energy poverty deprives 1 billion of adequate healthcare, says report', *The Guardian,* 7 March 2013.

Randerson, J. (2006) 'World's richest 1% own 40% of all wealth, UN report discovers', *The Guardian 6 December 2006* www.theguardian.com/money/2006/dec/06/business .internationalnews

Richards, K. (2010) *Life* (London: Weidenfeld & Nicolson, http://www.keithrichards.com/ life/).

Roberts, R., and P. Hirsch (2005) 'Evolution and Revolution in the Twenty-First Century: Rules for Organisations and Managing Human Resources', *Human Resource Management* 44.2: 171-76.

Roddick, A. (2005) *Business As Unusual: My Entrepreneurial Journey, Profits With Principles* (London: Anita Roddick Books).

Rushe, D. (2013) 'World Unemployment Figures Set to Rise in 2013, Claims UN Labour Agency', *The Guardian,* 22 January 2013, http://www.theguardian.com/business/2013/ jan/22/ilo-unemployment-numbers-rise-2013, accessed 5 November 2013.

Russell, T. (2012) 'Engaging Employees in Sustainability 2.0', Sustainable Brands.com, 26 July 2012, http://www.sustainablebrands.com/news_and_views/jul2012/engaging-employees-sustainability-20, accessed 8 November 2013).

Ryan, R., and E. Deci (2000) 'Self-determination Theory and the Facilitation of Intrinsic Motivation, Social Development, and Well-being', *American Psychologist 55*: 68-78.

Saddington, H., and P. Toni (2009) *Using ICT to Drive your Sustainability Strategy* (White Paper; Yelstra and WWF Australia), Executive summary at http://www.telstra.com.au/ business-enterprise/download/document/business-industries-sustainability-executive-white paper.pdf

Safaricom Ltd (2013) 'FY 2013 Presentation', Safaricom, http://www.safaricom.co.ke/ images/Downloads/Resources_Downloads/FY_2013_Results_Presentation.pdf, accessed 6 December 2013.

Sathe, V. (2003) *Corporate Entrepreneurship: Top Managers and New Business Creation* (Cambridge, UK: Cambridge University Press).

Sawyer, R.K. (2006) *Explaining Creativity: The Science of Human Innovation* (New York: Oxford University Press).

Schegg, R.M. (2013) 'Alternative Building Technologies for Housing the Urban Poor & the Development of Scalable, Sustainable Business Models', Hilti Foundation, presentation at Expert Group Meeting: *Regional Assessment on Increasing the Affordability of Sustainable Energy Options*, United Nations Bangkok, 19–20 February 2013.

Schein, E.H. (2004) *Organisational Culture and Leadership* (San Francisco: Jossey-Bass).

Schwartz, A. (2013) 'The League Of Intrapreneurs: 4 Changemakers Making A Difference Inside Big Companies', FastCompany Co.Exist, 10 April 2013, http://www.fastcoexist .com/1681796/the-league-of-intrapreneurs-4-changemakers-making-a-difference-inside-big-companies, accessed 6 December 2013.

Schwartz, P., and B. Gibb (1999) *When Good Companies Do Bad Things: Responsibility and Risk in Age of Globalization* (New York: John Wiley & Sons).

Singh, J. (2006) 'The Rise and Decline of Organizations: Can 'Intrapreneurs' Play a Saviour's Role?' *Vikalpa* 31.1: 123-27.

Sivers, Derek (2010) 'How to Start a Movement', TED talk, http://www.ted.com/talks/derek_sivers_how_to_start_a_movement.html, accessed 6 December 2010.

Sousanis, J. (2011) 'World Vehicle Population Tops 1 Billion Units', WardsAuto, 15 August 2011, http://wardsauto.com/ar/world_vehicle_population_110815, accessed 5 November 2013.

Spitzeck, H. (2009) 'Organisational Moral Learning: What, if Anything, do Corporations Learn from Ngo Critique?' *Journal of Business Ethics* 88.1: 157-73.

Spitzeck, H., C. Boechat and S. Leão (2013) 'Sustainability as a Driver for Innovation: Towards a Model of Corporate Social Entrepreneurship at Odebrecht in Brazil', *Corporate Governance* 13.5: 613-25.

Standard Digital (2013) 'Exporting M-pesa to India No Easy Game', Standard Digital, 7 May 2013, http://www.standardmedia.co.ke/business/article/2000083153/exporting-m-pesa-to-india-no-easy-game, accessed 7 January 2014.

Stone, C. (2001) *Networking: The Art of Making Friends* (London: Vermilion).

Stone, C. (2004) *The Ultimate Guide to Successful Networking* (London: Vermilion).

Stopford, J.M., and C.W.F. Baden-Fuller (1994) 'Creating Corporate Entrepreneurship', *Strategic Management Journal* 15.10: 521-36.

Stewart, E. (2013) 'How Does a Social Intrapreneur Add Value to a Business?' Guardian Sustainable Business Blog, 11 September 2013, http://www.theguardian.com/sustainable-business/social-intrapreneur-value-business, accessed 6 December 2013.

SustainAbility (2007) *Raising Our Game: Can We Sustain Globalization?* (London: Sustainability).

SustainAbility (2008) *The Social Intrapreneur: A Field Guide for Corporate Changemakers* (London: Sustainability in partnership with the Skoll Foundation, Allianz and IDEO).

Tapscott, D. (2003) *The Naked Corporation: How the Age of Transparency Will Revolutionize Business* (New York: Free Press).

Thain, M. (2013) 'Mark Thain, Barclays, on Competitive Edge and Long-Term Thinking', Shared Value Initiative, 23 May 2013, http://www.sharedvalue.org/resources/mark-thain-barclays-competitive-edge-and-long-term-thinking.accessed, 6 December 2013.

Thomas, D. (2012) 'Vodafone to Expand M-PESA Transfers', *Financial Times*, October 2012.

Towers Watson (2012) *2012 Global Workforce Study: Engagement at Risk: Driving Strong Performance in a Volatile Global Environment* (New York: Towers Watson).

UNGC and Accenture (2013) *UN Global Compact–Accenture. CEO Study on Sustainability 2013: Architects of a Better World* (UNGC?Accenture, http://www.accenture.com/Microsites/ungc-ceo-study/Documents/pdf/13-1739_UNGC report_Final_FSC3.pdf).

UNHCR (2013) *Mid-Year Trends, June 2013,* (UNHCR, http://www.unhcr.org/cgi-bin/texis/vtx/home/opendocPDFViewer.html?docid=52af08d26).

US EIA (Energy Information Administration) (2013) 'EIA Projects World Energy Consumption Will Increase 56% by 2040' EIA, 25 July 2013, http://www.eia.gov/todayinenergy/detail.cfm?id=12251, accessed 5 November 2013.

Valor Econômico (2003) 'Natura é exemplo de caso bem sucedido', *Valor Econômico*, 17 February 2003.

Valor Econômico (2008) 'Natura faz parceria com Amapá para repartir lucro', *Valor Econômico* 21 May 2008.

Van Riel, C.B.M. (2000) 'Sustaining the Corporate Story', in M. Schultz *et al.* (eds.), *The Expressive Organisation: Linking Identity, Reputation, and the Corporate Brand* (pp. 157–181). (Oxford: Oxford University Press): 157-81.

Wright, M. (2008) 'Shakti Power', *Green Futures*, 11 January 2008.

Wrzesniewski, A., and J.E. Dutton (2001) 'Crafting a Job: Revisioning Employees as Active Crafters of Their Work', *Academy of Management Review* 26.2: 179-201.

WWF-UK (2012) *Green Game-changers: Insights for Mainstreaming Business Innovation* (Woking, UK: WWF-UK).

Zadek, S. (2004) 'The Path to Corporate Responsibility', *Harvard Business Review* 82.12: 125-32.

Zahra, S.A. (1991) 'Predictors and Financial Outcomes of Corporate Entrepreneurship: An Exploratory Study', *Journal of Business Venturing* 6.4: 259-85.

Zahra, S.A. (1993) 'Environment, Corporate Entrepreneurship and Financial Performance: A Taxonomic Approach', *Journal of Business Venturing* 8.4: 319-40.

Further reading and resources

Austin J., and E. Reficco (2009), 'Corporate Social Entrepreneurship', HBS Working Paper 09/101; Harvard Business School, 3 March 2009, http://www.hbs.edu/faculty/ Publication Files/09-101.pdf.

Bode, C., and F. Santos (2013), *The Organisational Foundations of Corporate Social Entrepreneurship* (INSEAD Working Paper 15 January 2013; Fontainebleau, France: INSEAD).

Exter, N. (2013) *Employee Engagement with Sustainable Business: How to Change the World Whilst Keeping Your Day Job* (London: Routledge).

Hafenmayer Stefanska, J. and W. Hafenmayer (2013) *The Future Makers: A Journey to People who are Changing the World–and What We Can Learn from Them* (With an essay by Muhammad Yunus; Sheffield, UK: Greenleaf Publishing).

Marshall, J., G. Coleman and P. Reason (2013) *Leadership for Sustainability: An Action Research Approach* (Sheffield, UK: Greenleaf Publishing).

Miller, J. and L. Parker (2013) *Everybody's Business: The Unlikely Story of how Big Business can Fix The World* (London: Biteback Publishing).

Nijhof, A., J.K. Looise, J.K. and J. de Leede (2012) 'Social Intrapreneurship: A Conceptual, Theoretical and Empirical Exploration of its Meaning and Contribution', in 'Innovation, Social Responsibility, Creativity, Ethics and Olaf Fisscher', *Creativity & Information Management (CIM)* special issue, in association with University of Twente: 109-28.

Osburg, T., and R. Schmidpeter (eds.) (2013) *Social Innovation: Solutions for a Sustainable Future.* (Berlin, Heidelberg: Springer).

Useful websites

Business Fights Poverty: Intrapreneur Zone: http://businessfightspoverty.org/blog/category/ intrapreneur-zone/

CSR Europe Intrapreneurship Programme: http://www.csreurope.org/european-social-intrapreneurship-programme - .Ul_D-haffL8

Gifford Pinchot: www.pinchot.com

League of Intrapreneurs: http://www.leagueofintrapreneurs.com

Intrapreneurial Resources: http://www.intrapreneurialresources.info/

Blogs

The *Guardian* Sustainable Business, Fast Company, Forbes and *The Huffington Post* have all carried blogs and features about social intrapreneurship on their websites.

Index

About the authors

Prof David Grayson CBE is Professor of Corporate Responsibility and Director of the Doughty Centre for Corporate Responsibility at the Cranfield School of Management in the UK. He joined Cranfield after a thirty year career as a social entrepreneur and campaigner for responsible business, diversity, and small business development. This included the chairmanship of the UK's National Disability Council and several other government bodies, as well as serving as a joint managing-director of Business in the Community. He has also been a visiting Senior Fellow at the CSR Initiative of the Kennedy School of Government, Harvard 2006–2010.

He has Masters degrees from the universities of Cambridge, Brussels and Newcastle, and an honorary doctorate from London South Bank University. His books include: "Corporate Social Opportunity: Seven Steps to make Corporate Social Responsibility work for your business" (2004) and "Everybody's Business" (2001) - both co-authored with Adrian Hodges. David co-edited "Cranfield on Corporate Sustainability" (2012) and his last book: "Corporate Responsibility Coalitions: The past, present and future of alliances for Sustainable Capitalism" co-authored with Jane Nelson was published in January 2013.

Melody McLaren is Co-founding Director of McLaren UK, a creative business services consultancy, and is an Associate of the Doughty Centre for Corporate Responsibility at Cranfield School of Management. A graduate of the California Institute of Technology (BS, 1977) and Birkbeck College, University of London (MSc, Organizational Behaviour 2007), her eclectic career encompasses over 30 years of experience spanning a wide range of fields including research, writing, media relations, sales promotion, web development, social media and corporate responsibility campaigning in the US and Europe.

Trained as a classical pianist from early childhood to age 15, Melody was inspired to take up jazz piano in 2005 after attending a Global Music Foundation summer school. She continues to play the piano as well as supporting and documenting the work of the wider jazz community through photography and writing. In between her classical and jazz music stints she became World Hula Hoop Champion (1969) and set a Guinness World Record twirling 65 hoops simultaneously (1985) as well as playing competitive volleyball in the US and UK for over 20 years.

Heiko Spitzeck is professor at Fundação Dom Cabral in Brazil where he teaches strategy & sustainability to senior executives. His teaching experience includes courses for the boards of Nestlé Brasil, Michelin Latin America, Grupo André Maggi and senior executives at Itaú, Braskem, Petrobras, as well as other companies on Sustainable Business and Innovation. His teaching is informed by more than 12 years of consulting experience as well as academic research. His publications have appeared in numerous international journals as well as in several books published among others by Cambridge University Press. Heiko previously lectured at Cranfield University in the UK and held visiting positions at the University of California at Berkeley, Fordham University in New York (both U.S.) as well as the University of Extremadura (Spain). Heiko was educated in Germany, Spain and Switzerland. He received his PhD from the University of St. Gallen (Switzerland).

Printed and bound by CPI Group (UK) Ltd, Croydon, CR0 4YY
01/05/2025
01858459-0002